OVERCOMING

OVERCOMING

(Alone Against the world)

A Memoir

Hamid Zaher

Overcoming
Alone Against the World
A Memoir

Copyright © 2017 by Hamid Zaher

All rights reserved. No part of this book may be reproduced by any means, graphic, electronic, or mechanical, including photocopying, taping or by any information storage retrieval system without the written permission of the publisher except in the case of brief quotations embodied in critical articles and reviews.

Originally written in Farsi in 2009, in Toronto, Canada

First edition, 2012
Second Edition, 2017

Overcoming, by Hamid Zaher

ISBN: 978-1-304-33236-3 (sc)

Any commercial publisher willing to republish this book is welcome.

Facebook page: https://www.facebook.com/hamid.zaher.31

"Hamid's book is an impassioned and defiant attack on the conservative traditions and prejudices… Afghan human rights officials, contacted by the BBC, refused to comment on whether gay Afghans ever appeal to them for help. "Afghanistan is a no-go area for gays," said a human rights activist who asked not be named. "Hamid's revelation is revolutionary in today's Afghanistan.""
    —Tahir Qadiry, the BBC

"A remarkable, eye-opening autobiography that's as relevant as it is revelatory."
    —Kirkus Reviews

"These days a very shocking book has reached my hands that the study of no book has been as astonishing and confusing as this one; its events are legendary and even frightful… memories of his life by our fellow Afghan Hamid Zaher."
    —Maryam Mahboob, The biweekly Zarnegar

"One may say that this book has shocked its readers in a certain way. Everyone thinks whether they should pass it by silently and cautiously or talk about it freely and courageously without giving any complexity? I still believe that Zaher, with these memoirs of his, has courageously voiced a silent minority which hides itself in the closet for fear of ridicule, rejection, hatred and disgust of people and is forced to pretend it does not exist. He has indulged in a heroic act not only for the defense of his own identity but also for the thousands like him who continue to suffer silently and negate themselves."
    —Manizha Bakhtari, The biweekly Kabulnath

Hamid Zaher's memoir is fiercely intelligent and emotionally draining."
    —Michael Lyons, The biweekly Xtra

"Mr. Zaher says that he really had no idea how to go about the task of writing his memoir… he, whose story needs to be told,

has shown that he is a quick study and has written a very moving book that deserves a wide readership."
—Foster Corbin, the Amazon reviewer

"It's a bold, courageous and pioneering book that is worth reading... Zaher explains his story meticulously in detail. The courage, sacrifice, strength of character, perseverance and sheer determination that are essential when one is forced to leave one's homeland is not a small feat."
—Professional Student, the Amazon reviewer

"I feel that Mr. Zaher is a pioneer and will suffer and sacrifice much before the message really starts to get accepted."
—John Chancellor, the Amazon reviewer

"His story is interesting and informative. You will gain a perspective on many issues revolving around a person's sexuality. He offers us a glimpse into another perspective outside at least my circle."
—Okiedan, the Amazon reviewer

This book will make you realize that humanity still has a long way to come. Homosexuality while just being recognized in first world countries is far from accepted in the 3rd world. Zaher paints a terrible picture for those that are coming to terms with their sexuality in such countries but gives us all hope that if you persevere, you will succeed.
—Adrian Hutchins, the Amazon reviewer

Disclaimer

This book is a true story of my life. References to real people, events, establishments, organizations, or locales are all true and intended to provide a sense of authenticity. However, I have changed the names and important information of all real persons and characters, including my family members, in order to protect their identity and privacy.

Dedication

This book is dedicated to all gay and lesbian Afghanistanis so that they may live with pride and honor, in the absence of discrimination and contempt, and in all respects equal to the rest of society.

Contents

ACKNOWLEDGMENTS XIII
NOTE XIV
INTRODUCTION XV
PART ONE 1
   Babeh nadareh (?) 3
PART TWO 7
   Eezak (?) 9
   My Sexual Feelings 15
PART THREE 19
   The Spirit of Confusion 21
   The Ugly Truth 23
   Tradition and Sexuality 26
   Superstition 31
PART FOUR 33
   My Life Is Only an Example 35
   The Family Trap 41
PART FIVE 55
   Arrival in Pakistan 57
   My Marjan's Mental Sickness 64
   After September 11 Attacks 67
PART SIX 71
   Arrival in Iran 73
   My Conflict with My Marjan 77
   Shah Malang's Bitter Life 87
   My Acquaintance with Nawaz 94
   Money, the Key of Almost Everything 98
   I Was Zero 102
PART SEVEN 111
   Wandering 113
PART EIGHT 133
   The Spider's Web 135
   Qalandar's Lost Reputation 139
   My Acquaintance with Manouchehr 145
   Manouchehr's Broken Tooth 152
   Reaction of People in Van 155

April 2006 Van, Turkey	159
Manouchehr's Nose Breaking	164
Mehdi and Behroz	167
Yilmaz, a Turkish Gay	170
June 2006, Van, Turkey	173
My decision of Committing Suicide	176
In the Middle of the Intersection	180
Losing My Self-Confidence	188
My decision of Returning to Afghanistan	190
I Discovered the Secret of Asylum	197
The Police Officer's Crying Face	201
One-Week Protest	206
PART NINE	**221**
Ashakan Had Psychological Problems	223
Haider Was University Educated	227
The UN Representatives Creating Openings in the Schedule	236
My Journey from Van to Eskişehir	239
PART TEN	**245**
Arrival in Canada	247
Rahman Was a Lunatic	249
Toronto's Gay Parade	259
Afghanistan's Gay Closet	260
My Acquaintance with Hussain Zahedi	264
My Family's Reaction	267
CONCLUSION	**275**
MORE THINGS TO SAY	**279**
APPENDICES	**309**
Appendix 1	311
Appendix 2	313
Appendix 3	315
Appendix 4	317
Appendix 5	320
Appendix 6	322
Appendix 7	324
Appendix 8	325
Appendix 9	329
Appendix 10	331
Appendix 11	335
Appendix 12	336
ENDNOTES	**337**
Endnote 1	337
Endnote 2	339

Acknowledgments

My gratitude and thanks are due to the following that this book would not have been possible without the tremendous support of them:

Usman, my Sudanese friend, who was the first to suggest to me that I write this book,

Mr. Farrukh Duroudian, who took pains to translate this book into English,

Messrs. Anders Widmark and Kenneth Von Zeipel, and Ms. Helena Bani Shoraka, who took pains to translate this book into Swedish,

Mr. Gregory Terlecki, who wrote it as a screenplay,

Dr. Saboorullah Siasang, Ms. Manizha Bakhtari, Mr. Zia Afzali, and other critics and reviewers whose critical comments helped me improve this book,

Messrs. Hussain Zahedi, Ali Karimi, Haamed, Seyed and Fariburz Shagerd, whose insightful comments have benefited me immensely,

And last but not least, my gratitude and thanks are due to Ms. Maryam Mahboob and Mr. Zalmay Babakohi, whose unprecedented welcome warmed my heart.

Note

Because all the people of Afghanistan are not Afghans in terms of their ethnicity, as a result of the national identity they have been titled as "Afghanistani," so that all people are respected and their separate identities are not ignored. If one ethnic group is renamed after another, naturally the citizens are classified by the grade, and that will create the sense of ownership and monopolization in one special group. The main cause of riots and bloody war in Afghanistan in recent decades is largely on the same subject. Recently, a large number of Afghan nationals have chosen their national identity as "Afghanistani" to end Afghanistan's political tradition.

Introduction

The purpose of writing this book is to expose the existence of homosexuals in Afghanistani society and to draw the attention of the world to their plight. It was first published in 2009 in Farsi (See Endnote 1), under the title *Beyond* Horror; then it was translated into English in 2011.

In writing this book, I have started working on this issue at ground zero concerning Afghanistani society. All homosexuals in that society were hidden from every one; but their problem was beyond homosexuality—being bullied and humiliated for not marrying, and even for not begetting a child. As mentioned in the text of the book, there has been no awareness of the existence of homosexuals in Afghanistan before, and certainly nothing has ever been written to acknowledge their existence—until now. Despite this loud silence, same-sex and opposite-sex pedophilia has been a popular tradition in this society for centuries. This book is in fact the first message that introduces the existence of homosexuals in Afghanistani society. As the writer of this book, I am the first Afghanistani homosexual who has dared to come out of the closet.

Undoubtedly, only a small minority of medical professionals have been aware of this issue. Due that the subject is taboo, they have not openly discussed the issue and have not informed society of it. Only recently, have some Afghanistanis noticed that adult-to-adult homosexuality existed in Western countries; but they did not deem the matter as a natural disposition or even as a mental disorder or sickness—they only saw it as a Western lunacy.

With the subject matter being taboo, this book has had no positive or negative reaction in the Afghanistani society until several months after its publication, although it has been addressed to a multitude of people. No person has made any comments on it for fear of being labeled one way or another. Seven silent months after its publication, Ms. Maryam Mahboob, the editor of the bi-weekly Zarnegar, taking a great risk, introduced it to the people for the first time and gave it some exposure. I greatly value Ms. Maryam Mahboob's courage of conviction, and I express my heartfelt thanks for her act of courage. After her introduction of this book, some other Afghanistani critics, including Mr. Zia Afzali, Ms. Manizha Bakhtari, Dr. Sabourullah Siasang, Mr. Zalmay Babakohi, and one or two others under pen names, made their critique and expressed their views. I appreciate their attention and thank each and every one of them.

Dr. Sabourullah Siasang describes the depth of this taboo in Afghanistani society:

> "The book Beyond Horror by Hamid Zaher hit the market months ago, and there are abundant readers. Why, then, has no one come forward, save three or four distinguished Afghanistani writers, to speak out their mind about Beyond Horror?
>
> This "why" may have many "becauses": I have no time (although I can discuss it for two hours on the phone); I am afraid of getting involved with the phenomenon of homosexuality (although I have always said that I am not afraid of death); all humans, irrespective of their sexual orientations and ethnic roots, have equal rights in my eyes (still, it is better to remain silent and not to get caught up in this matter); I am still not prepared to accept homosexuals (if I put

it in writing, I would be labeled old-fashioned and a reactionary); and so on and so forth...

Of course critiquing Beyond Horror, under a pseudonym, even expertly, especially cursing, damning, praising, and acclaiming Hamid Zaher, who has bared his soul openly and under his real name, at least in this area, is not worth a penny."

Dr. Sabourullah Siasang said to me, "I sent this book to one of the most distinguished teachers of Afghanistan. After reading the book, he phoned me again and asked me not to tell anyone that I had sent this book to him, because no one should know that he had received this and had read it."

I sent a hard copy of the book and its PDF file to several local Afghanistani and foreign media, including the BBC and VOA, for their comments. None of them replied, nor did they have any comments, despite regularly introducing less voluminous and fictitious works of other writers. (Thanks to the BBC for their evaluation of this book after its English edition.)[1]

Perhaps it was egotistic of me to expect the media to give exposure to and critique my book. I requested several times for them to at least raise the issue of the Afghanistani homosexuals for the first time. Even this request was ignored. The Afghanistani media's indifference to this issue may be based on either the sensitivity of the issue or their contempt for homosexuals. In any event, this indifference expresses a kind of inappropriate treatment with the subject. Given the widespread indifference, it seems that the chance of a spontaneous transformation in the traditional society of Afghanistan, without the attention of the world society, is extremely weak. Consequently, it is predictable that violations of human rights and tragedies in this society will continue for the next several generations.

---

[1] The article of the BBC about this book can be found at: http://www.bbc.co.uk/news/world-asia-21426632

In relation to writing this book, I was interviewed in March 2013 by Ms. Jane Armstrong, a Canadian freelancer. But the editor of McLean's magazine, refused to publish that interview— only on grounds that the subjects of gays, Afghanistanis, and refugees are repetitive to Canadian readers. However, I express my gratitude to Mr. Dan Smith, the editor of the Toronto Star, who subsequently accepted the publication of my interview with Ms. Armstrong, even as a featured article[2]. My special thanks are due to Ms. Armstrong herself for her interviewing with me.

My question from the editor of McLean's magazine is: "are hundreds of other issues, including the white people, heterosexual stories, which are discussed every day, entirely new subjects, that a legal issue regarding a particular national and social group is labeled repetitive? What would honor and conscience mean, if one cannot distinguish a new subject from repetitive, as white from black, beyond one's color, race, and nationality? The white straight romance, fantasies, lyrics, and erotic poems which are made over and over into movies and songs, are never felt repetitive. Is the Afghanistani gay issue, while being raised for the first time, felt repetitive?"

Remark of Dr. Ali Shariati (1933 – 1977) is the answer to labeling such a legal issue repetitive, as he says: "If this world is such that one is forced to sing to death in order to obtain the most primary right of life, then this world is indeed a dirty world."

Notwithstanding the extreme wild prejudice against the Afghanistani homosexuals, even if just one person had spoken in their defense, perhaps my plea in this respect would have been one too many.

My request for reviewing this book was also ignored by the CBC Books, despite its being the sole movement towards founding rights for gay Afghanistanis in their most critical

---

[2] My interview with Ms. Armstrong, published by the Toronto Star, can be found at: http://www.thestar.com/news/insight/2013/03/17/gay_afghan_man_speaks_out_on_d eep_cultural_taboo.html

circumstances—While, the Canadian government itself allocates millions of dollars and hundreds of workers for the same cause in its own country and boasts of achieving this goal as a human development of its nation.

Ignoring of this book by Canadian sources can be for the reason to shirk the responsibility of acceptance of more Afghanistani gay asylum seekers. Otherwise, if it was worthless, why did the BBC pay attention to it? But if not, why, then, did the CBC Books and other Canadian literary sources ignore it, although it was written in Canada?

Part One

Babeh nadareh (?)

On one hot summer day in 1983, when I was a nine-year-old kid, I saw a poor, blind, old man in the Kheyrkhane neighborhood of Kabul. He had old, gray, worn-out Afghanistani attire on his body, a red-beaded Qandahari cap on his head, and worn leather shoes on his feet. He was sitting on the steps of a mud-brick shop with wooden beams, and the mud roof protruded outward, over the two steps to the door. The old man was sitting on the steps in the shade, resting for a while. Close to him were seven or eight naughty children, crouching and ready to take flight. They stomped their feet on the ground and shouted, "Babeh nadareh! Babeh nadareh!" (Dad has no! Dad has no!). They slowly crept toward the old man and threw pebbles at him. The old man was calm, patient, and so forbearing that as long as a pebble didn't hit him, he wouldn't move. A lot of pebbles lay close to him. When a pebble hit him, he would get up and run after the kids, who would quickly run away in all directions. The old man would sit down again on the steps, and the kids, crouching and stomping their feet, would sing again, "Babeh nadareh! Babeh nadareh!" and throw pebbles toward him. Thus, the old man's encounter with the kids had become a daily ritual, and anyone passing by the road would often see this incident. At first I thought that the old man's name was Babeh nadareh.

* * *

A few days later I was walking in the afternoon along the dirt road in the *Pansad Famili* neighborhood of Kabul, where high government officials lived. Heaps of rubble and garbage had formed along that road in the sewage bed, and each of those heaps blocked the sewage. Of course this was one of the rare parts in the northwest of Kabul that was equipped with piped water system, where sewage ran. There I saw another old man who entered that road from one of the alleyways on the left side. This old man was entirely different from the first one. He had dark brown skin and was taller and younger than the first one. He continued walking alongside the rubble and garbage dumps in the direction opposite me. About twelve dirty children, with dirty and sweaty faces and dirty and worn-out clothes, followed him. They shouted, "Babeh nadareh! Babeh nadareh!" and threw stones at him. The old man seemed in a great hurry and was agitated. Each time he stopped in panic and looked back, the kids would freeze in their places; as soon as he started walking, they would attack him like a swarm of bees. The tall, frightened old man walked quickly with his long legs, but the kids walked even faster, as if they had wings. I thought that the name of this old man was also Babeh nadareh. It was a bit strange for me that both men called Babeh nadareh were tormented by the children!

* * *

A few weeks after that, I was walking with my cousin Rakhshaneh, heading from my house toward her house. She was younger than me but smarter. My house was a couple of kilometers away from her house. This time I saw a third old man. He was walking along the road in our direction. Five or six kids were stalking him and shouting, "Babeh nadareh! Babeh nadareh!" and throwing stones at him. As we walked along, the number of children grew. We were close to him. Rakhshaneh, who had blue eyes, white skin, a large mole on her face, and blonde messy hair and blonde eyebrows, ran toward him and shouted, "Babeh nadareh! Babeh nadareh!"

This time it was hard for me to understand why children would torment anyone who had the name Babeh nadareh. I asked Rakhshaneh, "How many Babeh nadarehs are there? I saw one in front of your house. I saw another one in the Pansad Famili neighborhood. Now I see this one. Which one is Babeh nadareh?"

"None of them has any."

"What is it that they don't have?"

She looked at me with embarrassment, her eyes narrowed with wrinkles appearing around them, and her face became red with shame. She opened her mouth shyly, brought it close to my ear, and said softly, "They don't have a penis."

"Wow! I thought their names were Babeh Nadareh."

Rakhshaneh looked toward him and said laughingly, "Babeh nadareh! Babeh nadareh!"

I asked, "Why do they say that?"

"Because he did not marry."

"So what? Why they torment him?"

"Let's go and call him from behind!"

"Why call at him?"

"We'll have fun."

I didn't like this and said angrily, "No, it isn't fun for me."

Rakhshaneh, realizing my unhappiness, got embarrassed and did not speak anymore. That's how I learned both the meaning of Babeh nadareh, and that the children just wanted to have a little fun. I looked at the kids and realized that they were really having fun. Most of them laughed and shouted, "Babeh nadareh! Babeh nadareh!" and threw stones at him. But two of the kids looked angry and were aggressive: they came closer to him and hit his body directly with the pebbles. While we headed in the same direction, we saw the first pebble hit the back of his leg. He turned back angrily and ran after the children. All the children who were ready to escape took flight at once. But we did not intend to harm him and were not ready to run away.

When he turned back, the children ran further away, and we remained at a short distance from him. He had a few pebbles in his hand to defend himself. When I saw him up close with pebbles in his hands, I was frightened. I thought that the old man was mad and would hit anyone whom he could grab. He lifted his hand with pebbles in it, but when he looked into our eyes, he realized that we did not intend to bother him, and he ran after the children who were escaping. Every time a stone hit him, he angrily chased the kids, and the kids ran away with greater speed.

At first, seeing this adventure and the memory of Babeh nadareh was not so important and scary for me... until I noticed strange and gradual changes in my own body. Then all this became a permanent scare and a nightmare in my mind.

Part Two

Eezak (?)

The word *eezak* in colloquial Afghanistani Persian language actually means a neuter—that is, someone who is neither a woman nor a man. In other words, one with any kind of sexual problem who would not be able to generate offspring, specially not be able to engage in sexual intercourse, is called an eezak. But this word is used in several other meanings as well, such as a girlish boy, a boyish girl, an effeminate man, a sterile man, an infertile woman, impotent, lowly, coward, timid, a cuckold, or an incompetent. In the minds of most Afghanistanis, this word is extremely ridiculous and funny, and at the same time it is detested and loathsome. Children use this word to make fun of others. Elderly people use this word to taunt, to reproach, to insult, to humiliate, to belittle, to demean, to vilify, to ridicule, and to revile.

I had many feminine traits in my childhood, but others did not notice it because of my very young age. For instance, I always wanted to be in the company of girls, and I was interested in girlish games, such as playing with dolls, hide-and-seek, blindman's buff, and so on. I always wanted to be with girls inside my house or close to my house; I was afraid of going to faraway places and of playing aggressive boys' games. With the exception of a few neighborhood boys my own age, others did not know of these inclinations of mine. Neighborhood boys would call me to come out and play outside. I would open the door and peek outside, but I would not come out and would tell them, "I don't want to play."

They would say, "Why do you peek out through the door like a girl? Come on outside and talk to us, you bimbo! Why do you always stay at home like the girls?" Going out of my house with boys, alone and without girls, was frightful for me. Some of the neighboring boys called me "Hamid bimbo."

I not only had girly traits, but also did not feel like a boy. My male organ felt like an extra thing in my body, and I was ashamed of having it. I was envious of girls and thought to myself, *Lucky them! They don't have any extra thing hanging between their thighs to be ashamed of.* When I heard boys muttering things like "dick" and "fuck you," I wondered to myself, *How strange! They have a dick and are not ashamed of calling it a dick!*

As I grew older, my girly traits and habits gradually became clear to those around me. Whenever I spoke, neighboring children and extended family members immediately repeated my words like a girl and said in a soft drawn accent, "Oh, sister!"

My best memories of my childhood are of girls who were my adopted sisters. I always played with them, and whenever I saw one of them, I felt extremely happy.

Sometimes we played *jezbazi*: we drew blocks on the earth and jumped from one block over to another with one leg, and pushed one round pebble with one foot from one block to the other.

Sometimes we played *panjaq*: we threw up one of five small, round pebbles, and before it fell down, we would catch it together with the other four pebbles on the floor. Whoever won the game would throw up the pebble with one hand and, with the same hand, hit on the back or the hand the other girl, picking up the pebble before it fell on the floor. The game of panjaq was very exciting for me. Most of the time one of my adopted sister named Farzane, who was the daughter of my mother's uncle, would win the game, and she would hit the back of my hand or slap or claw my back. Each time she threw the pebble up and hit the back of my hand, I would be frightened to death and would scream.

Sometimes we played *Cheshm bandakan*, or hide-and-seek. We would go inside a room and close the eyes of one girl with a scarf, and other girls would run around the room away from her. The blindfolded girl would try to catch one of the others. When she touched one, it was the turn of the girl who was caught to close her eyes with the scarf. Whenever a girl with closed eyes came close to me, I would scream and would be so frightened, as if she wanted to eat me alive.

Sometimes we played *ghelghelak bazi,* or tickling one another. Some of the boys who saw me playing the tickling game with girls would become jealous of me and would say, "You are very clever, Hamid. You are tickling the girls by deceit and having fun!"

What they said would surprise me, and I would say, "What are you talking about? I have no idea what are you saying."

After hearing those words the girls, would be shocked and would keep their distance from me. But soon they would trust me again because they knew I had no feelings for them. I felt myself as a part of them, and they too felt as if I was a part of them, and they would tell the boys, "Get lost. What we do is none of your business." This retort by the girls would make me happy, and I would tell myself, *Well, it's nice that they consider me as one of them.* Some of the boys also wanted to play tickling with us, but the girls would strongly oppose it and would not allow them to come close. Sometimes they preferred to stop playing the game rather than allowing the boys to join them. I inferred from the girls' unhappiness that because the boys did not participate in other games of the girls and wanted to play only the tickling game, the girls didn't like it.

I always maintained a close friendship with a large number of girls. In later years, upon reaching puberty, each one of them would marry one after the other and go away from me; others who came from religious families would hide from me. Their distancing was unbearable for me.

* * *

In childhood, boys would call me Hamideh (a feminine form of Hamid), girl, bimbo, or eezak. Whenever I danced in parties, all men, young and old, would laugh at me and say, "Wow! He dances exactly like a girl!" Their laughter would sadden me; I would go and sit in a corner and would no longer dance. When people laughed at the way I spoke or acted and called me names, it would break my heart to pieces. I lost my spirit and my confidence day by day. I became a coward and was isolated. Some people commented on me and expressed their opinions. Some said, "He is eezak." Some said, "No, he is not eezak. He is sissy." Some said, "He is neither eezak nor sissy; he was a girl in his mother's womb, and later God changed his mind and converted him into a boy. God thought it was necessary for him to be born as a boy."

* * *

Spring 1988, Kabul
When I was in grade eight in school, Mazdak, my brother-in-law, was about thirty years old. Mazdak had earned a postgraduate degree from Kabul Polytechnic School in building roads and canals. One day when I was sitting at home and talking, Mazdak looked at me with extreme hatred and anger and said sharply, "Hamid, you are no longer a child. Don't speak softly like a girl. You are a man now, and you should speak like a man." His hateful glance and sharp tone hurt me a lot.

There was too much ignorance in society. Time was never favorable to me. Finally, time's cruelties forced me to adapt myself to society in order to avoid headaches. To achieve peace, I tried to change myself. As a first step, I always preferred to remain silent. If I had to, I tried hard to speak from the depth of my throat in a thick voice, so no one would mimic me. In my actions I tried to present myself as brave and bold so that no one would call me a girl *or eezak*.

As a result of a long period of play acting and imposing the play acting on myself, I gradually became an actor. But behind the play acting, the original character never changed and ultimately all the acting came to naught. Of course the hardships of life and hard physical work also hardened me. In economic terms, those were bad days indeed.

During the government of Hafizullah Amin in 1979, when I was five years old, my father was arrested on charges of opposition to the regime, and he was executed. My father was a military officer in the past. In those days the government of Afghanistan, after the death of military officers, gave their survivors full retirement salary plus a goods coupon for a lot of commodities. But after executing my father, the government gave us only half of the pension of a lowly government employee.

Even for that my mother had to run around a lot. Not even a good part of our mediocre life could be provided for with that amount. My mother used to run a bee-keeping business in the village, and she somehow managed to make ends meet. We come originally from the village of Chahardeh in the provincial town of Ghourband, in the province of Parwan, sixty-five kilometers northwest of Kabul. When I was seven years old, we moved to Kabul and settled there. Yet we did not have a source of income in Kabul and depended on the village. I began to do hard physical work from my early childhood. Each day after school closed, I worked as a porter with a one-wheel wheelbarrow.

In addition to play acting, the hard physical labor and long hardships of life enabled me to assume the appearance of a regular boy. Although I became "normal," and no one objected to the way I spoke or behaved, I did not feel like a man from the inside. If someone told me that I was a man or that I would marry in the future and would have children, I would feel unhappy. It was the same as if someone told a girl that she would marry a woman in the future and become a father.

My Sexual Feelings

When I was in grade eight, I saw my classmates and other boys of my age talking about girls and showing their interest in them. But I had no feelings for girls. I would think that perhaps a few months later I would take interest in girls. However, I noticed that, contrary to other boys, I was interested in older men. Even before this point, some older men seemed attractive to me. But then they were attractive to me physically, not sexually. In this period I became sexually interested in older men, especially those ten years or older than me. Older men, with large frames and hairy chests, seemed more attractive to me. Whenever I went to public baths or to the river for swimming in Ghourband, my birthplace, I saw older men in wet shorts with their organs showing, and I would stare. Some of them took off their shorts, and I saw their organs directly. This would make my heart throb, and my whole body would shake.

At first I thought that perhaps this was a temporary and reversible attraction, and in the future I would lose interest in them. I tried to help myself change my inclination from men to women. For this reason I tried to stay close to girls so as to develop an interest in them. But this made me feel like a fool; I felt no attraction to them because I felt myself as a part of them. If I tried to pay no attention to men so that my attraction to them would go away from my mind, but an irresistible attraction drew me to them involuntarily like a magnet. I felt pleasure from looking at them, and I felt the need to mix with them.

When I was in grades ten and eleven at school, my attraction to older men increased greatly. Wherever I went, I would gaze at the organs of older men. If I dreamed at night, I always saw men in my dreams having sex with me; I never dreamed of a woman. I would see myself in dreams like a woman, with whom the man was having sex. This would make me come.

Occasionally I felt like I was a woman while awake. Sometimes when I went to bed at night, I felt like having soft, large breasts that softly ached and made me restless. In such a state, I felt the need for the hands of a man who could press my breasts with his fingers and hands so that the pain in my breasts would go away. Out of unhappiness and restlessness, I would lie on the floor or press my chest against the mattress so that I no longer would feel those imaginary painful breasts. Gradually I forgot my painful imaginary breasts, but I started feeling my shoulders were curved and soft, and my waist was thin and delicate. Again, I felt the need for a man's hand to press my shoulders and waist so I could feel calm and peaceful. I would turn and twist out of restlessness, but the restlessness would reach its peak. At the height of my restlessness, I would feel a depression in place of my testicles. Again I would feel the need for a man who could insert his organ in my depression so that my restlessness would go away. In such a state, when I pressed my testicles with my hands, they would feel exactly like a vagina in place of that imaginary depression that I felt inside me.

In grade twelve my need for and my sexual inclination to older men increased severely and turned into an inevitable matter. In that state, when I looked at them fondly, some of them made offers of sex indirectly. But despite my strong need for them, I could not give a positive response to their proposal because of the cultural ignorance in Afghanistan. I would tell myself how hard it is. *I am inclined to them, and they want me, but I cannot accept them so that they can put me at ease.*

Overcoming

***

Fall 1993, Islamabad, Pakistan
When I graduated from college, I went to Islamabad for a few days to my sister's house. One day she showed me a promenade in the valley of a green mountain that was probably three or four kilometers away from her house. I went alone on foot to the promenade. When I arrived there, I saw a few men slowly pass me by. Among them I glanced at an attractive and rather chubby man who was probably around thirty-five years old. While passing each other I looked at him, and when we passed each other again I turned my head back to throw another glance at him. While I was staring at him, he noticed me and turned his head toward me. I stopped looking at him and continued to walk on the sidewalk. At the end of the sidewalk, I noticed that man coming toward me, smiling. He said hello and asked how I was doing in a familiar way, as if he knew me already.

One photographer was working there with his camera and took people's pictures. I wanted to take a picture of myself in that promenade, so I asked that man, "How much does the photographer charge for one picture?"

He ignored my words as if he did not understand me. I repeated several words to make him understand: picture, photo, photograph... No matter what I said and pointed to the photographer, he ignored me and continued to talk to me. I spoke a little bit of Urdu, and he spoke a little bit of Pashto. We started talking to each other in our half Urdu and half Pashto. The sun was setting and it was getting dark. While talking to me, he slowly took me to a lonely corner. On a rock we sat side by side as if on a bench. He asked me, "What does your father do?"

"My father died."

He put his hand on my head, pressed his mouth on my face, and kissed me. I thought he was doing it because he felt pity for me.

Again he asked, "Your father is dead. Then how do you make ends meet?"

"It is a hard time, and life is difficult."

With his hand on my shoulder, he again kissed me longer, sucking my lips deeper. While I felt pleasure from what he was doing, I said to myself, *What a strange sense of pity! How he kisses! I wish everyone were sympathetic like this!* When I looked at him and compared myself to him, I didn't expect him to have any interest in me because I was a rustic Afghanistani, and he was a Pakistani—and from Islamabad, at that! And the attractiveness that I saw in him! I never expected that he would want or could take pleasure from my body. He asked me a few more questions, and after the answer to each question, when there was no longer any sympathy or pity, he kissed me quickly and in a strange way. I was now sure that he meant something. Finally, he no longer would let me talk. As soon as I tried to speak, he would start sucking and licking my face and mouth. My heart was throbbing from passion and desire, and I was trembling from head to toe. He said to me, "You want to take a picture?"

I was surprised that he knew from the beginning what I was saying but said nothing at that time.

"Yes, I want to take a picture."

"How many pictures do you want to take, one or two?"

I did not know how to respond quickly and was thinking what to tell him, and he looked at my eye eagerly. At last I said, "One, or maybe two."

As soon as I said one or two, he again pressed on my lips. He said, "Come with me. Let us go get your picture."

He took me with him. It was the very first time in my life that I experienced sex.

I returned to Afghanistan again, and for a long time I had no sex. I always suffered from sexual deprivation.

Part Three

The Spirit of Confusion

In light of the understanding from and the approach to the word *eezak* in Afghanistani society, one may say that it precisely means homo or homosexual, although *apparently* neither eezaks nor homosexuals exist in the Afghanistani society. Because the word eezak in the minds of most Afghanistanis is an undesirable word and is used to taunt, to insult, to revile, and to ridicule, all unfortunate homosexuals, *without exception,* hide their identity from everyone so that no one knows. Gays marry women, lesbians marry men, and even transsexuals marry women. In short, no one knows a homosexual except himself or herself. At the same time, the word *homo* in Afghanistani literature is considered an immoral and dirty word, and writers are wary of even mentioning it. Instead, they use the word *namard,* or impotent. The word *namard* has the prefix *na,* or no, and the adjective *mard*, or male, which means someone who is impotent or sterile.

Afghanistanis extensively use the word *homo* obscenely and the word *impotent* rather politely to insult and to humiliate. Yet they do not know the meaning of homosexuality; to them it is just synonymous with pedophilia. Their understanding of the word *homo* is not that of a homosexual but only the lacking of sexual tendency and sexual power. It is the root cause of their despising the word *homo.* Accordingly, the reason why the words *homo* and *impotent* are regarded as obscene and offensive is not the sense of homosexuality but only the sense of absence of sexual inclination and manliness.

In traditional Afghanistani morality and literature, honor and prestige are summed up in the male sexual power and manliness more than anything else. Therefore, addressing a person as a homo or impotent and accusing him of lacking sexual power and manliness is considered the utmost insult and disrespect. For this reason some Afghanistani men try to present themselves to other people as macho and sexually powerful, and they engage in polygamy in order to acquire more respect and prestige. At the same time, pedophilia—which is synonymous with homosexuality in the Afghanistani mind-set—is not considered a vice because men who engage in this act prove their machismo and manliness. Some feel even proud of themselves and openly keep or associate with young boys. However, if there is a sexual relationship between two adult men, their manliness is questioned, and it becomes the greatest vice and sin in society. Having an adult homosexual relationship in Afghanistani society is absolutely impossible. As soon as the young boys that were once a partner of a pedophile become an adult, they no longer remain with the man because their continued association becomes their greatest vice and shame for both. They are handed over to the law and are forced to cease their relationship. This undoubtedly seems contradictory: how are two adult men handed over to the law for having such a relationship, but an adult man and a young boy can escape the law? But law is nothing other than what the people want it to be. When an adult man enters into this kind of relationship with a young boy, the boy, in light of his soft body and the absence of a beard, is allowed to maintain this relationship as the opposite sex, and the adult man is also allowed to use him as the opposite sex.

The Ugly Truth

The truth exists despite all of its ugliness. Sometimes the truth is so ugly that you do not want to smell, see, or touch it. But with the hiding of the truth or escaping from it, we will not remedy the suffering of needy people.

In the traditional society of Afghanistan and the anarchy state of the government, there are too many people for which faultfinding, ridiculing, and laughing at other people is one of the best pastimes. With this habit they often create tension and violence in society. In such conditions the life for the people with diversities—especially for the weak—has turned to hell. Traditionally, those who do not ridicule others are considered coarse, isolated, and unsocial. Those who ridicule others to make people laugh are considered intelligent, social, and cheerful. But, in the long run this popularity and intelligence turns into hatred and insanity. This kind of pastime becomes habitual for them, and they create many antagonists among the people—even among like-minded others. Often the outward appearance and character of the other party, or their family members and relatives, are used as the source of ridicule. For instances, blindness, deafness, defects in hands and feet, and the like are used to ridicule others.

Many families, villages, regions, and ethnicities are given one or more ridiculous names, and when these names are used, people enjoy and laugh at these jokes. Our family and the families of our uncles and others around us are known as "the crazy Qaleye Niazi." The family of my maternal uncles is known as "the muddle-headed Khaje khil," and all the people of our village are known as "the frog-eater Saghayi."

Several other families and villages in our neighborhood are known by such names: the dog-sucker Mazanchi, the clumsy clod Baghbalayi, the four-legged Sayed Ahmad khil, the paste dough–eater Ferenjali, the garlic-eater Gudareyi, Tah Qaleyi Payinokhor (one who drinks downstream water left after irrigation), Bakhmi Moorkhor (one who eats worms). Many other families and villages are known by such names.

In all parts of Afghanistan, the Uzbeks are known as the feebleminded and the devastator; the Tajiks as the water porter and the milk seller; the Afghans (Pashtuns) as the donkey Avghan, the idiot Avghan, and the tabarghan or jackal Avghan; and the Hazaras as taghare (uneven earthen tub) the nose-less, and the flat-locked Hazara. Many other ethnic groups and regions have been labeled by such silly names. Hindu and Sikh minorities have become isolated for fear of being ridiculed and reviled; they are not seen even in the most modern neighborhoods of the city, and they cannot go to schools and universities.

In these circumstances, if one is identified as a homo, it would become doubly vexatious.

Although making fun of people and creating tension is the habit of ordinary people, they have partisans in the government and the police so that nobody can complain against them.

Even in the 1990s, one professor of Kabul University himself, in collaboration with one or two other distinguished scholars, wrote a book under his nickname about Burhanuddin Rabbani's government. Because Burhanuddin Rabbani was the second Tajik president in the contemporary history of Afghanistan, the professor wrote his book under the title *Dwahume Saqavi*, or *The Second Water-Portership*. Instead of that, if he had written it under the title of The Second Dictatorship, it would not be seen as funny by a university professor and his coauthors; although in that book, they very clearly advised the strategy of ethnic cleansing to the Taliban regime to prevent another repeat of water-portership in the future. (See also Endnote 2 about "The Ariana Encyclopedia" and the "Ethnography Atlas of Non-Afghan Ethnic Groups Living in Afghanistan")

Tradition and Sexuality

In Afghanistan the word *homo*, which is considered as the lacking of sexuality, or without sex, is like the words genie or demon in that no one has ever seen one, but it always remains on the tips of people's tongues. When some people hear or say the word *homo*, they make funny faces, as if they have heard or said something very dirty and nauseating. In Afghanistan I never saw anyone who had been identified as an actual homo. But if someone is identified as an actual homo by the people, he will become the most shameful buffoon of the century. He will be ridiculed and vilified to death—and not only he, but his entire family and his relatives.

* * *

Summer 1998, Kabul
One day in Kabul I was sitting with and talking to two of my neighbors. One of them, in his midthirties, was one of the noble residents of Kabul and was quite a cultured person. He had passed twelve grades at the school and had lived for a period in Pakistan. Because he had lived there for some time, he said about Pakistan, "Wherever you go in Pakistan, you will see lots of homos. But in our dear Afghanistan you will not see any homo at all. So far I have not seen even one in Afghanistan."

Overcoming

I was sitting there, and I said to myself, *Can a homo breathe in this atmosphere of terror? Here, among these three men, at least one is a homo. How can you speculate that there is not even one in the entirety of Afghanistan?*

* * *

Fall 2000, Kabul
I come originally from the village of Chahardeh in the provincial town of Ghourband in the Province of Parwan. When I was seven years old, we moved to Kabul and settled there.

In the year 2000, the total population of Chahardeh was no more than four or five thousand people, of which only 10 percent actually lived in the village; 90 percent were in various cities of Afghanistan and overseas. One of those families, whom I had never seen and did not know, had left Chahardeh several years ago and moved to the Balkh province, in northern Afghanistan. One of the boys of the family married a girl, and three or four months after their marriage she left her husband and came to her mother's house. She did so because the boy had failed to consummate their marriage. After the return of the girl to her parents' house, this news circulated among the people of Chahardeh, and soon many of those living in various cities of Afghanistan, and even overseas, learned of this news.

We lived in Kabul and they lived in Balkh. I did not know their family at all. Yet I heard several people say, "The son of so and so married the daughter of so and so in Balkh. For four months he could not have sex with his wife. Ultimately the girl became unhappy and returned to her parents' house."

When people heard this news, they were so surprised, as if the poor boy had developed two horns on his head. Some would say, "Wow, he couldn't do anything to his wife? What a shame!"

When people showed such a reaction behind his back, one can only imagine how he would be treated face-to-face. Would such a childish behavior not result in his facing the stone-throwing children?

This boy had married for fear of being ridiculed as a homo by his own people. I told myself that he was a fool to marry because of peer pressure, and I promised never to make a laughingstock of myself because of what people would say.

* * *

Spring 1999 – Kabul
I was invited to a marriage ceremony of one of my classmates in the Cheharqale neighborhood of Vazirabad. About twenty people were sitting in a large room before the dinner was served. Most of them were educated and so-called intellectuals. No one spoke; there was absolute silence in the room. Suddenly a transsexual, who looked half man and half woman, entered the room and said in a soft, feminine voice, "Hi everybody!" He walked coquettishly like a woman and sat in a corner. As soon as he said hello, the silence was suddenly broken, and everyone started laughing. Groups of two or three people started whispering to each other.

A very close friend of mine from the university, named Saleem, was sitting beside me. He laughed, brought his mouth close to my ear, and started talking about another transsexual. He said, "One homo lives close to our house in the neighborhood." He wanted to continue his story, but I became very angry by the foolish laughter of the party. I angrily disrupted him and said, "I don't like fault-finding and backbiting."

When I said this, Saleem felt ashamed and said nothing more. I sat on the left side of Saleem, and there was another person sitting on his right side who knew this transsexual. When he heard the word *homo* from Saleem, he said, "No, he is not a homo. I know him. He is our neighbor. He is married, and a year has passed since his marriage."

Those words made me very sad. I felt a lump in my throat and wanted to cry. I said to myself, *I have quite a manly appearance, and no one has any doubts about me, yet I cannot marry. Whereas this man, who is altogether feminine in appearance, did marry. Why did he make his life even more hellish?* I saw such rudeness in this party, where the majority of people were university-educated intellectuals. What could one expect from the people who were illiterate and whose hobby it was to ridicule others?

It was not the first time that I saw such rudeness and impudence in this party where the majority of people were university educated; I had seen even worse in the university environment and in other places. But it was the first time where they pretended to be so highbrow, yet they behaved in such a lowly and shameless manner.

How the transsexuals suffer in Afghanistan may not be comprehensible for some. But if one imagines oneself to be a man with all the habits, behaviors, and face of a woman living among the traditional society of Afghanistan, one might better understand how they suffer in their lives.

This transsexual who had married a girl was a genuine Kabuli and was among the most cultured people of Afghanistan. When a Kabuli transsexual gives in and marries a woman to escape ridicule, imagine the pressure transsexuals and homosexuals face from villages, especially those living in far-off villages of Afghanistan, where no one is literate!

* * *

Summer 1999, Kabul
Various types of violence are another example of mistreatment that give greater dimensions to the limitations imposed on this group, in addition to the mental pressures arising from social maltreatment. Apart from the fact that they are subjected to violence in society by traditionalists, not even because of their acts of sexuality but also because of their feminine habits and conduct, at the same time they are also subjected to violence by their own family due to disrepute and shame.

During the rule of the Taliban, when the Taliban set fire to villages and towns in the region of Kohdaman and expelled the people from that place, we assigned one room to a woman from

Kohdaman who had become displaced, and she started to live with us at that time. One day that woman was talking to my mother together with two or three other guests. I did not notice what initially made them talk about the homos, but I heard the woman talk about one in her own old neighborhood. She said, "There was no homo in our neighborhood. Only years ago there was one who acted like a homo; he spoke like the girls, was coquettish, wore a scarf, and sometimes put on the clothes of his mother or sister. Because of that habit, his brothers beat him up whenever they got angry. Because his brothers used to beat him a lot, he ran away from his house one day and came to Kabul. Nobody knew his whereabouts for some time, until his brothers found out his address and came to Kabul and killed him."

* * *

Circa 1994 or 1995, Kabul
One of the main reasons for the complete disappearance of transvestites and transsexuals in Afghanistani society may be the fact that they are subjected to violence by their families because of the supposed disrepute and shame brought on the family; quite possibly many of them are killed by their own family during the early years of the appearance of their feminine and transsexual habits and behavior. But I have also seen some disturbing cases among the mentally ill people: those who were confused and were not sure whether they were men or women.

I remember neither the exact time nor the place, but when I saw one of those mentally ill people for the first time and doubted whether he was a man or woman, I thought that perhaps mental illness had gradually affected his face and changed it so much that even his gender had become ambiguous. But soon I thought about myself and said, "No, from the beginning he had a feminine condition more than I have, and for that reason has been ridiculed and hurt and humiliated so much that he has completely lost his nerves and has become completely insane." I then said to myself: This is your future; the sooner you come out of the closet, the sooner your future will be here.

Superstition

Superstition is the other side of the coin. While Afghanistan is still steeped in superstition, sexual discrimination and sexual humiliation are on top of the list of its superstitions. Most Afghanistanis believe that bears and pigs are the meanest and dirtiest animals on earth. At the same time they believe that a man without hair and a woman with hair, on face and body, are worse than the bear and pig.

I had a Hazara friend named Feda. He was in his late twenties and had a college diploma. Most Hazara people are hairless, but Feda was hairy. He used to say, "If you spit on a hairless man or a hairy woman, it has a lot of divine reward. But you have to do it in such a way that they don't realize it."

With the problem I had in Afghanistan, I understood the problem of the hairless men and hairy women. I replied to Feda, "I don't believe these old wives' tales, and there is no divine reward in work."

Feda retorted, "Do you know about the divine reward, or does God know? Are you more intelligent than God? He says there is a divine reward, and you say there is none!"

* * *

Spring 1998, Kabul
One day during the rule of the Taliban, I heard that the Taliban in the Maryam College market had painted the faces of two

young men with motor oil, had put them behind a pickup truck, and drove the truck slowly down the street. The two young men called out, "Anyone who commits pederasty will have a fate worse than ours!" The truck moved by, and they continued to repeat this sentence. When I heard this, I asked myself, *If you do nothing, these ignorant people should not ridicule you as a homo.*

Of course this has been the ancient law in Afghanistan, and it will always be there. This law did not come into effect with the coming of the Taliban, and it will not go away with the Taliban's departure. The Taliban displayed this kind of punishment to serve as an example to others. The men they arrested as pedophiles were punished on Fridays after the prayers by pulling down a wall on them. The Taliban announced on the radio the execution of pedophiles and other criminals one day before Friday. I heard this announcement several times, "Tomorrow, after the Friday prayers, Sharia punishment for pedophiles will be executed in a public space in such and such city."

In addition to pedophiles, the Taliban punished other criminals on Fridays after the prayers in gyms, hanging their dead bodies and their severed hands or legs for several days or even one week in intersections and heavy traffic thoroughfares, so that people would draw a lesson from it. Sometimes they even hung the bodies of those who had committed no such crimes—for example, people like Dr. Najibullah and his brother, who were hung on the gallows for a few days in an orchard in downtown Kabul. There was no lesson to be drawn in their case.

Part Four

My Life Is Only an Example

When I realized that I was attracted to my own sex, first I thought that perhaps my attraction would change in the future to the opposite sex, and I would become straight like others. Sometimes I wanted to tell others that I was attracted to men and had no feelings for women. But because I lived in Afghanistan and was quite familiar with the thoughts and habits of people, I knew that if I spoke one word in this respect, I would face a host of difficulties. I feared that not only would people make fun of me, but also my own family would think I had psychological issues, and they would take me to a psychiatrist every day until I actually became psychotic. I was not sure that I would face any violence upon disclosing my sexual orientation, but if I had come out of the closet, it was quite possible that I would have been subjected to violence. I could not trust anyone, not even the closest members of my family.

At that time, when I knew nothing about the outside world, I thought that perhaps all the people of the world were at the same intellectual level as the people of Afghanistan. Of course my perception of the outside world at that time was not too far-fetched, because human thought has changed very rapidly during recent years; yesterday's world was backward, and today's world is progressive. But unfortunately far-flung and poor countries like Afghanistan have not been able to bring about rapid intellectual change. People of poor and backward countries are still centuries behind the developed and prosperous countries. It is not an exaggeration to say that in poor countries, including Afghanistan, there has been some intellectual growth—albeit slow growth—but still there are innumerable issues that need to be addressed.

At the time when I was thinking whether or not to come out of the closet, people's thinking in Afghanistan was so horrible that if someone said something out of the ordinary that people had not heard before, the speaker would face violent opposition or would be labeled crazy. I myself was called crazy for expressing my views on economic, social, and other issues, and many of my friends and family ridiculed me as a wacko. Even at the university, many of my classmates called me crazy. There were others who shared the same fate, and no one listened to us in the educational circles. At that time, people in Afghanistan believed that one must not get too much education, or else one would go crazy. I had seen a number of educated people with different views on certain intellectual issues who were regarded as mad. But others who were not educated were popular among the people because of their traditional views. I had heard a lot about the Dark Age in Europe from my teachers during my school days. They said that the European ignorance ultimately came to an end under the influence of the Arabs in Spain and France. This surprised me so much, and I would say to myself, *How strange! They talk of the Dark Age in Europe, but no one says in what age we are living now!*

People were very sensitive about sexual issues. I had become known as crazy or mentally retarded for speaking out on everyday issues. If I spoke out on sexual issues, what infamy would I acquire? Perhaps they would call me the craziest, the most disgraced and most ridiculous person on earth. I had joined an English learning center for a time. To some, this action seemed extremely ridiculous—how can a mentally retarded person learn the English language?

Overcoming

* * *

I used to think that perhaps my sexual orientation would change in the near future, but with the passage of time, not only did it not change, it became stronger. Finally, by the age of nineteen or twenty, I lost all hope of change in my sexual orientation, and I started to think of finding a way to save myself from a terrible future in backward Afghanistan. By this time, I had graduated from college and was preparing to go to university. But the buildings of Kabul University and other universities had by this time turned into the front lines of war between various warring factions, which used those buildings as bunkers. Those skirmishes lasted three years in Kabul, after which the faction led by Burhanuddin Rabbani, who headed the government, drove the competition out of Kabul, and the university opened again.

At that time I decided to seriously pursue my education and to make up for my neglect of the past. During my entire college courses, I had neglected my studies and passed with poor grades. Due to war conditions, teachers hardly failed any students; everyone passed with minimally acceptable grades. In order to prepare myself for the competitive entrance exams, I enrolled for mathematics, physics, and chemistry with a teaching institute. I also thought of my bleak future due to my sexual orientation. I thought that because I would not be able to marry in the future, people would constantly ridicule me until I became psychotic. At that time, psychological problems in Afghanistan were contagious like influenza, and those suffering from it affected others too. The culture of ridicule reflected the fact that people were indeed psychotic—by ridiculing others, they turned them into psychotics.

To avoid ridicule in the future for not marrying, and to have an excuse for not marrying, I figured perhaps it would be better to remain uneducated, unemployed, and poor. If people asked me why I did not marry, I could say that I had no money or income, and I could not afford a wife. Again, I would think that if people found out in the future that I was attracted to men or that at least I was not attracted to women, they would ridicule me. Children would follow me everywhere and hit me with stones. This triggered the childhood memory of *Babeh nadareh*. I remembered the old men whom children followed and pelted with stones. I had other terrible memories too, but the memory of *Babeh nadareh* was the first one that had shaken me to the core; seeing any other terrible event only reminded me of that one.

To avoid ridicule, I thought of leaving Afghanistan in the future. Of course sexual deprivation was also unbearable, but ridicule was the greater evil. I thought of going to Pakistan or Iran because other countries were beyond my means and out of the question. I thought, *if I go to Pakistan or Iran, why pursue education? It would do me no good. Whatever I may be here, there I would be nothing but a laborer. Why work hard for education?*

Then again, I thought to myself, *if I go to Pakistan or Iran, my education may do me no good, but at least they would not humiliate me for being uneducated. So, as long as I am in Afghanistan, I will study so that if anyone humiliates me in Pakistan or Iran, I can say to them, "If I am not more educated than you, at least I am no less educated than you. If you think you are superior to me, perhaps you are here in your country, but outside it, you are exactly as I am."*

* * *

Finally I decided to go to university, and after I had completed my education, I would leave Afghanistan and go to Pakistan, or preferably to Iran. I prepared for the competitive entrance exams. The number of participants was very low, so the possibility of acceptance was high. I was accepted in the field of pharmacy and pursued my studies to the end for four years.

I finished my first year at the university during the rule of the Mujahedin. When I was halfway through the second year, the Taliban arrived in Kabul. With their arrival the university remained closed for several months. Based on my earlier decision to leave Afghanistan, I wanted to leave Afghanistan right away before completing my university course. The arrival of the Taliban or the Americans or any other group made no difference for me; I had to leave Afghanistan. Whatever change in regime, the people were the same people, and they were driving me crazy.

After the university closed, I wanted to leave Afghanistan and go to Iran. I had no money to go to Iran, but among the people of our village there was one human trafficker who took people to Iran without charging any money in advance; he took it from them later in Iran.

When I decided to go to Iran, I said to my maternal uncle, who was three or four years younger than me, "I want to go to Iran. Do you want to come with me?"

He said, "What will we do in Iran?"

"We'll work in Iran for some time, and when we have saved enough, we will go to Turkey. We will work in Turkey for a while and save money and then move on to another country. Ultimately, we'll go to a very good country."

"When do you want to leave?"

The trafficker was named Vahid. I said to my uncle, "Vahid has come from Iran and is taking men there. If you don't have money, he'll take you there without money. He'll collect his fee from you in Iran."

"Okay, let us go to Vahid and talk to him."

We went to see Vahid. He said to us, "Get ready to move by next week. Other travelers are ready to move. We'll start next week."

My and my uncle's problem was that people in our family would not allow us to go to Iran. If we did so, we had to run away from the family. If the family got any hint of our plans, they would tell Vahid the trafficker not to take us with him. Without the family's permission, he would not dare take us with him. My uncle said to me, "It is better not to tell them at all. We'll go without telling the family."

There were lots of young men in Afghanistan who suddenly disappeared after fighting with the family, and some who left without any fight. Months or years later, they reappeared in Pakistan or Iran.

I replied to my uncle, "I am already known as crazy. I don't want to go any further and be known as raving mad. I won't go until I get my family's permission."

"My family will not permit it. We have no choice but to go without their permission."

"I will get permission from my family; you tell nothing to yours."

"Fine. Even if they don't allow you, I'll go alone, by myself."

I told my older brother and my mother that I wanted to go to Iran, but they did not allow me to go. I insisted and they wouldn't budge.

My uncle was still going to leave home without his family's permission. I thought that if something happened to him, they would blame me. Thus, the day he was to leave, I told my older uncle what was going to happen. My older uncle told the trafficker not to take my younger uncle with him. Thus, he too did not leave.

The Family Trap

March 1999, Kabul

Long before I went to the university, I had made a serious decision to leave Afghanistan. But after I graduated my mother and I remained alone in our house, and her responsibility fell on my shoulders. I had seven brothers and sisters. According to seniority in age, the oldest among us was our sister Hangameh, the second one was our sister Afsaneh, there were our two brothers, Navid and Valid, and then there was myself. At the end was our younger sister Jananeh, and the youngest one was our sister Mastaneh.

At the time when I wanted to go to Iran but could not, two of my brothers, Navid and Valid, and two of my sisters, Hangameh and Jananeh, immigrated to Moscow first. After some time Navid and Jananeh left Moscow for London, and Valid and Hangameh immigrated to Netherlands. My two other sisters, Afsaneh and Mastaneh, married in Afghanistan. Thus, my mother and I remained alone at home.

We brothers and sisters did not call our mother Mom, but we called her by her honorific title, Marjan. My mother's actual name was Gowhar, but after her marriage my grandma gave her the honorific title of Marjan. Before that, the wives of four of my older uncles were given the titles of Deljan, Guljan, Shirinjan, and Parijan. Rhyming her name with their names, my grandma called my mother Marjan.

In Afghanistan, people usually give honorific titles to their daughters-in-law and sons-in-law; usually rhyming names are considered. Rhyming is also generally used in naming their children. In the villages of Afghanistan some people call their mother and father by the titles given to them. We did this in our village. All relatives from my father's side addressed her as Marjan and spoke of her to others as Marjan. But if we spoke of her, we said Marjanam (my Marjan); if we addressed her directly, we said Marjan only. Thus, it will be easier for me to speak of my mother as Marjanam or my Marjan.

* * *

When all of my brothers and sisters either left Afghanistan or married, my Marjan and I remained alone at home. Therefore, I could no longer leave her completely alone and depart Afghanistan. I was afraid of having a terrible future in backward Afghanistan, so I wanted to leave my Marjan with Afsaneh and move out of Afghanistan. Meanwhile, Navid, who had immigrated to London, and I hoped that he would help me financially and I too would immigrate to London. I had no expectations from Valid because he was a self-centered and money-loving person from his childhood; he always took care of only himself and cared for no one else. Jananeh was careless and did not even take care of herself. Hangameh was selfish and contradictory; she wanted to be unique in all respects and could not see anyone in the family at her level. In short, Navid was my only hope for financial support, without which I could not move to London. But my Marjan was by no means ready to let me go and leave Afghanistan.

She had built a house in Afghanistan, and we lived in our privately owned house. Afsaneh lived in a rented house. I repeatedly told my Marjan that Afsaneh and her husband should move their furniture to her house, and I should leave Afghanistan. But my Marjan opposed their joining her. She wanted me to live with her until the end of her life. She never said to me directly that I should stay with her to the end, but that's what she wanted. She would say, "Don't hurry to go overseas; with the passing of time, everything will be okay." Hangameh, who was in Netherlands, was opposed to me in her heart, but she pretended to support me. She told me not to hurry and that she would arrange for me in the future to join her in Netherlands. But no energy and desire was left in me to remain in Afghanistan. My past experience and my Marjan and Hangameh's behavior toward me told that they were not sympathetic to me. But I was not cheeky enough to talk to them seriously. They had won Navid's heart tactfully and persuaded him not to give me any financial support from London.

Ignoring my Marjan's wishes was the greatest challenge for me. After years of pain and suffering, she had recently achieved the greatest desire of her life: she lived in her own house, some of her children lived overseas and sent money for her, and she had another one living with her to serve as her servant. She was living in such comfort that she could not have imagined it in her wildest dreams, and she was not at all prepared to let go of this situation. My Marjan was an illiterate woman, but she was exceptionally tactful in her acts and deeds. She knew perfectly well that if she openly opposed my going overseas and did not allow Navid to give me financial support, I would still leave. She also knew that for me, Afghanistan was hell, yet she and Hangameh always delayed my departure from Afghanistan by making empty promises.

With the passing of time, their actual intentions became clearer. More or less, all human beings have a sixth sense in them. My sixth sense told me that even if my Marjan and Hangameh owned this world, still they would not do the favor of sending me overseas. Nevertheless, I completely complied with their wishes, thinking their promise would perhaps be fulfilled one day. Thus, after my graduation from university, I was forced to remain in Afghanistan for two full years and to put up with the backward Afghanistani traditions and culture.

* * *

I had concealed my feminine traits to some extent by play-acting, but I was not at all like a normal man in terms of manliness. Although homosexuals in Afghanistan did not have an external existence, the people who find faults in others are very competent in their skills. Some people were not completely sure about me, so they hesitantly called me eezak and sister. The fact that they called me eezak and sister was not important for me, but what offended me in the extreme was my fear of coming out of the closet and the resulting ridicule for the rest of my life.

I became depressed with every passing day. I was afraid that if I did not marry in the future, people would realize that I had a sexual problem, and I would become a laughingstock. This thought always triggered the childhood memory of *Babeh nadareh*, which made me even more depressed.

During the Taliban government, when I remained alone at home with my Marjan, all family and friends told me every day that my Marjan was alone and had no one to help her in her daily chores, so I should marry immediately so that she had some help.

I was already worried about my future, but now, in the age of twenty-three, the loneliness of my Marjan became doubly vexatious for me. She and others told me every day, "Why don't you marry? For how long you wish to remain single?" And each time I made one excuse or another to not listen to them.

* * *

Any time I asked my Marjan to allow me to leave Afghanistan, she would say, "If you want to leave Afghanistan, don't ask for my permission. Go to whichever country you can on your own. I have not chained your feet."

I had no money to go anywhere, and my Marjan saw me at the edge of the precipice. She knew that if I left Afghanistan without the financial support of Navid, a difficult future would await me. If my Marjan did not allow it, Navid would not help me in any way. Thus, she would frustrate my plans but would not admit that she was stopping me from leaving.

Once I said to her, "I foresee a very bad future for Afghanistan. War will turn Afghanistan from bad to worse. If the war comes to an end, Afghanistan has nothing to fall back on for its economy. At that time the consequences of the past war will appear. Now, when there is a war in Afghanistan, foreign aid is coming here for the continuation of the war; people are living off the war. But in the future, when the war is over, foreign aid will cease. The only way I see for the salvation of Afghanistan's future is the control of the growth of population. Today, when the people do not have peace and all of them are displaced and scattered all over, the population is increasing twofold every ten years. Tomorrow, when the war is over and the people have peace, the population will multiply tenfold every decade. It is then that life in Afghanistan will become really hard. Today, when Navid can and wants to help me go to London, you do not allow him to help me. Tomorrow, when he can't and won't want to help me, you will not accept the fact that you have ruined my life."

My Marjan, who had never listened to anyone in her life, said to me, "Listen, son! Don't tell me anything about any decisions you have made for your future. Do whatever you think is best for you. If you have any problems in the future, don't bother me about it every day. You are nagging me so much now and making my life so miserable. God knows what problems you'll cause me in the future."

"But you don't allow Navid to help me to leave Afghanistan."

"Go wherever you want to go—I haven't chained your feet. You are not so important that I would depend on you and would not let you go. If you want to go, then go. I won't say anything to you or to Navid."

"So if I tell Navid to send me money to leave, you'll agree to live with Afsaneh, so that Navid will accept my departure?"

"You are in such a hurry and so jealous. You think that everyone left and became rich; you remained here and did not become rich. So go. I don't depend on you or on Afsaneh. I can take care of myself, and I will live alone."

"Okay. Then I'll tell Navid to send money for me, and I'll leave. Don't tell him that I left without your permission."

"You and Navid and Afsaneh be damned! I do not depend on anyone, and I will not talk to any one of you."

* * *

One day I told my Marjan, "If you expect me to marry and bring you a helper, I'll never marry in my life. What you expect from other people's daughters, you should expect the same from your own."

She replied, "I am not so shameless that I will bring water for my son-in-law to take a shower."

This is what My Marjan always said that, *I have my pride and would not bring water for my son-in-law to bathe.* What she meant was that she didn't want to see him sleep with her daughter and then take a shower in her house!

Had I left Afghanistan without my Marjan's permission, people would have said that I deserted my old mother and left her alone, and at the same time Navid would not have helped me. I was caught in a dilemma: People told me my Marjan was alone and I should marry, but I wanted to leave Afghanistan.

* * *

Because I regarded my Marjan as the only obstacle for my salvation from a terrible future in Afghanistan, I unconsciously treated her badly, and our life together became stressful for both of us. I hurt her like crazy: I would pick fights with her every day without any reason. She too would make no concessions. Most of the time we would not tolerate each other and would argue about the smallest things.

Overcoming

I always tried to hurt her financially. Sometimes when she spoke of money, I would say in front of others, "You are a very materialistic person. Have you worshipped the carpets and utensils in the house today?"

I enjoyed cheating my Marjan and taking her money, due to the conflict we had with each other. I always got money from her via one excuse or another. At the beginning, she did not realize that whenever I got money from her on whatever excuse, it was always more than what I needed. Later, when she realized it, she became more careful about me. But I thought of stranger excuses and took more money from her. Ultimately, it came to a point where my Marjan had no faith in me and never sought any help from me in any matter. If help was needed in shopping in the market, she would seek help from my uncle's or aunt's family or even from strangers—but not from me.

One day my cousin said to me, "When I see you and Marjan, I don't believe that you are mother and son."

I asked, "Why don't you believe it?"

"Because I haven't seen any mother and son treating each other the way you do."

"So what kind of relationship do you think we have with each other?"

"You seem quite like a young sister and brother who always oppose each other and have no forgiveness."

* * *

Summer 2000, Kabul
When I could not leave Afghanistan, I thought that I was stuck there until the end of my life and that people would ridicule me because I could not marry. I knew that there were many other people like me who had the same problem that I had, but they married so that people would not belittle them as *eezak* or a homo. Ultimately, I decided to test myself with a woman. If I was able to have sex with her, I would marry; if not, I would leave Afghanistan one way or another.

In terms of sex, men stimulated me sexually. If I wanted, I could act like a butch toward my men. But acting as a dominant partner in sex gave me no pleasure; I only wanted to have passive sex with men. I had no sexual feelings for women. When I decided to test myself with a woman, I was imposing this as a task on myself; I had no interest in having pleasure with a woman.

While I was thinking of testing myself, my neighbor Jooya said to me one day, "The widow sister of the street tailor is depraved."

"What do you mean by depraved?" I asked.

"She wanted me to fuck her, but I didn't."

When he said those words, I thought of trying it myself with her. I asked. "Why didn't you fuck her?"

Hearing my words, Jooya's mouth watered and his throat dried. He gulped air and said. "No particular reason."

"If you are really sure that she is depraved, let's both fuck her."

My words were music to Jooya's ears, and he said. "I didn't think you liked to fuck; otherwise, I would have asked you. Actually, there is no place to fuck her, either in my house or in hers."

Only my Marjan and I lived in the house. She often would go to my sister's and my aunt's house, and I would be alone at home. I said to Jooya, "Here, we have a place in our house. You know that my Marjan is often out of the house, and I am alone."

We agreed that whenever my Marjan was not at home, Jooya would bring the tailor's sister with him to my place.

Two or three days later, my Marjan went to see Mastaneh, my younger sister, and I remained alone at home. I told Jooya to bring the tailor's sister with him. When they came, I was afraid of trying it myself, but Jooya took off his shirt immediately and went inside the room with the tailor's sister. Hardly two or three minutes had passed when he opened the door and came out.

I asked, "What did you do?"

Jooya replied, "Our job is done."

"So quickly?"

"I don't know why. As soon as I inserted it in her, I came. You go too, and finish it quickly."

I went inside the room with the tailor's sister. My feet moved, but not my heart. Jooya, who had come quickly, did not satisfy the tailor's sister; she was still hungry and expected me to satisfy her. But when I looked at her hungry face, I felt disgusted to touch her body. In whatever way I tried to stimulate myself, I could not get it on. She wanted to help me, but the more she "helped," the worse it became. Finally I put on my clothes and opened the door.

Jooya asked, "Job done?" I said nothing. He asked me again emphatically, "Have you finished your job or not?"

"Yes, I have."

"I gather from the way you said it that perhaps you have not been able to do it. Have you or not?"

"Yes, I made love to her."

He asked the tailor's sister, "Is he telling the truth?"

She was still in need of a fix and said, "No." She immediately went to Jooya and embraced him. As soon as she embraced Jooya, he got excited again and said to me, "Hamid, go outside."

I went outside the room, and this time he satisfied her. She stayed with us for two hours. Jooya wanted to force me to make love to the tailor's sister. I tried two more times, but each time I lost my spirits and became more disgusted. At the end, Jooya made love to her one more time. I came to the conclusion that I should never marry and should leave Afghanistan to avoid people's ridicule.

* * *

December 2000, Kabul
Two years had passed since my graduation from the university. My Marjan's stubbornness continued, and I was still stuck in Afghanistan. As the saying goes, "Goat, goat, do not die, since Solomon's barley will come." It simply means that patience is a

virtue. But I thought that if I kept waiting and hoping for Solomon's barley to come, my Marjan would keep promising to send me overseas at the appropriate time, a few more years would pass, and I would not be able to recover the time I had already lost. So I thought to make use of the remaining time and of my own abilities, as to escape the hell that was awaiting me. I thought of the best and most respectable way of leaving Afghanistan. I said to myself that during the past two years, my Marjan and Hangameh had fooled me by their cunning; now it was time to pay them back in their own coin. If I acted obstinately, Navid would become difficult and would not help me.

I thought of finding a few fierce-looking Taliban and bribing them to come to my place and to pretend to arrest me on charges of political offense. If my Marjan saw them, she herself would ask me to leave Afghanistan. In fact, the Taliban were not local Kabulis but were essentially from the south. However, some local Kabulis had also joined them. I spoke to one of them whom I knew, but he freaked out and did not agree to do it.

I also spoke to my cousin Siavash in this respect and asked him to help me if he could. He laughed and said, "Very interesting; it is the best scheme to escape from Afghanistan. If you don't succeed in this, there is no way out for you."

I said to him, "If I can't escape from the trap of these simple Afghanistanis, how can I escape from the trap of foreigners if I ever go to a foreign country?"

Siavash laughed and said, "You are right, indeed."

Siavash and I shared the same views in every respect, especially about the elders of our family, whom we held responsible for our miserable lives. One of the classmates of Siavash had joined the Taliban, and luckily he was one of those tramps who feared nothing. He had assumed a very fierce Taliban-like appearance, which in the view of the Kabulis was completely barbarian. Siavash and I spoke to this classmate of Siavash and said to him, "We'll give you two million Afghanis if you come to my house to arrest me, and let me escape from the house."

He showed us two of his friends who also looked fearsome like the Taliban and said, "The three of us will appear at the front door of your house and let you escape from the back door."

I knew my Marjan's stubbornness too well; I knew only one threat of arrest would not convince her to let me escape. Therefore, I planned it in such a way that the Taliban would arrange my escape in three stages. I thought that if I left Afghanistan, I needed to get my passport ready in advance. I told them about this and said, "Give me a few days time so I get my passport and obtain a Pakistani visa as well. Then you proceed with the plan."

In the past, those Taliban who wore their special garments and turbans and applied *sorme* or kohl to their eyes seemed barbarous and terrifying to me. When I first saw Siavash's classmate and his friends in the Taliban garments, I became happy and thought that if my Marjan saw them like this, she would be afraid of them and would force me to leave Afghanistan. From the day I arranged my escape from Afghanistan with the help of the Taliban, the more I saw them in the terrifying Taliban outfit, the more they seemed gentler and nicer. Now I needed their fierce Taliban appearance so that my Marjan would be frightened and would let me go from Afghanistan. I came to the conclusion that external beauty and ugliness was nothing; it was the internal appearance that mattered.

I obtained a Pakistani passport and visa. At that time Pakistan, Saudi Arabia, and the United Arab Emirates were the only countries that recognized the Taliban government; they had their embassies in Kabul. I obtained my passport and visa, and at the initial stage, the Taliban brought a fake warrant of arrest at my house and served it to my Marjan. The summons read, "Hamid must appear before Police Station Four within forty-eight hours."

My Marjan took the letter from the hands of the Taliban, looked at it, and immediately realized my scheme. She said to me, "I know that this letter is nothing but your own plan. I'll go and talk to the Taliban myself. You always tell me you don't like to live in Afghanistan."

In order to stop her from taking the fake letter to the police station and showing it to them, I said to her, "Let me see what it says in the letter, and why do you say that it's my plan?"

I took the letter from her hand, threw a glance at it, tore it to pieces, and said, "The Taliban are crazy. Why should I go to the police station? I'll never go."

My Marjan went to the police station and made inquiries. They told her that they do not know anything about the summons, but if there is one, the party concerned should appear before the police station so they could speak to him. My Marjan returned and told me, "You can't deceive me—you sent that summons through someone so as to escape on this excuse. I raised you so you would be some help in my old age, and I am a proud person and won't live with my son-in-law."

I didn't reply but said to myself, *All right, say whatever you want to say. Later we'll see who is more stubborn.*

Three days later the Taliban soldier with two of his friends knocked on the door. My cousin Siavash, who was a part of this plan, was already at home. It was agreed that when the Taliban knocked at the door, we'd let my Marjan open the door, and then Siavash would join them and talk to the Taliban in the presence of my Marjan. But when they knocked on the door, the woman who was our neighbor and lived in our house opened the door before my Marjan could open it. When Siavash went to talk to them, the Taliban grabbed Siavash by the collar of his shirt, hit him and kicked him several times, and took him with them. The woman came running and recounted for my Marjan how Siavash was beaten and kicked and arrested.

A little later Siavash returned and said to me in the presence of my Marjan, "The Taliban asked me where you were. I told them that you had disappeared and we have no news of you for the last three days. I said that I did not know your whereabouts. They took me with them and threatened to put me in prison unless I found you for them. Later they released me and said that you should report to them personally. As long as you are being pursued by them, I'll not be able to come to your house."

I did not look at my Marjan but said to Siavash and the woman, "The Taliban might come back. I'll escape from here and will go to Afsaneh's place."

I jumped the wall of the back neighbor and went to Afsaneh's house from the back alley. A little while later my Marjan, accompanied by my aunt and grandmother, came after me; she had decided to go to the police station and pick a fight with them. But Afsaneh, my aunt and grandmother, scolded my Marjan and did not allow her to go to the police station. They said that I should escape from Afghanistan. But my Marjan still persisted and would not allow me to leave. Sometimes she would say that we would go to Mazar Sharif, and sometimes to Herat. In short, she wanted to move from one place to another, but she would not permit me to leave Afghanistan.

Now that I had outwitted her, I told her seriously, "I will no longer allow you to make decisions about my life. I know where to go. I'll go to some place where the danger of the Taliban will not threaten me."

When I spoke seriously, Afsaneh's husband, Zahed, who was sitting there, yelled at my Marjan and said, "Why do you want him to fall in the hands of the Taliban? There is no difference between Kabul, Mazar Sharif, and Herat. Wherever you go in Afghanistan, the Taliban are there. He has no choice but to leave Afghanistan."

My aunt, grandmother, and Afsaneh also supported Zahed and scolded my Marjan. At that point in time, going to the regions under the control of the Taliban's opponents and crossing the frontlines was more difficult and more dangerous than escaping overseas. Otherwise my Marjan would have insisted that I go to those areas under control of the Taliban's opponents. Thus, I outmaneuvered my Marjan... but she did not let me escape alone from Afghanistan. I stayed in Afsaneh's house for several days while my Marjan obtained a passport and a Pakistani visa. She joined me in the minibus, and we set out for Jalalabad and from there to Pakistan. Zahed accompanied us up to Jalalabad. My passport with the Pakistani visa was in my pocket, and she had no knowledge I'd prepared it.

When we arrived in Jalalabad, I left my Marjan and Zahed in a hotel and said, "I am going to the passport office to see what is going on, and whether I can get a passport." I went outside and walked on the streets for a couple of hours. When I returned I told my Marjan, "Getting a passport from the passport office is a tedious job. I have found out a man who charges five thousand *kaldars* and gives the passport quickly. He also gets Pakistani visas."

The Pakistani rupee is known as a *kaldar*. Due to instability of the Afghani currency at that time, the Pakistani rupee was more popular in Afghanistani markets.

When I said five thousand *kaldars*, her eyes popped out from their sockets, and she said, "Wow, wow, five thousand? Don't get the passport; it's not worth it. I'll rent a house here in Jalalabad, and we'll stay here."

Zahed, who was sitting there, suddenly became furious and said, "What is five thousand, for which you are so stingy? Actually it is quite cheap if they give him a passport and visa quickly for five thousand. If the Taliban arrest him, can you get him out for five thousand? Give him the money immediately and let him get the passport."

My Marjan's hand reluctantly went inside her purse, and she gave me five thousand Pakistani rupees. I put the money in my pocket, went outside, walked for a couple of hours, and returned, showing the passport to my Marjan and Zahed. The sight of the passport made Zahed very happy. We got up and set out toward Pakistan. Zahed accompanied us up to the Pakistani border. When the Pakistani police allowed us to enter the Pakistani territory, we said good-bye to Zahed, who returned to Kabul.

Part Five

Arrival in Pakistan

29 January 2001, Peshawar, Pakistan

After our arrival in Pakistan, we headed to the city of Peshawar. We had a few family and friends there. We temporarily moved in with a friend who was from the same village as us, and our two families knew each other. When we came to their house, first we sat down and talked to them for a couple of hours. Then my Marjan took the telephone and spoke to Hangameh in Netherlands. "The Taliban came to arrest Hamid, but luckily they could not. We escaped and came to Pakistan. Now we cannot go back to Afghanistan. Right now we are sitting in Dr. Mubin's house. You know their telephone number. I'll hang up so that they don't have to pay. You call us again!"

When my Marjan finished and hug up the phone, Hangameh and her husband Mazdak were on fire. They immediately dialed back, and while the conference button of their phone was on, they taunted and reproached my Marjan and said whatever came to their mind right in front of Dr. Mubin's family.

They said to her, "You are lying. You think we are so stupid we'll believe you? The Taliban came to arrest Hamid? Has he become so important that the Taliban would want to arrest him? You have fabricated a lie for us, and you want to stay in Pakistan on this excuse. What did you lack for in Afghanistan? Go back to Afghanistan quickly! Hamid boy is not such an important person that the Taliban would want to arrest him. Do you think it's cheap to live in Pakistan? Has your good fortune blindsided you? With the money you could live comfortably in Afghanistan, you can't live there, can you? If you want to live there, you have to pay rent and for utilities. You think we are sitting on a treasure trove so we can send so much money for you? We cannot afford to send you any money. We have a responsibility for our own kids. How much should Navid and Valid suffer for your sake? They too have a future. Do you want them to suffer for your sake and do nothing for their own future?"

When Hangameh said that life in Pakistan was expensive and we had to pay rent and utilities, she was right because there was no water, gas, and electricity in Afghanistan for which we had to pay. For over half an hour, Hangameh and her husband exhorted my Marjan. Both of them put her under so much pressure that when she wanted to talk, she couldn't. Her throat was dry, and she had lost her voice.

Finally, I could take it no more and took the receiver from my Marjan. So far I had behaved formally toward Hangameh and Mazdak; I thought I depended on them and never spoke sharply to them. Now I took the receiver from my Marjan and said to Hangameh, "I'll not permit you to say anything about my life. I'll live wherever I want to live. Where I wish to live has nothing to do with anyone."

Hangameh had grumbled so much at my Marjan that she had lost her voice and breathed heavily because of the excitement. She said to me in a cracked voice, "You are not an important person. I don't care where you choose to live. But you should know that living in Pakistan requires money. We cannot afford to send you money to live in this expensive country. You have learned that we have bought a car here, and so you think that we have become rich. We wouldn't have bought this car if we didn't have to. We pinched pennies and saved money to buy the car. I don't want to interfere in your life, but you should know that we cannot send you money."

Some time ago I had heard that they had bought a car, but I was so terrified in Afghanistan that I had forgotten my own name, let alone remembering their car. I replied, "You are not supposed to play God and give us our daily bread. Don't think that people are looking at you to receive their bread from you. I have not asked you for money, and I do not expect any money from you."

"I for one cannot send you any money. You don't even feel sorry for Navid and Valid, who are under so much pressure."

"I told you that I don't expect any money from you. You are not supposed to provide people their daily bread."

"I am not talking about myself; I am asking how Navid and Valid can send you money."

"When I say 'you,' I don't mean you alone—I mean all of you. You have nothing to do with our life and the high prices in Pakistan. I will go to Iran and will work there."

"Loud mouth! You should know that even going to Pakistan is not easy; everyone can't do that." What she meant was that were it not for her money, we could not have come even to Pakistan. But my words had shut her up. Hangameh was one of those highbrows; she wouldn't talk to anyone easily. If she did, she did so in a way as if she was doing them a favor. Often she talked in a patronizing way.

When I took the receiver from my Marjan, Mazdak knew I was on the line. Initially he grumbled a little bit, but when he saw that I wouldn't shut up like my Marjan, he gave up. In the past I was always at odds with Hangameh and Mazdak; we were like water and oil. When we talked to each other, even their nice words seemed sarcastic to me, and my kind words were rude to them. Mazdak was from the province of Laghman. He had first met Hangameh at the Kabul Polytechnic School, where they were classmates. Hangameh and Mazdak were both very intelligent and clever, but Mazdak was the better of her.

When we came to Pakistan, Mazdak immediately realized that I wanted to go to Europe. Mazdak took the receiver from Hangameh and said to me, "Hamid, I know you want to come to Europe. If you come here, life is really easy in Europe. But don't think that you can do it with the help of others. Anyone who has done it has done it on his own. Go to Afghanistan, work there, earn money, and come to Europe with your own money. If you come here with your hard-earned money, it will be more satisfying. No one helped me, and I came here on my own, and for that reason I really enjoy living here. If you come here with the help of others, you should know that you won't be able to find work, and you won't be happy."

"Fine. I'll come with my own hard-earned money. But there is no work in Afghanistan. I'll go to Iran, work there for a while, and gradually move out to other countries."

"You are completely wrong. If you cannot find work in Afghanistan, you can't find it in Iran. Thus, if you come to Europe with the help of others, you won't find work in Europe."

"That's my final decision. Everyone's thinking is good for him. I cannot use your advice."

* * *

When Mazdak said that he had immigrated to Netherlands on his own, he was right. Mazdak was indeed very intelligent, clever, and ambitious. In all circumstances he was able to find for himself the easiest and high-income jobs. His outward appearance was impressive too: he was tall and had a manly appearance. He attracted people to himself like a magnet, and they entrusted him with responsible jobs. He deserved such trust. As long as he was in Afghanistan, he worked with foreigners in a renovation firm. He was the boss and had the authority to employ individuals in other positions. He rented a house in the best location in Islamabad, and he lived there with his family.

Later, with the fortune he had made for himself, he moved with his family to Moscow. At that time the Russians were used to the communist way of life and were not familiar with free trade and private business. After the collapse of communism, Mazdak started business in Moscow without competition and earned a handsome profit. He had two garment boutiques and brought Navid, Valid, and Jananeh to help him run the shops. Then, with the huge fortune that he had made by selling garments in Moscow, he flew by airplane to Netherlands, and there he first acquired permanent residence and then Dutch citizenship. After his immigration to Netherlands, he still operated his boutiques in Moscow.

When Mazdak told me to go to Europe on my own, he didn't realize that I was not comparable to him in any way whatsoever: I was short, thin, timid, a clumsy clod with a womanly appearance, and as they called me, an eezak or a homo. I had no job experience, and in terms of age I was at least fifteen years younger than him. Everyone knows that no one trusts and gives a responsible job to a young, short, thin man, especially if he is feminine too. But Mazdak had compared me to himself and had asked me to work in Afghanistan like him, to earn money and go to Europe on my own!

* * *

When I arrived in Pakistan, did not plan to stay there but wanted to leave immediately for Iran. But my Marjan started looking for a house and wanted us to stay in Pakistan. When Hangameh and Mazdak said nasty things to us, it made me happy because it ended the diplomatic maneuverings and the veil of modesty. I too broke the chains of formality, and the conflicts between me and them came into the open. I used their noises as an excuse and said to my Marjan, "I do not want to live in Pakistan because I don't want to listen to their shameful words. I will go to Iran to work and earn my living."

At that time I was looking for excuses so as to prevent my Marjan from growing roots in Pakistan and sticking to me—which would waste a few more years. But all my excuses were useless, my Marjan rented a house, and we settled down in Peshawar.

Hangameh and Mazdak were unique in mischief-making. They naturally harbored malice toward me and didn't want others to be on good terms with me. After talking to me, they brainwashed Valid in Netherlands and convinced him not to help me. I for one had no expectations from Valid, because all our life we were neither good nor bad to each other. A few days after this event, Navid contacted me and repeated all those things that Hangameh and Mazdak had told me. He also said, "Pakistan is expensive. We cannot send you money to support you there. If you want to come to Europe, go to Afghanistan, work there, make money, and come to Europe with your own money."

"I will go to Iran, will work there, and will move out to other countries with my own money."

"If you are competent to work, you can work in Afghanistan; if you are not competent, you cannot work anywhere. People have worked hard in Afghanistan, earned money, and come from there to Europe. If your mind doesn't work to make money in Afghanistan, your mind wouldn't work anywhere else."

"It's clear that Hangameh and Mazdak have taught you these words; I have heard exactly the same thing from their mouths. Can't you speak out your own mind? Who has made money in Afghanistan other than thieves and extortionists? If there is work in Afghanistan, why then are the foreign countries helping the poor in Afghanistan?"

"You complain so much. Okay, don't go to Afghanistan; stay here. I will send you money, and you should no longer talk of going to Iran."

"I for one cannot go to Afghanistan; if I go, the Taliban are pursuing me, and they will arrest me."

Talking of the Taliban made me sad because I used to tell myself that those living outside Afghanistan told stories to foreigners so that they would not send them back. Now I was telling stories to my own family so that they wouldn't take me back to Afghanistan. I always used to tell my Marjan, "On the Day of Judgment, when you and I will go to hell, I will need no guard to stop me from escaping from the hell, because as long as you are with me, you will prevent me from escaping."

* * *

When it was decided that we would live in Pakistan, Navid said to me, "Have patience for two years; I'll arrange for you to come to London. In order not to waste these two years time in Pakistan, go to a body shop and work without wages as a repairer of cars. When you have learned it, you can use this skill here and can earn your living."

Navid insisted several times on my going to a body shop and learning to repair cars without wages, so as to acquire the skill. Physically I was not at all fit to engage in car repair. Even if I was given the highest wages, I didn't want to work in the field. But in order to let Navid help me go to London, I did not oppose his proposal and began to work in a body shop owned by a man from Jalalabad. I worked there without wages for about nine months. During the hottest days of summer in Peshawar, when a man's clothes were soaked in sweat from top to bottom, I worked from the morning till sunset. I had no intention of learning anything. I only wanted to make Navid happy so he would help me go to London. When I got to London, I'd do something that I was really willing and able to do, not the job of repairing cars.

My Marjan's Mental Sickness

We rented a house in Peshawar and settled down there. I kept the five thousand rupees that I had taken from my Marjan on the pretext of a passport in Jalalabad, because she never gave me any pocket money. In Afghanistan I supported myself entirely with the money that I made there. After graduating from university, I worked in a private pharmacy and earned a monthly salary. During my days in the university, we had a roughly 250-square-meter piece of land in front of our house. Before the arrival of spring, I would cover this land with plastic and would plant flower saplings, peppers, eggplants, and tomatoes. I would sell the samplings to someone who would resell them to others. From this work I earned my entire university expenses.

When we set out toward Pakistan, I thought that my Marjan would not give me any pocket money in Pakistan, and I would have problems in this respect. For that reason I took that money from her on the pretext of the passport. My Marjan and I never trusted each other. When we rented the house in Peshawar, I concealed that money in the lining of my jacket, so that she would not search the pockets of my clothes and find the money. I intended to take that money out gradually and spend it. The weather was hot in Peshawar, and it was not necessary to wear the jacket. I hung the jacket in which I had concealed the money inside the closet.

Overcoming

In our early days in Peshawar, my Marjan developed a mental sickness for a period due to the ill will between me, Hangameh, and Mazdak. Sometimes when she pondered on it too much, she would automatically take deep breaths. Gradually her breathing would become heavier, her body would shiver, and she would cry louder and louder. She would continue to shout out loud until she became tired and fainted. Where she fell, she would go to sleep. When she got up from her sleep, her nerves would be soothed, but she never remembered what had happened to her. This happened to her several times. In those days we had a telephone at home, and the situation had become so critical that Hangameh, Mazdak, and Navid would call us and try to convince us to go back to Afghanistan. They would say that nothing would happen to me and that we must return to Afghanistan. Hangameh and Mazdak had set up barricades against me on the other side so as to stop me from moving toward Europe. They had started a counterattack so as to gain the lost territory—that is, Pakistan. On this side, I was not prepared to retreat, and my attacks to move forward toward Europe continued. Thus, the situation at home was in serious disarray. In those circumstances, the mental sickness of my Marjan intensified.

One of our relatives, a lady in her midthirties, lived alone in Pakistan. During the illness of my Marjan, that lady would come to our house to visit with Marjan. One day she came over, and I went outside for a walk. My Marjan was conscious and was in good spirits. When I returned I saw that she had had a nervous breakdown and was lying unconscious in a corner of the house. When I entered the room, I saw that the lady was removing clothes from the closet. When I opened the door, she was taken by surprise, and her unmoving eyes became fixed on me. The closet door was still open, and her hand was inside the closet; she was frozen and could not move. I was so simpleminded that I thought that because I opened the door unexpectedly, she was taken by surprise and froze. I thought that because my Marjan had fainted, she was perhaps looking for something.

The next day when I searched for the money under the lining of my jacket, I saw that the lining was torn and the money was gone. But two days ago it was there. I remembered that when I had entered the room yesterday, that lady was taken by extreme surprise. Perhaps she had removed the money before I came in and was looking for a bigger sum. When I did not find the money, I was seized by a headache and high blood pressure, and my head hung heavy. I sat down and rubbed my forehead with my hand to calm down. I said to myself, *Now that you have lost the gamble, do not lose your opponent. It's better to just keep quiet. Now that the money is gone, our friendship with that lady and her family should not be destroyed because of the money.* I pretended as if nothing had happened and soon enough forgot everything altogether.

That lady was previously a teacher in Kabul. At first when I saw the money gone, I said to myself that this lady was one of those teachers who told their students that they had no morals from family upbringing, but she herself was without any character. *On second thought, bravo to this lady. Well done! She does have character and personality. She lives here alone and no one helps her. But we receive help. I am without honor and without conscience. I never thought of giving that money to her in the first place. She was justified in getting it herself. Well done, lady!*

After September 11 Attacks

About eight months had passed since I'd come to Pakistan when the events of September 11 occurred. The United States soon started its attacks against the Taliban in Afghanistan. At that time two of my sisters, Afsaneh and Mastaneh, also escaped from Afghanistan for fear of war, and they came to Pakistan and stayed with us. Navid knew that I had no attachments to Afghanistan; in fact he was planning to get me out of Afghanistan, but due to my Marjan's loneliness he could not take any action.

A few days after Afsaneh and Mastaneh came to our house, Navid thought that the time was appropriate and said to my Marjan, "You live with Afsaneh and Mastaneh, and so I want Hamid to join me."

My Marjan was always looking for excuses to prevent me from leaving her. When I left Afghanistan, she deliberately came with me to Pakistan so that I could not go anywhere else. Now that Afsaneh and Mastaneh were with us in one house, she had no excuse, but still she tried to exert more pressure on Navid to make him change his mind. She said to him, "If you want Hamid to join you, Mastaneh has a future, too. If you want Hamid, arrange for Mastaneh as well so that she comes to you along with Hamid, and she is not left to rot in Afghanistan."

Mastaneh was not alone—she had her husband. If she came with me, her husband had to join her, too. Navid said, "I don't have enough money to support three persons. Let Hamid come, and later I'll do something about Mastaneh."

She replied, "No, if she does not go with Hamid, I do not think you will do anything for her later on. Whenever you can bring them together, go ahead; if not, talk no more about Hamid."

It was decided that I would leave with Mastaneh and Arman for Iran, and from there I'd go to Turkey and then to Europe. At that time my Marjan became depressed and said that if Mastaneh left her, she would not be able to endure separation from her. We all thought that she would be depressed for only a few days after Mastaneh left, and then she would get used to it. But my other brother Valid in Netherlands said to my Marjan that if she was not able to endure separation from Mastaneh, she should leave with us. If Navid paid for us, he would pay for her.

My Marjan accepted Valid's proposal. Before we got ready to set out for Iran, I said to Navid, Valid, my Marjan, Mastaneh, and Arman, "This secret should remain with us; no one should know that we intend to go to Iran. Especially say nothing to Hangameh and Mazdak in this respect, because I do not wish them to know about my plans."

I knew that if they learned anything about our plans, they would meddle and make mischief and create discord among us. With the slightest discord our plans to depart could be disrupted. No one said anything to Hangameh and Mazdak until one day before our departure, when Valid could no longer resist and told them about our plans. However, he told them only about Iran and said nothing about our plans afterward. He did it so that they would not complain.

They made a desperate effort to disrupt our plan. They immediately convinced Valid to withdraw his support. They quickly phoned Valid in London to brainwash him. They called us in Pakistan to convince us to change our position. We intended to go unlawfully with the help of a trafficker. They tried to brainwash my Marjan and dissuade her from leaving.

Overcoming

They said that land mines were planted across the entire border of Iran, and that if we tried to enter Iran, we would walk on mines and put our lives in harm's way.

But now it was too late. We were completely ready to go. They could not persuade us to do their bidding. I told them seriously that I would not allow anyone to interfere in my affairs. Finally, the next day the four of us—my Marjan, Mastaneh, Arman, and I—set out from Pakistan to Iran.

Part Six

Arrival in Iran

Fall 2001, from Peshawar to Tehran

We took a bus from Peshawar and headed toward Iran. After two days and nights of travel, we arrived at the Iranian border. The border area of Iran and Pakistan was a complete desert; there were no villages and no trees. We were close to the Pakistani border where there were many human traffickers who helped illegal travelers from the borders. We spoke to one of them to take us to Tehran. He said, "My area of operation is from Taftan to Zahedan only."

Taftan was this same border area, and Zahedan was the first city of Iran on the other side of the border. We paid the trafficker twenty thousand *toman* per person, so eighty thousand *toman* for all of us, which was equal to one hundred US dollars. He took us to the city of Zahedan.

I said to the trafficker, "We do not know anyone in Zahedan. If the police catch us, they will expel us from the border."

The trafficker replied, "I'll take you to a safe house where they rent out rooms to illegal travelers; they will introduce you to other traffickers who take people to Tehran and other cities."

In the city of Zahedan, the trafficker took us to the house of an Afghanistani refugee who used to live in Helmand, Afghanistan. He introduced us to another trafficker to take us to Tehran. Before departing for Tehran, we waited for three days in his house so that the second trafficker could take us to Tehran. During those three days, Arman and I stayed in one room with the menfolk at the house, and my Marjan and Mastaneh stayed in another room with the womenfolk. During those three days their women spoke to my Marjan and Mastaneh about their culture, customs, and common practices. The provinces of Helmand and Parwan, although not one of the well-known provinces of Afghanistan, were as different from each other in terms of their culture and customs as the sky from the earth.

In this family one woman, among others, lived with her two daughters-in-law and one daughter. The woman pointed out her senior daughter-in-law to my Marjan and Mastaneh, and she said, "I bought this daughter-in-law six years ago for the price of four hundred thousand *kaldars*."

My Marjan and Mastaneh were shocked to hear those words. The woman pointed to her junior daughter-in-law and said, "I bought this daughter-in-law one year ago for seven hundred thousand *kaldars*." Then she pointed to her thirteen-year-old daughter and said, "We have sold our daughter for six hundred thousand *kaldars*."

This thirteen-year-old girl, who was still a child, had been sold in advance but still lived in her parents' house until she reached the age of fifteen or sixteen, when she would go to her husband's house. My Marjan and Mastaneh were quite shocked, but the woman continued. "Don't be surprised; it is our custom. We do not want to send our daughter valueless to her husband's house. It is our custom to take money from our son-in-law so that he appreciates our daughter and values her."

The thirteen-year-old girl felt proud of herself and said to my Marjan and Mastaneh, "Yes. They have sold me for six hundred thousand *kaldars*. One of my sisters went to her husband's house. We sold her for five hundred thousand *kaldars*. We sold another elder sister eight years ago for one hundred and fifty thousand *kaldars*." Also, the daughters-in-law were proud that their prices were not cheap.

Overcoming

Later, Mastaneh summarized what she heard from the woman. I did not believe Mastaneh's words and said to her, "No way. How simpleminded are you? This is not true at all. They said something, and you just believed them."

When I did not believe Mastaneh, she told me all about their customs, and I had to believe that it was indeed true. When I was in Kabul and Parwan, I had heard people say that in certain regions people sold their daughters for money. But I had never believed what people said; I thought that due to regional and ethnic differences, people of one region slandered people of other regions and ethnic origins. Even when I was in Kabul, I once heard a man say bad things about the culture of his own region. He said that if one had money there, one could marry any girl—and nothing else mattered. But I did not believe him, and believed that he thought evil of his people and slandered them for no reason. Here, for the first time, I did believe that such a culture did indeed exist in Afghanistan.

After three days' wait in their house, we boarded a bus with the second trafficker, who took us first to Shiraz and then to Tehran. After forty-eight hours, we arrived in Tehran and gave two hundred thousand *toman* to the trafficker.

* * *

Fall 2001, Tehran, Iran
We had our maternal uncle's address in Tehran and went straight to his house. It was fall, and the weather was getting cold. We were in a hurry to move toward Turkey before the arrival of winter. Coming to Tehran from Pakistan was easy and did not cost much. We paid seventy thousand *toman* per person for travel from the Pakistani border to Tehran. But going to Istanbul, Turkey, was not easy and not cheap. From the day we arrived in Tehran, Arman and I tried to find a trafficker who could take us to Turkey. There were many traffickers who worked on this route, but finding a trustworthy one was not an easy task. Wave after wave of illegal travelers left from Tehran to Turkey, which had tightened its borders. Seventy to eighty

percent of the travelers going to Turkey were repatriated to Iran. On their way back to Iran, they got lost in the mountains and faced many hazards.

Arman and I looked for a trafficker for over one month, but we wanted to leave for Turkey before the arrival of winter and snow. We saw many travelers who, after their departure for Turkey and after suffering many hardships, came back to Iran. In these circumstances everyone told us that regardless of the emergency, women and children should not take this route. Thus, my Marjan and Mastaneh decided not to go, and Arman remained in Iran because of Mastaneh.

My Conflict with My Marjan

My family withdrew from going to Turkey for fear of getting involved with danger and difficulties. But I was still determined to go and said to my Marjan, "It is not appropriate for you to leave in this scandalous situation. You stay here with Arman; I will leave alone."

What we should or should not do was entirely up to my Marjan. She replied, "You are not more important than us that we will stay here and you will go to Europe and have a good time there. If we go, you will come with us; if we don't, you'll remain here with us."

The conflict that began slowly between me and my Marjan came into the open. Previously she wanted to outmaneuver me diplomatically, but now, when the conflict was open, it turned into martial law. Now all secrets hidden in my heart and of my Marjan would gradually come into the open. Our plans to leave together were defeated. We rented a house in the Afsarie neighborhood in Tehran and settled down there illegally.

***

One day when we were sitting at home, I told Navid on the phone, "Now that my Marjan, Mastaneh, and Arman cannot leave in these scandalous circumstances, I'll set out alone and leave."

Navid replied, "If you can find a trafficker who would charge more money but would take you to Europe directly instead of Turkey, that would be better."

My cousin was at home. I asked him if there was a trafficker who would take people directly to Europe. He said, "They do not take you directly to Europe, but there are traffickers who would take you to Moscow for four thousand dollars."

I relayed this information to Navid, who had lived in Moscow for two years. He said, "It would be much better if you go to Moscow. You can come from there to London for another four thousand dollars. If you live in Moscow for some time, the job market there is not bad. Afghanistani refugees have good jobs and income there; you can work with them. Presently I'll send you four thousand dollars. You talk to a trafficker, and I'll send your pocket expenses to you later on."

When I was talking to Navid, my Marjan sat there and listened to me. She took the receiver from me and said to Navid, "Because of the danger and difficulties involved, I do not want him to go to Turkey. If he can go to Moscow without any danger or problem, that would be fine. You send the money so that he can leave for Moscow."

When I heard my Marjan talk to Navid, I instantly knew that she wanted to grab the money and put it in her purse. She wouldn't allow me to go. Conflict between me and my Marjan was almost in the open. We argued with each other every day, wanting to impose our wills on the other. As soon as I realized that she wanted to grab the money and keep it in her purse, I started planning for myself. Navid had sent money for us once before, through a money exchanger. Navid always sent money both in Pakistan and Iran in my name, and my Marjan would take it from me and keep it in her purse. She was the sole arbiter as to how to spend it. She never gave me any pocket money, not even bus fare, so I was forced to work and earn my monthly allowance. I felt shame to complain to Navid in this respect. I knew that if that money got into her purse, I would never achieve my goal and would never get any part of that money. I thought of keeping it in the trust of the money exchanger until I found a trafficker; then I would negotiate with him about his fee, and I'd transfer the money to the trafficker's account directly from the money exchanger.

* * *

Navid sent the money, and like an experienced hunter, my Marjan prepared to go with me to the money exchanger and take the money. When we left home to go to the money exchanger, Mastaneh's husband Arman also accompanied us. The money exchanger had already informed us on the phone that the money had arrived. I wanted to go to the money exchanger to talk to him about the trafficker, because money exchangers, like realtors who were well-informed about real estate and related laws and regulations, acted as a guide for illegal immigration and human traffickers. But my Marjan's only intention was to take the money. When we arrived there and the money exchanger wanted to give the money to me, my Marjan wanted to count it. I said to him, "Is the money in your hands?"

"Yes."

"I do not want to take the money from you now. Keep it in trust with you. I want to go to Moscow and am looking for a trafficker. Keep the money with you until I find a trafficker. Do you know any trafficker who would take me to Moscow? If so, please introduce him to me. In this deal you will be trusted by both parties."

Those words threw cold water on my Marjan. Her eyes came out of their sockets, the color of her face changed, and she stared at me with surprise. I threw a sideways glance at her and pretended as if there was no discord between us. Although we pretended as if all was well, we knew what was going on in each other's minds. I continued to talk to the money exchanger, who said, "I know three or four traffickers. The most trustworthy of them is Mr. X, who is currently in Mashhad. He will return in a couple of days, and then I will talk to him about it."

When the money exchanger uttered those words, my Marjan became even more surprised and alarmed. I stole a glance at her and saw that she was watching the money exchanger and Arman like a hawk. She had been put in a bind and was thinking of using her diplomatic maneuvers. At last she couldn't hold it any longer and said to the money exchanger, "Presently we will take the money while you talk to the trafficker. When we reach an agreement with him, we'll bring the money back to you so that he takes Hamid to Moscow, and you transfer the money to his account."

In order to not be outmaneuvered, I said quickly to the money exchanger, "No, it's not necessary to take the money once and then bring it back again. The money is for my trip; we will not use it for any other purpose. You can charge your fees from the trafficker, and you may work with it until you transfer it to his account."

The money exchanger said, "No, I'll charge no commission to him. I will introduce a trustworthy trafficker to you only for humanitarian reasons. But as long as the money stays with me, I'll work with it."

My Marjan said, "We'll not take the entire amount; we'll take two thousand, and the other two thousand will remain with you. If more money is required, we'll bring it to you."

The money exchanger said, "It doesn't matter to me. If you want two thousand, I'll give you two thousand. If you want the entire amount, I'll give you all your money."

My Marjan repeated, "No, we'll take only two thousand, and the other two thousand will remain with you. If more is required, we'll bring it to you."

This made me think that by taking two thousand dollars, my Marjan wanted to make a lame duck out of me so that I wouldn't be able to move. I said to the money exchanger, "We trust you; taking two thousand makes no sense because we do not intend to spend it. We do not need it at home, so why take it from you and let the money remain idle?"

Overcoming

Whatever reason my Marjan put forward, I gave her a stronger reason. The exchange of words increased. Eventually, my Marjan was defeated in her maneuvering against me and came home with apprehension and anxiety.

* * *

At home, my Marjan's efforts continued; she was thinking of other diplomatic maneuvers to defeat me. She phoned Navid in London and said to him, "Look at this stupid thing Hamid did: he left the money with the money exchanger. Can one trust a stranger money exchanger? Tell Hamid to take the money from him. Is it not better to keep the money at home rather than with a stranger? Maybe he takes the money of many people in trust and runs away one day from all of us; or maybe something happens to him, and we no longer see him."

Navid insisted that I take the money from the money exchanger and keep it at home. I tried to wait for the return of the trafficker from Mashhad. I procrastinated for a few days on one excuse or another and did not take the money back from the money exchanger, until my Marjan lost her patience. I took the trafficker's phone number from the money exchanger, phoned him, negotiated with him about my journey to Moscow, and agreed to go to the money exchanger and sign a contract in his presence. My Marjan still insisted on taking the money back. On the appointed day, she came with me to the money exchanger's. She accompanied me with the intention of taking the money, but I intended to sign the contract. I prayed that the trafficker came on time so that the money did not fall in my Marjan's hands.

When we arrived at the money exchanger's, my Marjan was eager to count the money, and I was eager to see the trafficker. The trafficker was a little late. I told my Marjan, "Let's wait for him. He'll be here any moment; I want to talk to him."

She shot back, "Taking money has nothing to do with the arrival of the trafficker. Take your money and talk to him when he comes."

"Do not hurry for taking the money back. I have an appointment with the trafficker. I will wait for him. At the end, everything will be done together."

A half hour later the trafficker arrived. We agreed with him that he would take me to Moscow through Azerbaijan. If I did not arrive in Moscow, he'd not be entitled to receive any money, and the money would remain with the money exchanger. Either I would go to Moscow and he'd receive the money, or I'd return, and the money would be mine. We decided that the money would remain with the money exchanger, and I got ready to go. My Marjan was about to be defeated in this plan.

We returned home, and I got ready to leave the next week. My Marjan was restless. She said out loud she had no strength to stay away from all of her sons—at least one of them had to remain with her. But in fact she was concerned about losing the money.

The day of my departure was coming quickly. My Marjan thought of how to retaliate against my plan. At this point she picked up the phone, and called Navid, and told him, "Why don't you understand me? If Hamid leaves me, I will go crazy like last year and will become a lunatic."

Navid said, "Why are you worried about his joining me? Now he is not going through Turkey, which is dangerous and risky. He is going through Moscow. On the road to Moscow the police take the money from the traffickers. The job will be done with money; there is no danger involved."

"There may be no danger. He may go to London; he may stay with you. But I will be alone. What about me?"

"You are not alone; you are living with Mastaneh. If you go back to Afghanistan, Afsaneh will also be with you."

"When a daughter marries, she belongs to others. One cannot depend on one's daughter."

Navid told her, "There is no difference between daughter and son. Whether you live with your daughter or with your son, it makes no difference at all."

"How come it makes no difference? How is it possible to be no different! One may have three sons, but not even one will stay!"

"What do you expect from the son that you don't expect from the daughter?"

"If I die, not even one of my sons will be beside me for the funeral!"

"Don't worry. I will arrange for you to join us lawfully in the future and live with us."

"If even one of my sons does not stay with me, I am done. I will have a nervous breakdown and will die before then."

"Then what do you want? Do you want Hamid to cancel his trip?"

"Yes! He doesn't listen to me. You ask him to cancel his trip."

"Okay. Give the receiver to him. I'll ask him to cancel his trip."

Navid told me to cancel the trip and to go get the money back from the money changer.

* * *

I was supposed to undertake this trip with Navid's money. However, I would not go without his consent, even if I had money from him enough to go to the moon. Thus, we decided to go to the money exchanger and take the money back. I made an appointment with him. Earlier my Marjan had become weak and lifeless; now no spirit was left in me. I was completely confused and sluggish. While my head spun, my eyes lost their luster, and I did not know what went on around me, we set off with my Marjan.

When we arrived at the money exchanger's, a Hazara woman was sitting there. Her sons had sent money for her from Europe, and she was there to collect it from the money exchanger. When we talked to the money exchanger about changing our mind, the Hazara woman realized that I wanted to go to Europe but that my Marjan would not allow me. She said to my Marjan, "Your son wants to go to Europe, but you do not allow him to go?"

My Marjan replied, "Yes, it is very hard for me to be alone."

"If he goes, he'll be saved from a miserable life in Afghanistan. It will be good for him."

"Perhaps, but if I am left alone, I'll go crazy. I have suffered a lot in my life; I have no nerves left in me. If he goes away from me, I will become insane."

"I too have suffered a lot. It's a miracle that I am still alive. If I sit down with you and tell you about my past, you'll agree that you haven't suffered as much as I. I have four children, but I live alone. I thank God that all of my children are in Europe and have escaped from their miserable lives in Afghanistan. I am happy that my children will not suffer from the misery and pain that I have suffered. They study in Europe and send me money. You let your son go and save him from the horror and misery of Afghanistan."

I said to the Hazara woman, "My mother is not alone. Two of my sisters live with her, but she says that she doesn't want to live with her daughters."

"Wow, lucky you!" the woman said to my Marjan. "You have two daughters with you? Why then do you say you are alone? Let him go. I have no one and am entirely on my own. I live with two women like me who are alone. You and I have suffered from all the miseries of Afghanistan. Why do you want to destroy his entire life? Let him go and be saved."

My Marjan said nothing, and I asked her, "Do you mind if we do not collect the money, and I leave with the trafficker?"

She said meekly, "Well, if you want to be saved, then go ahead."

"All right, then. The money will remain here, and I will leave on the appointed day with the trafficker."

My Marjan unwillingly accepted this sacrifice in the presence of the Hazara woman—that is, she let me go and sacrificed her own life for my sake. We did not take the money back from the exchanger and returned home.

Overcoming

* * *

My Marjan knew full well that I was not prepared to return to Afghanistan, but on her part she was by no means ready to give up. Upon our arrival in Pakistan, I had told her about the Taliban episode and that it was my own creation. I did so in order to convince her that I was serious and hoped that she would leave me alone. Whatever I did increased her stubbornness and resentment. I told her in the presence of others, "You know that I do not wish to live in Afghanistan. You saw that I even brought the Taliban in front of our house. Why then don't you give up your stubbornness? Why do you want me to do something to make you the butt of jokes for the people?"

She had a stubborn pride. Whenever she refused obstinately to agree, she would show no flexibility. She thought that if she showed flexibility, her pride would be broken. Here, what was important for her was her insistence on her stubborn pride—and getting hold of the money left in trust to the money exchanger.

The day of my departure was coming close. Only one day was left, and the day after that I would leave with the trafficker. My Marjan had no peace and was restless. She walked around the house and stared at me grudgingly. The sun was about to set. Suddenly my Marjan began to shout out loud and curse me, Navid, and the Hazara woman. "Oh Navid, I wish you were dead! I wish God had not given me such stupid children! Your stupid father died and left me alone, and now you are leaving me alone! Oh, Hazara woman, I wish that you live to hear all your children have died! May you bereave your offspring!"

Our neighbors on the ground floor heard her voice. While she shouted and yelled, she picked up the phone and called Navid. When Navid answered, she continued to curse for a couple of minutes without talking directly to him. Finally, when she started to speak into the receiver, she said, "If Hamid leaves me, get ready my burial shroud. If he goes, I'll die."

Thus my Marjan became the ultimate winner and disrupted my departure. We took the money back from the money exchanger, and my Marjan got her wish, which I had worried would happen from the beginning. She took the money and put it in her purse. From the moment she got hold of the money, she stopped talking to me for a couple of months. We lived together under one roof, but the house had become a prison for me. Her grudge against me could be seen clearly on her face. Every time I looked at her face, my wounds became fresh. Financially those were the worst days of my life. I only ate at home with them; I had neither proper clothes nor shoes, and not even bus fare. Thus, I began to look for work here and there.

Shah Malang's Bitter Life

I became acquainted with one of my fellow countrymen named Shah Malang, who used to live in a neighboring village in Afghanistan. I began to work with him in the shoe market. Shah Malang had a shoe shop in the great bazaar of Tehran. I would take two or three pairs of shoes from him and would sell them to people on the sidewalk. I was a hawker, and it was a difficult job without much income.

I had never thought that anyone other than me would leave Afghanistan because of the problems arising from popular culture and the traditions of Afghanistan. But when I came to Iran and became acquainted with Shah Malang, I heard from him that he had left Afghanistan because of people's taunts. Shah Malang had come to Iran six or seven years ago. I had seen him several times in Afghanistan in the Chahardeh market area and at the bus terminal in Kabul, but I had never talked to him, and I did not know his name. A few years ago when Shah Malang was in Afghanistan, I heard people say several times that the daughter of Shah Malang had run away with a boy from Panjshir. A little later I heard that Shah Malang had gone to Iran. I never knew who Shah Malang was, although I had seen him in person. At the beginning I did not know that Shah Malang's going to Iran had something to do with his runaway daughter. When I got to know him, I heard it from him that he had left Afghanistan because of his daughter and the taunting of the people. He had escaped from Afghanistan to Iran, and yet he had still not escaped from people's taunts.

When I was working with Shah Malang, I became acquainted with him and his family; his son, Shah Darvish, became a close friend of mine. Shah Darvish and I liked to talk to each other every now and then on the phone and shared some laughs.

One night my cousin Fahim came to our house. The same night Shah Darvish phoned me, and we talked to each other and had some laughs. Fahim, who was sitting there, asked me, "Who are you talking with?"

"With Shah Darvish."

"Who is Shah Darvish?"

"The son of Shah Malang."

"Which Shah Malang?"

"Shah Malang, the same person who owned a mechanic's workshop at the bus terminal in Kabul."

"The person whose daughter ran away with a Panjshiri boy, and he came to Iran?"

"Yes."

"Where did you find them? What relationship do you have with them?"

"My uncle knew him and introduced me to him. I work for him at his shoe shop."

"Why do you work for him? Can't you find work anywhere else than Shah Malang?"

I was at home with Fahim, my Marjan, Mastaneh, and Arman when Shah Darvish phoned me again a few moments later. I picked up the phone, and we began to talk and laugh with each other. Fahim asked, "Is it the son of Shah Malang again?"

"Yes."

"Don't let him talk too much. How can you bear him?"

"While he is talking to me, I cannot interrupt him and say good-bye."

"Don't say good-bye. Just hang up and don't listen to him."

Overcoming

"I cannot do that. How can I hang up without saying good-bye?"

"If you cannot do it, give me the phone, and I'll talk to him."

I did not give him the receiver because I was afraid that if I did, he would say something nasty to Shah Darvish, who would then be unhappy with me. When Fahim interfered while I was talking, it made me panicky, and I said good-bye quickly and hung up the phone.

Minutes later I went to the washroom, and while I was in there, Darvish phoned me a third time. This time there was no one to stop Fahim. He picked up the phone and spewed venom. As soon as I came out, I saw that Fahim had done the job and was sitting in a corner. Arman, who was also sitting in the room, had heard Fahim and told me that Fahim had taunted Shah Darvish about his sister. I was surprised that he could do it, and how quickly! I was afraid from the beginning that Fahim might say something nasty to make Darvish unhappy with me. Now the situation was bad beyond expectation. Five minutes later the doorbell rang. I picked up the intercom receiver and asked who was calling.

Shah Malang, breathing heavily, said in an angry tone, "Who is the mother-fucker who insulted me? Kick him out of your house immediately. I will tear his ass up to his mouth."

Arman said to me, "Don't open the door. They will come up and start a fight."

We were on the fourth floor, and he was on the ground floor behind the door. I wanted to go down and apologize to him and to ask him to forgive Fahim for his rudeness. But I did not realize that he was so angry, he had come there only to fight and nothing else. He was also not alone. When I went down, the four of them rushed in as soon as I opened the door and started to climb the staircase quickly. I tried to run quicker in order to stop them, but no matter how fast I ran, they were ahead of me, blocking my way. The four of them and myself hurriedly climbed the stairs. I was third in line.

At first when I opened the door, I wanted to stand up in front of them and have a conversation with them. But as soon as I opened the door, Shah Malang and Shah Darvish immediately ran past me, and I followed them quickly. The other son of Shah Malang and another person who had accompanied them wanted to get in front of me. I tried to block him, but I did not succeed. Ultimately we arrived at the third floor. The two individuals who were ahead of me were only one step ahead. I called out from the third floor, "Arman, close the door! They are coming. Arman, close the door quickly, or else they will beat up Fahim!"

When we arrived at the fourth floor, I saw that Arman had only half closed the door and was trying to shut it completely. Shah Malang pushed the door to open and enter. I went ahead of Shah Darvish and pushed the arm of Shah Malang to the side, knocking his hand away from the door. Arman closed the door. The group knocked, yelled, and shouted, trying to break in and beat Fahim into pulp. Up to that moment I had no idea what Fahim had said to them on the phone and what they had told Fahim. I started a conversation with them, and they explained the story, which I will sum up below.

Fahim asked, "Yes, who is calling?"

"Hello, excuse me, please give the receiver to Hamid."

"You are the same person who spoke to Hamid earlier?"

"Yes. Please give the receiver to him and tell him that Shah Darvish wants to speak to him."

"Aren't you ashamed of yourself, to bother other people?"

"Are you meddlesome? Give the receiver to Hamid. I need to talk to him."

"Asshole. Put the receiver down and stop bothering people."

Fahim hung up on him and did not allow Shah Darvish to speak. His words made Darvish angry, and the hanging up added insult to injury. Darvish started saying nasty things in a foul language. His father, Shah Malang, who was there and noticed Darvish using foul language, became extremely angry. Malang picked up the phone to call again, to apologize for his son. No more than a minute had passed since the previous call.

Fahim picked up the phone and said, "You won't behave, asshole! Put down the phone and stop bothering people."

"My dear, don't be angry. I am not Shah Darvish; I am Shah Malang. I do not know what this young man has said to you. Tell me what he has said so that I can break his jaw."

"Put down the phone, you asshole."

"My dear, you are mistaken. I am not Shah Darvish. I am Shah Malang. You are speaking to me."

"I know you are Shah Malang, whom a Panjshiri boy has fucked. A Panjshiri boy has fucked you, you asshole! I am telling you to put down the receiver and stop bothering people."

Fahim spewed more venom and hung up on him. Shah Malang had escaped from Afghanistan to Iran because of people's taunts. At this moment the venomous taunt pierced his brain and nerves so deep that it filled him with insane rage. They already knew where our home was because they had visited us previously. At the height of his rage, Shah Malang immediately set out by car, accompanied by his two sons and a friend. They came to our house to beat Fahim into a pulp. Somehow I calmed them down a bit and did not let them beat up Fahim.

Shah Malang swore, "By God! By my honor! I escaped from Afghanistan to Iran because of my daughter's eloping and people's taunts. But they still taunt me, as you have seen, here in Iran where my past should be behind me. I am not like other people who have left Afghanistan and come here because of poverty and hunger. When I left Afghanistan, I had fifty thousand dollars with me. I am not a political refugee, either. I was somebody in Afghanistan; I had honor and respect. There, for me, it was not like Iran, where one is humiliated by everyone like a stray dog for being an Afghanistani."

Shah Malang addressed me and said, "You see it yourself that here, we Afghanistanis, as aliens, are not treated like a human being by the xenophobes. I accepted all this humiliation and degradation in this country because of my daughter's elopement, and yet this shameless boy taunts me like this."

Shah Malang did not have a work permit due to his illegal stay in Iran. He started a business with his money, in partnership with an Iranian. His sons could not go to school because he did not have legal residence in Iran.

What misery and misfortune can one girl's elopement bring for an Afghanistani, and what consequences does he have to endure! Shah Malang's life was destroyed, and his sons were deprived of education forever!

The story of his daughter's elopement goes like this. His daughter had a boyfriend from Panjshir, but Shah Malang had betrothed her to another man. For this reason the girl was not happy and eloped with her fiancé from Panjshir. After her elopement, nothing was heard of her for the next three months. Then it became known that she had run away with her boyfriend. The boyfriend, who helped her escape, did not marry her but forced her to marry his elder brother, who was handicapped and had lost both legs in a war.

According to Afghanistani tradition, a girl who establishes her first sexual relationship with a man has to marry that same man. The Panjshiri boyfriend was a married man, and the very first night after her elopement, he did not establish sexual contact with her but made her available to his older brother. Thus, the girl was forced to marry that older, handicapped man. The Panjshiri man was recognized as the culprit here.

Shah Malang complained against the man's family and demanded to have a girl from his family in order to erase the disgrace, according to Afghanistani tradition. The disabled man was a widower and had a seven-year-old girl. As the punishment of his crime, he gave away his seven-year-old daughter in marriage to Shah Malang's family. This trade-off is known as "*bad va radd*" in Afghanistan.

In order to erase his disgrace, Shah Malang gives the seven-year-old girl in marriage to his thirteen-year-old son. Nevertheless, people continued to taunt him. Thus, he was forced to escape from Afghanistan with his entire family and to go to Iran.

Overcoming

Shah Malang said to me, "You see, I took back a girl and erased my disgrace. And yet people taunt me so much! Had I not erased my disgrace, and had I not taken back a girl, God knows what they would have said to me!"

* * *

I worked with Shah Malang as a peddler for a couple of months. Peddling was a troublesome job without much income; I could not earn my pocket allowance from this job, let alone save any money. Finally I was forced to look for another job.

I started working in a shoe factory as a packer. The factory production was high volume, and I worked twelve hours a day so as not to get backed up. Despite this hard work I earned 2,500 *toman* per day, which was equivalent to three US dollars. If I did not sleep and eat at home with the family, I could not have run my life with this money. Nevertheless, with penny-pinching every step of the way, I was able to save about forty thousand *toman* (about fifty US dollars) per month. I worked in this factory for about three months.

My Acquaintance with Nawaz

Summer 2002 – Tehran, Iran

In jobs at the traffic circle, where one could often find construction work, one could earn four thousand *toman* a day for eight hours of work. I left the shoe factory job and went every day to the traffic circle to find a job. Some days I got a job, and sometimes I didn't. Sometimes I got a one-day job and sometimes I got a multiday job. We used to live in the Afsarie area, where the jobs were few and far between. I started going to Tehran Pars on a minibus, where jobs at the traffic circle were more frequent.

Once I got a three-week-long job at the Tehran Pars traffic circle. There I met an Afghanistani laborer named Nawaz who was in his late thirties. Nawaz was also a security guard at a building. He had a wife and children in Afghanistan, and he had left them there and worked in Iran. One day I was sitting with Nawaz in his guard's room and talking to him. He smiled at me and said, "You have beautiful eyes!"

When I heard him say this, I told myself not to let go of him. I stared at him and said, "Really? You are telling me seriously that I have beautiful eyes?"

"By God, I am serious."

While we stared into each other's eyes, I asked him, "How are my eyes beautiful?"

"Well, they are beautiful. I see them as beautiful."

"How are they beautiful?" I repeated.

"By God, exactly as a girl's eyes."

"Oh, like a girl?"

Yes, by God, like a girl."

"So will you marry me?" I joked.

While he was staring at my eyes, he said nothing. I asked him again, "Well, will you marry me or not?" He smiled but said nothing. I said, "My eyes are like those of a girl. So will you marry me or not?"

"If I marry you, what do I do then?"

"I don't know what you will do. What do you want to do?"

"When people marry each other, what do they do?" Nawaz asked.

"I know what they do. And if you marry me, what will you do?"

"If I marry you, I will…"

"It's okay. Do you want to … now?"

"Yes, by God, if you want, I want to, right now."

"Take off your clothes. We'll see if you are telling the truth." He languidly looked into my eyes but said nothing. I said, "By God, I am serious. Take off your clothes so I can see how serious you are." He removed his shirt. I said, "Take off your pants." He opened his belt and took off his pants, leaving his shorts on. I said, "Remove your shorts, too."

He took off his shorts, looked at me, and said, "You should also remove your clothes."

I took off my clothes, and we had fun together. That's how we got to know each other closely, and during our friendship in Tehran, we repeated this several times.

*　*　*

My older sister Hangameh came with her two children from Netherlands to Iran during summer vacation, and they stayed with us for one month. One day she was talking of freedom in Netherlands and said, "There is so much freedom in

Netherlands that men marry men, and women marry women, and they live with each other."

When I heard her say this, I said to myself, *I'm sure they are homosexuals like myself.* No one in our family knew that I was a homosexual.

I saw in Iran that displaced Afghanistanis contacted the office of the United Nations High Commissioner for Refugees (UNHCR), applying for refugee status there, and the UNHCR sent them to immigrant-accepting countries. Only important political and social cases were accepted by the UNHCR; they turned down cases of refugees who had no important problems. I always said to myself that I had a real problem in Afghanistan. Others were accepted and sent overseas by the UNHCR on important political and social grounds, but I was neither a political activist with political grounds nor an important person on social grounds. I used to think that the UNHCR accepted only cases of important persons who were very intelligent and capable as social refugees, and they paid no attention to people like me. But this speculation of mine was not far from the truth.

One night I was lying awake on my bed and thinking. I remembered Hangameh, who had said that marriage between two men or two women was legal in Netherlands and was recognized. I said to myself that if the Europeans have given this freedom to their people and also talk of human rights, if they actually believe in their rhetoric, then they must accept me as a social refugee. Thus, I decided to apply to UNHCR on grounds of homosexual marriage. I thought to myself that although I was not an important person, still there was a 1 percent chance that they would accept me as a refugee.

The next morning I went to Nawaz and spoke to him about this matter, and I said, "I want to apply to UNHCR on the grounds of marriage with you. Thus, you and I could be accepted, and we can go to Europe."

At first Nawaz did not accept, but eventually he said, "Apart from the fact that we will lose face in society, it is simply not possible for us to go to Europe through the UNHCR."

Overcoming

But I insisted and convinced him to try this possibility. Nawaz said, "All right, go and see how it works out. If they accept to interview us, I will come with you for the interview."

I found out the address of UNHCR, went there, and made inquiries to the officials about seeking refugee status. They told me that I should write down whatever problems I had in a letter, bring it there, and drop it in the mail box. A decision would be made about it subsequently.

I wrote a letter, included my address on the envelope, and dropped it in the UNHCR mail box. I waited one month for its reply, but no reply came. After a month I wrote a second letter and dropped it in the UNHCR's mail box. Again I waited for one month to receive a reply, but none came. I wrote a third letter, and still no reply. Finally I went to the office of UNHCR and made inquiries. They told me that if I had dropped my letters in the mail box, I must wait at least for one year for the reply. This was during a time when the government of Iran had put the displaced Afghanistanis under extreme pressure to leave Iran. The police arrested displaced Afghanistanis everywhere and deported them from Iran. Likewise it had applied many other pressures on them to make them leave Iran voluntarily.

Thus I decided to apply directly to the embassies of countries that accepted refugees. I wrote my letter, made ten photocopies of it, and sent them to ten different embassies simultaneously. Perhaps one of them would give me a positive reply. The Austrian embassy sent me a refugee form. I immediately filled out that form and sent it back. My address that I had given to the embassy changed quickly, and I did not follow the matter anymore. The Swiss Embassy sent a negative reply. The Norwegian Embassy wrote a negative reply on my own letter and returned it to me (see Appendix 1).

I achieved no result from my actions. For me, there was neither the UN nor the embassies of refugee-accepting countries. I forgot such fanciful acts and dreams, and I continued my efforts and work in this wild world.

Money, the Key of Almost Everything

I saved 350,000 *toman* from construction work. I had heard from people that if a person did not know how to use a computer in this day and age, he was considered illiterate. For that reason I was looking for an opportunity to take computer lessons. I had money, so I decided to join computer classes. I thought to myself that by taking lessons, I would not become proficient in the use of the computer unless I had a PC at home. I decided to buy a computer from my money and take the tuition fee from my Marjan. I said to her, "I want to take computer lessons; give me money to pay my tuition fee."

"Don't ask me for money. You work and have the money. Pay it yourself."

"I want to buy a computer from my money, because if I do not have a PC, joining the classes won't do me any good."

"Go away. You can't fool me with your words."

"Navid and Valid have been sending money to me and to you for years, but you have never given me any money, and I have never asked you to give me any. I have never complained to them about you. If you don't give me the tuition fee, I'll complain to them."

She pondered for a few moments. Although she had several thousand dollars in her purse, she started to cry. My sister

Mastaneh, who was at home, reproached my Marjan and said, "Why do you cry? He has said nothing to make you cry."

"See how much patience I can have? He argues with me all the time."

"There was no argument. All he did was ask for his tuition fee." Mastaneh shot back.

"He always tries to extort money from me on whatever excuse."

"So you are crying for money? Is money so important that you would cry for it? Money is for spending. Give him the money to take computer lessons."

My Marjan took out thirty thousand *toman* from her purse and gave it to me. I took tuition fee for two semesters from her. When I asked about the price of a computer, the seller told me it would cost 500 thousand *toman,* but I had only 350 thousand *toman*. I said to my Marjan, "Give me 150 thousand *toman* which, combined with my own money, would be 500 thousand. That's the price of a computer."

"I gave you the tuition fee, for which you should be thankful. You said you'd buy the computer from your own money."

"My money is not enough."

"If you don't have the money, keep quiet."

I decided to plot against her to get the computer money from her. A man named Yusuf, who came from one of the villages close to our own, used to live in Tehran. I used to socialize with him and sometimes brought him home with me. My Marjan hated to see him there. She would not say anything in his presence, but behind his back would say to me, "Mastaneh lives with us; you should not bring a stranger here." I would tell her, "I am already captive enough because of you and cannot go anywhere. You cannot impose your views on me."

One day I said to Yusuf in the presence of my Marjan, "I want to buy a computer, but I do not have enough money. You pay half of the money and I pay the other half. Let us buy it jointly. I will keep it at home with me. You can come here anytime you wish, and I'll teach you how to use it."

Yusuf agreed before my Marjan. "Okay, we'll buy it jointly."

When Yusuf said those words, I looked at her face and noticed that she was extremely angry. She said nothing in Yusuf's presence, but when he left, she said to me, "If you buy the computer jointly with Yusuf, don't keep it at home, but take it to wherever you want. If the computer is at home and Yusuf comes here every day, I'll break the computer to pieces as well as Yusuf's head." When I saw her so serious, I knew that with this plot I wouldn't be able to get the money from her.

One of my maternal uncles lived in Tehran and had eleven children. Both he and most of his children were interested in learning to use the computer. One day I said to my uncle in my Marjan's presence, "Do you want to buy a computer jointly with me? We'll keep the computer here. Whenever you or the children wish to use it, you can come here, and I will teach you how to use it."

My uncle said, "It's really a good idea. People pay a lot of money to computer centers but do not learn enough. If the computer is at home, it will be enough that only you go to the computer center and teach us the lessons you learn there."

My Marjan said nothing but thought to herself that if I bought the computer jointly with them, her house would become a school, and they would come there every day to learn. Because my uncle was her brother, she could not oppose the idea; if she did, I could start mischief. When my uncle left our home, my Marjan gave me two hundred dollars and said, "Go get a computer for yourself."

I took the money from her and bought a computer.

* * *

I do not know why my Marjan was opposed to my going to Europe. Perhaps it was important that I stay with her. But the fact of the matter was that my separation from her was not the reason for her opposing the idea—it was the money that had to be paid to the trafficker. It was intolerable for my Marjan to give away the several thousand dollars. She herself said openly to me one day, "Don't think that you are important to me! By God you are not, and by God I am not happy with your being alive."

My Marjan was not only a miser; her obstinacy and stubbornness knew no bounds. She was unique in confronting others and raising controversy. Whoever she opposed was certain to lose. In the past, when she defeated some of my uncles, relatives, and friends, I enjoyed it. But this time it was my misfortune; she opposed me until she completely isolated me. For a long time nobody even spoke to me.

My Marjan, Mastaneh, Arman, and myself lived in the house. All of us had come to Iran with the intention of going to Europe. But when we could not go, we stayed in Iran for one more year. Ultimately, Mastaneh and Arman decided to go back to Afghanistan. I thought that if Mastaneh and Arman went to Afghanistan, my Marjan would remain with me, and our life together will become more difficult each day. She had no forgiveness for me, and I did not have magnanimity for her. I had to leave home before Mastaneh and Arman left for Afghanistan. In this situation she might go with them.

For that reason I left home and started to work for a construction company in the north of Tehran, which was located far away from home. At night I slept in the laborers' room at the job site. Thus, my Marjan was forced to go to Afghanistan with Mastaneh and Arman. When they decided to return to Afghanistan, my entire family—my Marjan, Navid, Valid, Hangameh, and even Mazdak—insisted that I go to Afghanistan too. If I did so, they promised to send money for me to open a pharmacy and buy a car; they would even pay for my marriage expenses. If I did not go and paid no heed to their words, they would abandon me and would not talk to me. I said to them that if they helped me without preconditions, I would be thankful to them; if they set conditions for me, I couldn't care less.

After buying the computer I became jobless for a time and borrowed two hundred thousand *toman* from my friends, becoming indebted to them. I did not have proper clothes and shoes to wear. At this time when my Marjan left for Afghanistan, she had several thousand dollars in her purse, but she did not give me even one *toman* out of it. I was left alone and empty-handed in Iran, and I began my life from zero.

I Was Zero

So far I was hopeful that ultimately Navid would help me and that I would immigrate to Europe with his help. The day he landed in London, I was as happy as if I were there. But now I realized that my situation was more precarious than I had imagined. I began my life of loneliness coupled with confusion. In the early days when I saw myself in that situation, I lost all hope. But soon enough I thought that this change should be the beginning of success in my life. I did not realize my true situation earlier, but my eyes were open now, and I knew where I stood. In a way it was good to know that I had to start my life from scratch.

In the early days of my independence I began to work in the construction industry together with my Afghanistani friend Hamed, whom I got to know in Iran. It was cold during the winter. Hamed and I lived in a half-finished labor room in an incomplete building; there were no doors or windows in the room. Only the walls inside the room were plastered, but on the outside hollow bricks were exposed to the elements. The days were cold and the nights were freezing. We had covered the window hole with a plastic sheet and hung a plastic curtain on the door space. Inside the room there was nothing except three or four dirty, worn-out blankets. The blankets were so dirty, as if they had been used in a mechanic's workshop. We worked eight hours each day in addition to a couple of hours of overtime. Day was our shelter, because it kept us warm while we worked, so we did not feel cold. But at night we huddled under two dirty blankets. We had no pillows on which to rest our heads; I would put a brick or tile underneath the lower blanket and put my head on it. We ate only bread and cheese for breakfast, lunch, and dinner. I had no money for food and had a debt of two hundred thousand *toman* on top of that. Hamed paid for my food. The only thing that I owned was a computer which I kept in trust with my cousin. I was not willing to sell it.

After twenty days of labor work, I received my first wages from the company and I gave a part of it to Hamed to buy groceries. Every day after work, Hamed and I walked on the streets and sifted through garbage to find blankets, a mattress, carpet, pots and pans, clothes, and shoes. At first I felt ashamed of myself, but Hamed would smile and say, "Come on, don't be shy. Let us face our fate. It is much better than to die of cold at night." Soon enough we found carpet and pots and pans, and clothes and shoes in relatively good condition. We furnished our room with secondhand items.

I worked for a few months for the company, paid my debt, and saved a little money. I decided to go to Turkey with the money that I'd earned by working as a laborer. I needed about eight hundred dollars to go to Turkey; I'd saved about a hundred each month. Labor work was backbreaking, but for me it was better than the family life. At home with my family I had no control over anything; even for eating food, my Marjan and Hangameh would remind me that they were doing me a favor. Most workers were unhappy with their working life and always complained. Not me. I enjoyed those days when I thought of *Babeh nadareh*, the Afghanistani culture, and the treatment my family meted out to me. As the saying goes, "One who has not suffered pain will not appreciate good fortune."

* * *

During the period of my working in Iran, I became familiar with various peoples and their cultures. I learned more about the people from Afghanistan here than I knew about them while still in Afghanistan.

Once I worked on a house for twenty days with seven or eight other boys from Herat province who came from the town of Adraskan, in Herat Province. When I asked them the name of their village, they said "Zalalgag." All of them, without exception, were engaged to marry a girl from the ages of three or four. From what they told me about their customs, I understood that it was their custom to be engaged to a girl during the first few days immediately following her birth. The father of the boy pays a certain amount of money to the father of the girl on this account. When the girl and the boy reach the age of puberty, they marry each other.

I told them that this custom did not exist in my village. They were surprised and wondered how people married if this custom did not exist. I was horrified by their custom. I thought to myself, *If a homosexual fell in this trap of engagement, how could he get rid of it in the future?*

* * *

Once again I was waiting for work at the traffic circle. A man came by who needed two laborers. I and an Uzbek boy from Faryab Province in Afghanistan were hired. We went with him and worked for him for a few days. The Uzbek boy was sixteen years old and had come to Iran six years ago; he had run away alone at the age of ten. He spoke Persian with a perfect Iranian accent. I asked him why he had run away from his home, and he replied, "When I was seven years old, my father engaged his friend's daughter to me and gave a considerable amount of money to his friend for this purpose. Initially my father had agreed with his friend that we would not marry soon and would wait for a few years until we became older. But when I turned ten, my father hastened, held the marriage ceremony, and brought the girl to our home. When I married, I was ten years old and the girl was seven. I was not at all prepared to marry, and because of the marriage I became very melancholy. Twenty days after the marriage, I ran away from my home, got on a minibus, and came to Iranian border. There I mixed with other passengers and came to Iran with them."

"With whom did you live when you came to Iran?"

"With nobody—I lived alone."

"You were only ten years old. Who paid for your living expenses?"

"I worked and earned my living."

"When you arrived here, didn't you regret it?"

"No, not at all. I never regretted it."

"Do you wish to go back home to your wife and your parents?"

"No, I'll never go back."

"You never want to go back?"

"Never."

"Until the end of your life?"

"Yes, until the end of my life," he said firmly.

"Do you think that your wife is at your place, or has she returned to her father's house?"

"I have no clue."

In those days, when I was working as a laborer, I did not have much time to ask him about the details of his lonely life in Iran. Besides, I was afraid that if I asked him more questions, he might be offended. God only knew how he had lived his lonely life in Iran. But living alone in Iran was nothing new for boys; there were thousands of Iranian street children who lived alone without any guardian.

* * *

I lived in Iran alone for one year; I was not in contact with anyone in the family. At that time, my Marjan lived in Afghanistan with my elder sister Afsaneh. The relationship between my Marjan and Afsaneh and her husband, Zahed, slowly deteriorated. My Marjan owned a house in Kabul and received money from Europe, but Afsaneh and Zahed's financial condition was not good, and they lived with my Marjan in her house. Perhaps because of this, my Marjan expected them to obey her in every respect, but they didn't. Ultimately, my Marjan thought of coming to Iran and taking me back with her to Afghanistan. She expected me to do her bidding and make no decisions about my own life. However, she knew that I would not return to Afghanistan even if they gave the entirety of Afghanistan to me. Yet she wouldn't leave me alone.

One day I heard that my Marjan had come to Iran and, from my uncle's house, had inquired after my health and asked me to go to her, so we could decide about our life. I said to myself, *It's a mistake to try the option that has already been tried.* In order for her to understand my position, I did not visit her for the next ten days. After ten days I went with a bouquet of flowers to see her. When she saw me, she said, "Go clear your account with your employer; if he owes you money, take it and come home. We will look for a house, and then at the appropriate time we'll decide about our life."

I said, "I cannot settle my accounts so quickly. I need to work there for a while."

"Why do you need to work for some time?"

"Because I need money." I thought that if I raised the issue of money, she would ask me how much money I needed and would volunteer to either give it to me herself or ask Navid to send it to me. But she said nothing.

Presently she complained to me about Afsaneh and her husband Zahed. "Afsaneh and Zahed have become extremely selfish; they expect me to do nothing but appreciate them every day. They argue with me all the time, and their children have also become rude and misbehaved."

When my Marjan complained to me about them, I said nothing, but inside I felt very happy and said to myself, *Now they will know what I put up with for so many years.*

She complained to me about Hangameh and Mazdak as well. "Hangameh and Mazdak are so much at odds with you that they don't even like to hear your name—they hate you."

When I heard this, I said, "You just learned that they are at odds with me? You don't need to tell me that; I know everything. If they don't like me, they do it openly, and they don't want to abuse me. But you do it indirectly, and you abuse me. Their enmity is better than your 'friendship.'"

My Marjan listened to me carefully and did not reply. I said good-bye to her and returned to my workplace.

I did not visit her again for the next twenty days or so. She asked several times why I didn't visit her. Ultimately I went to see her again and stayed for a couple of hours. Then I did not visit her for the next three weeks. Again she inquired after me, but I did not visit her. Ultimately she came to see me. When she saw my room, she said, "Why didn't you come? We could have looked for a house."

"You go rent a house for yourself. I'd like to stay here."

"Why do you like to stay here, in this small and dirty room! Come and let us rent a house together. Only then will you realize that you have a life."

"Do you think I felt very happy when I lived with you in the house?"

"You are comparing this place to our house? There, your meal and tea were ready. There was no shortage of anything."

"You rent a house for yourself. When you live there, I'll come to visit you," I repeated.

"Get up right away and let us go. I haven't come here to argue with you; I have come here to take you with me."

"Go and stop talking. I'll come to see you later."

* * *

During one year working as a laborer, I saved enough money to pay the trafficker to take me to Turkey illegally. It was winter time and the weather was cold; for that reason, those back roads to Turkey were not suitable. I was waiting for the warmer spring weather to arrive so that I could leave for Turkey. I did not intend to rent a house and live with my Marjan because I thought that if I lived with her for some time and then left for

Turkey, people would say that I'd left my mother alone and deserted her. Meanwhile, I picked a fight with someone at my workplace and was forced to leave that place. So I rented a house with my Marjan and lived with her for a couple of months, until the spring.

I negotiated with the trafficker, and he agreed to take me to Turkey for nine hundred dollars. I had not informed my Marjan of my decision to go Turkey, but when I finalized my deal with the trafficker, I told her that I was going to Turkey. She said, "What will you do in Turkey? I have come here to take you back to Afghanistan."

"Now I am not going with Navid's money, so you can't make him change his mind. This time I am using my own money, and I know what I will do in Turkey."

"You are not so rebellious that you would go anywhere you like."

"I have my own money, and I do not depend on anyone."

"Will Hangameh and Navid let you go?" my Marjan asked.

"Hangameh and Navid are nobody to give me permission. If they have money, it is for them, not for me. I will not be their captive."

I had paid the money to the trafficker. My Marjan contacted Navid and Valid to tell them to forbid me to go to Turkey. She thought that I still listened to them, and if they didn't permit me, I would take the money back from the trafficker. Navid and Valid contacted me and said that if I went to Turkey and left Marjan alone, I would not be recognized as a member of the family—they would abandon me. I told them, "If you would abandon me, so be it. All the favors you did me in the past are appreciated, but you don't need to do any in the future. For the last several years you have worked for your own future, and Marjan was left with me. Now it is your turn not to leave her alone."

My Marjan also asked Hangameh and Mazdak to talk to me, but they actually didn't want to speak to me. Mazdak said to my Marjan, "You know it very well, Marjan, that so far as Hamid is concerned, even my good advice falls on his deaf ears. Talking about him is extremely tiresome for me. I do not wish to interfere in any of his affairs. If he does not listen to you, his mother, he wouldn't listen to me. Don't tell me to ask him not to go to Turkey."

I made my preparations to leave. Hangameh, Valid, and Mazdak no longer spoke to me, but that wasn't a big change: in the past, too, they did not make direct contact with me. They would talk to me once in a while just because they had called Marjan, and I was home with her.

Only at the time of my leaving did Navid call and say to me, "Now that you have ignored our word and are moving toward Turkey, call me when you arrive there. I'll try to help you come to Europe."

* * *

During the last days prior to my departure for Turkey, I spoke to my Marjan and told her the reason why I was leaving her alone, so that she would not feel bad. I said, "I have sexual problems. I cannot marry a woman, and I cannot have sexual intercourse with her. You know how it is in Afghanistan; if one does not marry, people revile him. If I go to Afghanistan, they would ridicule me every day until they drive me crazy."

"Why? Are you not a man? Why can't you marry?"

"No, I am not a man; I am an eezak (a homo). If I go to Afghanistan, people would taunt you because of me. They would say that your son is a homo," I explained.

She didn't believe me. "You brought the Taliban in front of the door of our house in Afghanistan in order to escape from there. Now you are just giving this bad name to yourself in order not to return to Afghanistan."

"No, by God I am telling you the truth. I am telling you this so you will not feel bad about why I left you alone. Otherwise I would not tell it even to you. If I go back to Afghanistan, people would ridicule you because of me, saying that your son is a homo."

"I don't believe you at all. You can no longer lie to me. You brought the Taliban to our door, and now you're faking this scandal and calling yourself a homo."

"I told you the truth in order not to disappoint you. You may accept it, or you may not." When I said those words, I felt a lump in my throat and I cried. My Marjan cried with me.

I knew what I faced back in Afghanistan, and I couldn't return. All sexual problems, from the Afghanistanis' perspective, invoke ridicule and sarcasm. Even men who marry a woman but do not have children are ridiculed. Those who have only daughters but no sons are taunted as "daughter-begetting" and "female-back." Many of those who do not have a son dress up one of their daughters as a boy and present her to all the people as a son to escape ridicule.

I knew even a daughter of one of our close friends that she was nine years old when she first knew that she was not a boy but she was a girl, although her mother was a teacher and her father was a doctor. Then she became very much disappointed when she knew she was a girl. Their coming out of the closet is as scandalous as that of the gay people.

I set out for Turkey, and my Marjan returned to Afghanistan. She lived there for some time with Afsaneh, and then Navid arranged for her to join him lawfully in London. Overall, I had lived in Iran for two and half years before my departure for Turkey.

Part Seven

Wandering

May 2004, from Tehran to Istanbul

In May 2004 the trafficker took me and two other passengers from Tehran to Istanbul. We boarded a bus in Tehran and arrived at the Turkish border without any trouble. At the border we joined others consisting of Afghanistanis, Iranians, Pakistanis, and Bangladeshis. We were told that from the border to Istanbul, we would cross several border and inspection posts. In addition to those hurdles, there would be police patrols that searched the roads twenty-four hours a day to arrest passengers travelling without a passport.

In order to hide from the police during our journey, we started after sunset and walked on foot all night: in clear and moonlit weather, in cloudy or rainy weather, in muddy fields or irrigated farms, in brooks and still waters, downhill and uphill, on mounds and mountains, on precipices and snow-covered peaks. We walked for hours on end. During the days we stopped at rough places for fear of police. We stopped four five days in barns, four five days in mountain caves, and one day under a low bridge through which a river crossed.

At nights when we walked, I recalled an Iranian song that said, *"Lucky the caravan that passes the night, and arrives at the destination at the break of the dawn."* But the destinations we arrived at the break of the dawn were barns where humans and the chicken and cattle were together. Once, when our caravan of thirty-five individuals entered a barn in the twilight of the dawn, it frightened the chickens and the cattle, who made strange noises. Seeing the frightened chicken, one of us laughed and said, "The chickens are afraid of us. They think we are a horde of strange two-legged animals which has encroached upon their barn."

Inside the barn there was no dry place to sit. After walking from dusk to dawn and being dead tired, we had no choice but to sleep on the damp floor. Insects crawled inside our clothes. One night we walked on foot from sunset to sunrise, for ten long hours. During those ten hours it rained cats and dogs continuously, and all our clothes and shoes were drenched by the rain. Because of the cold I had put on a velvet jacket, which after soaking in water became quite heavy. The next morning we were tired, desperate, and wet, and we arrived at our destination: a cold and damp barn. We slept in that barn with our wet clothes on until the sunset, when we resumed our journey. Those days were so painful that one day felt like ten. In Tehran the trafficker had told me to be prepared for long hikes; I had bought hiking boots for such occasion. Now they were filled with water. Even at nights when there was no rain, sometimes we had to walk through water with our boots on. Where the risk of encountering the police was high, we walked on foot; where the risk was low, we rode trucks. Finally, after a journey of fifteen days, we arrived in Istanbul.

* * *

June 2004, Istanbul, Turkey
I did not know anyone in Istanbul. When I arrived there, I walked around the streets for several hours. I was looking for a hotel where I could spend a few days. Hotels ask for ID and passport, but I had come here illegally and had no passport.

Overcoming

Ultimately I found an Afghanistani man who had rented several rooms in an apartment building, and he had converted it into an illegal hotel. He rented them out to those travelling without a passport. I spent three nights in that makeshift hotel. Then I found two Afghanistani men who lived in a bachelor suite, and I joined them.

When I was in Istanbul, I saw a large number of Afghanistanis who knew no one in Istanbul; some of them had no money and had come empty-handed. In the summertime, when the back roads of Turkey are more suitable for illegal travel, hundreds of young, penniless Afghanistanis arrive in the Zeytinburnu neighborhood, which is the gathering place of Afghanistanis in Istanbul. They wander about on the streets aimlessly, looking for shelter. Those without money look for jobs and food. Many of them sleep for several nights in parks and streets. I saw eight of them who slept in the sewing workshop of an Afghanistani who lived in Istanbul. Inside the workshop there were no beds; they slept on the floor at night and wandered about during the day. They had no money and found food with difficulty. I said to them, "I thought that I was the craziest person in the world to come to Istanbul without address; but you are crazier than me. You have come here without money and without an address."

One of them laughed and said, "No, mister, you are wrong. There are people crazier than you. And there are many more who are even crazier than us."

* * *

July 2004, Izmir, Turkey
I was in Istanbul for a month or two when I decided to go to Europe. Together with three Afghanistanis, whom I had met in Istanbul, I bought an inflatable boat with oars that could be folded and put inside a suitcase. After inflating it, it became the size of a two-person bed. We put the boat in the suitcase and went to the Izmir coastal area, in the west of Turkey, so as to row the boat to Chios Island in Greece. We inflated the boat at

night on the beach and set out for Chios Island. We rowed for four hours in the sea and came close to the island, when the Greek coast guard spotted us and stopped us. We were forced to return to Turkey. We rowed until dawn and came back to the Turkish coast. From there we returned to Istanbul.

I remained in Istanbul for a few days and then decided to go to Greece once again. I had no money. I contacted Navid in London and asked him to send me money. I asked for one thousand dollars, and he sent me exactly that.

* * *

July 2004, Bodrum, Turkey
I gave seven hundred dollars to a trafficker to take me to Greece. The trafficker sent me by bus with a group of eighteen persons, all of whom were Afghanistanis. The bus went to the coastal area of Bodrum, in the west of Turkey, and from there we were to go to one of the Greek islands. We boarded the bus in Istanbul, and after about fifteen hours we arrived in Bodrum. Upon our arrival the weather was stormy and the waves were high. We had to sleep for five nights in a jungle close to the shore, waiting for the storm to subside and the waves to calm down.

I was wearing thin summer clothes for the summer weather. The days were hot, but the nights were cold and freezing. Every night the storm would begin after sunset and gradually would whip into a frenzy until dawn. At night I took refuge in the slope of a flood watercourse to escape from the cold storm. The slope was three to four spans beneath the earth's surface. I slept in the watercourse without anything but a three-liter plastic bottle that I filled with water and used as a pillow; whenever I moved in my sleep, the screeching noise of the bottle hurt my ears.

Here was one of the passages of immigrants from the Middle East toward Europe. Some escaped from the oppression of the Middle East to stay alive; some went to earn a living. But I escaped from the ridicule and revilement of my culture. Here was a road that passed through the mouth of death. News arrived every day about the drowning of poor passengers and weak ships.

Ultimately the storm subsided on the sixth night, and the coastal waters became completely calm. We boarded a small, old boat that was as long as a bus; its motor made a noise like an old generator. We set out for one of the Greek islands, but on an indirect and long, winding course. The captain of the boat who steered was one of the Afghanistani passengers. After two hours of sailing indirectly, the captain changed the course of the boat toward a small and lit island. With the speed of the boat, I thought that we would arrive there in an hour. But the more the boat sailed, the more distant the island seemed, instead of coming closer.

We left the harbor when the ocean was calm, but in the middle of the ocean the storm slowly awoke from its slumber. At first, small waves covered the surface of the ocean, and the boat passed them smoothly. Small waves gradually turned to waves the size of rolling hills, and the ship floated on them helplessly like a matchbox. Then the large waves gradually turned into crazy, whirling ones, pouncing the ship like a hunter. Every wave that reached the boat hit it hard, but the boat limped on and stayed her course. Each time lots of water sprayed into the boat, and the salty water poured down from our heads and faces like torrential rain, burning our eyes and lips. Each wave violently pushed the boat up, but she would come down quickly at an angle of thirty-five to forty degrees. The next wave, following the first, would hit the boat almost vertically. Each time the boat descended, the height of her hull would become level with the surface of the ocean, and I would think that we would surely be devoured by the ocean. But before the water tanked up the boat, she would balance herself. The ocean was getting more violent when the boat suddenly dropped down from the crest of a high wave. This time the boat's hull was pulled downward to a depth of more than twenty centimeters. For the first time a sheet of water entered the boat from the front. But before the water filled it completely, she balanced herself again.

At this time a boy from Panjshir, who did not have a life jacket on, had hidden himself under the hull of the boat so as not to see the dangerous waves. But the thick wall of water that entered the boat drenched him from head to toe. The boy was suddenly shaken up and sat back in alarm. He refused to take a life jacket at the shore and said God would save him. The alarm with which he jumped made me laugh, although I was as terrified as him. But I said to myself, *What are you laughing at? At your death, when the boat is going to sink in a moment?*

Several other waves also filled the inside of the boat with water. There was a room at the lower level of the boat, which could be accessed from the middle of the boat where the captain sat and navigated. The room was now filled with water, and the captain's feet were in it. The captain called, "My feet are in water. Pump the water out quickly." I immediately started to pump out the water together with another person with the help of a hand pump. But it was no use; I thought that a large wave would drown the boat any moment and send her to the ocean floor. All passengers prayed to God to save them from drowning. The boat and the ocean were not friends anymore; now they were at loggerheads with each other, like sheep and wolves. Cruel ocean waves attacked the boat like a pack of wolves.

We sailed for five hours, and the island came closer. Buildings became visible, and the lights of honking cars coming toward us lit the boat. If the boat reached the shore while the ocean was stormy, she could hit the rocks on the shore and sink. This thought made me afraid of reaching the shore. I said to myself: *The island is very close, but before we arrive there, either the boat will sink or the coast guard will catch us.*

As soon as this idea hit me, I heard machine-gun fire. A Greek navy ship was speeding toward us. Our captain immediately turned the boat off and destroyed its motor so they wouldn't be able to turn us back. The navy ship stopped close to us. It was a warship, and a soldier who stood on the upper deck

Overcoming

with an RPG missile aimed at us issued the warning, "Go back to from where you came. Otherwise we'll sink you in the ocean."

Our captain replied, "I have destroyed the motor of the boat." But the soldier did not believe him. They continued to issue warnings for five minutes, after which the warship, which was modern and speedy, circled around us and created a whirlpool. The inside of the whirlpool had become deep like a pit, and we were inside it. If they had strengthened the whirlpool a little bit more, our boat would have drowned.

Some passenger shouted, "For God's sake, do not drown us. Have pity on us! We are Muslims. Have pity on us, we are Muslims..."

The word Muslim frightened me, and I shouted at them, "Don't say Muslim, for they will surely drown us."

But nobody listened to me, and they continued to shout. "Have pity on us, we are Muslims."

I said to myself, *We're lucky that these soldiers don't speak Farsi. If they did, they would drown us.* The warship distanced from us and then fired at us, hitting the gasoline tank. The gasoline spilled all over and covered the water. When I compared our boat to their warship, it seemed to me that our boat was like a malnourished child standing before a large WWF wrestler.

Soon a civilian ship arrived and towed our boat to the waters between Turkey and Greece and left us there. We remained afloat for about five hours, between Turkey and Greece. Ultimately a Red Cross boat came from Turkey and returned us to Turkish territory, where they handed us over to the Turkish police. We remained in Turkish prison for one week, in the city of Bodrum, and it was decided that all of us would be deported to Iran.

* * *

A number of Afghanistanis were sitting around me in the prison, and one of them was interpreting my statements to the police. I hoped that the Turkish police would not deport me to Iran, and

I said, "I am a gay. If I am repatriated to Afghanistan, they would kill me there." When the Afghanistanis understood the meaning of the word gay, their sense of honor was hurt, and they wanted to beat me up in prison, but they did not do it for fear of the police. One of them, named Barialay, who was extremely mindful of honor and pride, took my being gay seriously, and he became very angry.

During the one week we were in prison, the Afghanistanis were at odds not only with me but with each other as well. The prison was full of noise, and the Afghanistanis aggravated the situation. Prior to us a group of Iranians were in the prison. They all sat in a corner and seemed dejected and bewildered. The Afghanistanis were loud and noisy, and the Iranians were confused and perplexed.

As long as I was in the prison, I had no peace at the hands of some Afghanistanis, especially the man called Barialay. They wanted to pick a fight with me and constantly asked me why I called myself a gay, giving a bad name to all Afghanistanis. There was a middle-aged, firebrand Iranian who incited them to acts of violence against me. Whatever he said made Barialay twist with rage and want to attack me. In order to address Barialay indirectly, I said to the Iranian man, "Afghanistanis are intellectual people and respect the character of every human being." As soon as I finished my sentence, the Iranian man sniggered and looked at other Iranians. Barialay took notice neither of my words nor of his snigger—he just wanted to attack me.

In order to calm him down, I told him an anecdote from my past. "I had a sincere friend in Iran, and there was another person who did not want us to be sincere with each other. In my absence he told my friend every day to pull my hair, and in my friend's absence he told me not to allow him to pull my hair. He ultimately succeeded in his trick and caused a fight between me and my friend. When we made friends with each other again after the fight, we told each other about the instigator. My friend wanted to discipline the instigator by beating him up. But I said no; if he was a civilized person, he would be ashamed of himself. If he was not civilized, we couldn't make him one by beating him up."

The Iranian man asked, "Then what did he say? What did you say?"

I said to him, "My answer to you is silence."

There is a saying in the Persian language to the effect that silence is the answer to a fool's question. By using those words, I had made an indirect reference to this saying. When he heard my response, he was taken aback, and this shut him up.

During the one week we were in prison, we had no place to sleep at night. Everyone slept on the floor haphazardly. Some knocked into me on various excuses and harassed me. During the day they pestered me with questions about my being gay. There was no peace in prison.

* * *

After a week, we were handcuffed in groups of two and put onboard a bus heading toward the Iranian border. The handcuff of the man who was tied to me was loose, and he was able to get his hand out of the handcuff. The bus set out from the city of Bodrum, and after a couple of hours it stopped in the dark of the night in a market filled with people.

The man who had removed his hand from the handcuff said to me, "Let us go and run away."

I replied to him, "My handcuff is tight. Wherever I go, I'll be recognized as a criminal and will be rearrested. If you want to escape, go and run away."

He got off the bus. There were a few soldiers and police officers inside the bus. When he was getting off the bus, one police officer saw him, but because he was alone and had no handcuff, the police officer did not immediately realize that he was a prisoner and wanted to escape. After a few moments the police officer became suspicious and looked back; he saw me sitting alone on a seat. He came to me and asked me in Turkish, "Who was sitting beside you?"

I said, "I don't speak the Turkish language."

Other passengers acted as an interpreter between us. Ultimately I said, "The one who was sitting here has gone to the washroom."

By now about two minutes had passed since the man got off the bus. The police officer looked outside through the bus door but could not spot him in the crowd. He came to me, held the collar of my shirt, and dragged me out of the bus to beat me up. While there were people all around the bus, he kicked me in the back and punched me in the chest. I immediately grabbed my belly, which was not hit at all, fell on the ground, and rolled around while holding my belly. I pretended as if I was suffering from extreme pain in my stomach. The officer grabbed my collar again and tried to lift me up in front of the people to take me again inside the bus, but I made it look so bad as if I could not lift my weight from the ground. Now the officer felt ashamed in front of the people, and he put his hands under my arms and lifted me. He took me inside the bus and put me on my seat. If I had not done so, he would have beaten me up to his heart's content.

Among the passengers there was a man about forty years old who was sitting on a seat beside his wife. His hand was cuffed to the bus seat, but his wife was free. He had two children who were sitting on another seat, and they were also free. I was alone on my seat. The officer unlocked his handcuff, brought him next to me, and handcuffed his hand together with mine.

When he sat down beside me, he was angry at first and said to me, "Why did you let that boy escape? Now they have handcuffed me to you instead."

I said, "You were handcuffed anyway. What difference does it make if you are tied to the seat or to me?"

He pointed to his wife and said, "At first I was sitting there. Now they have brought me here."

"Here or there makes no difference. Wherever you may sit, they'll deport you all the same."

He laughed and said, "Here is no different from there?"

"No."

During the next leg of our trip, I noticed several times that he was looking at me. A little later he put his hand on my thigh. This did not make me suspicious, because all these days he had been with his wife, except this one week when we were in prison. Moments later he began to press and to massage my thigh with his fingers. Now I understood what he meant, but I ignored him. A little later he suddenly put his hand on the back of my hand and massaged it. Again I said nothing and ignored him. Whatever he did, I remained passive and did not stop him. From here to the Iranian border was a twenty-four-hour journey, and during these twenty-four hours he had a good time beside me.

* * *

We arrived at the Iranian border. There, the Turkish police, without coordinating with the police of Iran, drove us illegally toward the Iranian territory and ordered us to walk straight ahead; if we walked to our right or left, they would open fire on us. The man who was sitting beside me on the bus gave me two bags of his belongings and said that he would accompany me wherever I wanted to go. Since I was afraid that some Afghanistanis might beat me up at the border, I intended to run away and did not want to take the bags from him. But he insisted and gave me the bags. His wife and children were with him. We crossed the border with other passengers and moved toward Iran.

I separated myself from the rest in the dark of the night and set out alone, walking about a hundred meters away from them. Then I determined the direction of my path. I looked around me in order to see a city to walk toward, but wherever I looked I saw no lights; there was not even a small village to walk to. The terrain was completely mountainous. I was in the middle of mountains that had surrounded me on all four sides. I was in the lower slopes and should continue my journey in that direction. I had to walk on foot for hours in this region in order to find a city or a village. The problem was that I was wearing light summer clothes and only sandals on my feet. It was cold, and it was hard to walk on foot in sandals in the mountains. I started walking up the mountain to see a city or a village and then follow that direction. When I walked up the mountain, I saw no city or village, just more mountains. I decided to descend on the other side of the mountain.

On my way down I saw a valley. I walked for an hour along the valley and saw a light on top of one mountain; I realized that it was a border post. I did not know what else to do, so I thought I would give myself up to the border guards. I started walking up the mountain toward the light. When I came close to the post, I thought that land mines may have been laid around it. I did not know where the main road was, so I started whistling continuously from a long distance, hoping that the soldiers would hear me and come out of the post. On a corner of the post there was an observation deck. When the soldiers heard my whistling, they came on the observation deck and looked at me. I was quite far away from them, so they could not talk to me. By signals they showed me the road to the post.

When I came close to the post, the soldiers guided me calmly inside. But when I entered inside, I saw that an officer was sitting there. He looked at me and shouted, "Hands up. Don't move." I put the two bags down on the floor and raised my hands. He ordered two soldiers to search me. The soldiers came and searched me. I had two hundred Euros in my pocket. They removed the Euros and showed them to the officer. The officer took the money. They imprisoned me at the border post for twenty-four hours. The next night they cut the barbed wire at the border and turned me toward Turkey once again.

On this side of the border I had previously experienced the hardships of going to Istanbul. Now that I was alone and had no money with me, I didn't want to go to Istanbul. I preferred to go to Iran again. The border areas were laid with landmines, so I crossed the barbed wire and started to walk again toward the mountainous regions of Iran. I set out on foot up the mountain, and after two hours of walking I came to the top of the mountain and saw an illuminated village on the other side. I descended happily from the mountain toward the village.

The village alleys were full of trained dogs. The main occupation of the people of this village was cattle breeding. When I came close to the village, all the dogs started barking and moving slowly toward me. I had not yet reached the village when the dogs came to me. They were hairy, large, and terrifying. About eight to ten dogs blocked my way and would not allow me to get close to the village. Nevertheless, I continued walking toward it. The closer I got to the village, the more dogs from the village that would come running toward me. The dogs tore the bags in my hands. I threw the bags on the ground to keep them busy so that they wouldn't follow me, but they did not even look at the bags and surrounded me on all sides with their mouths open. They put their teeth on my shank but did not bite me, though they tore my pants a little bit.

Finally I reached the village. The dogs' barks reverberated so loudly in the valley that all the village people awoke from their sleep. Some people came out of their houses and hushed away the dogs. For fear of the police and of being accused of trafficking, the village people did not allow me to stay in the village, but they showed me the way leading to the city. From this village to the nearest city in Iran, which was Khoy, the distance was about seventy or eighty kilometers. I walked this distance with difficulty, and without a passport, ID, or money. The village people gave me food. The people living in this border area are Kurds. They are oppressed people themselves, and they understand strangers and help them without expecting anything in return.

I arrived in Khoy after suffering a great deal of hardship. I walked around in the city without a penny in my pocket, looking for a vehicle that would take me to Tehran. Finally I saw a group of people sitting by the roadside, waiting. A bus came and stopped close to them. They started to board the bus. I was quite far away from them, and due to exhaustion, I had no energy left in me to walk. I had originally decided to sit down for a while to rest, but seeing the bus, I forced myself to run and got on the bus without talking to anyone. I said to myself that wherever the bus goes, I will go with it. When I was on board, I saw that all the seats were filled except one, in the last row. I sat there. A man was sitting on my left side, and I asked him where the bus was going.

"To Tabriz," he replied.

"I have been deported from Turkey and have no money with me. I have boarded without paying the fare. I don't know what the driver will do about me."

"Where are you from?"

"I am from Afghanistan."

"Your Farsi accent is like that of the Kurds. I thought that you were a Kurd. I myself am a Kurd."

Most people in Iran thought that I was either a Kurd or a Lor because of my accent. Sometimes even Kurds or Lors thought that I was one of them, and they would immediately start talking to me in their own language. The man who was sitting by my side took out five hundred *toman* from his pocket and said to me, "The bus fare is eight hundred *toman*. When the driver's assistant asks you to pay the fare, give him these five hundred *toman* and tell him that you have no more money."

The Kurds are very generous people. Before arriving at Khoy, a Kurdish taxi driver brought me from a long distance to the city of Khoy and gave me a thousand tomans. I walked around in the city of Khoy for four or five hours and spent those thousand tomans there. The driver's assistant came inside the bus and demanded fare from me. I gave him the five hundred tomans and told him that I had been deported from Turkey, that I had only that five hundred tomans and nothing more. He accepted the five hundred tomans, and I came to Tabriz with that bus.

At the Tabriz terminal I was looking for a bus that would take me to Tehran free of charge, without demanding the fare. I asked a driver to let me get on the bus for free. He asked, "Where are you from?"

"Afghanistan."

"I am a driver. I do not own this bus, so I cannot allow you to get on the bus for free. Ask other drivers. If they own the bus, one of them might let you get on the bus."

I asked the second driver to allow me on board for free. He said, "I cannot do that." I asked about fifteen other drivers, to no avail.

Finally, one Tabrizi driver guessed from my accent that I was an Afghanistani. He asked me in his thick Tabriz accent, "Are you a *vatandar* (compatriot)?"

"Yes."

"Now that you are a compatriot, you pay no money; get on board."

The word *vatandar* in the colloquial Afghanistani language means a *hamvatan,* or a fellow countryman. Some Iranians address Afghanistanis with this colloquial Afghanistani word. The driver let me on without paying a fare, and the bus moved out. Halfway through the bus stopped for lunch. One of the passengers had seen the driver let me get on the bus without paying the fare, and he realized that I had no money for food; he bought me a meal.

* * *

August 2004, Tehran, Iran
Despite all the coming and going, I was back in Tehran. On the first day I was happy to be in Tehran because I had escaped from the hardships of the road. But the day after, when I got up from the bed, I saw myself in Tehran again, which made me extremely melancholy and depressed. I felt that I had returned to a desert full of dust and sand—the same desert full of dust and sand that did not accept me as a part of itself. I should have returned to the hell that would ridicule and revile me, but would accept me as a part of it. Sorrow and pain had wrecked my nerves, my heart was broken to pieces, and my eyes were hazy

and I saw everything gray. My visit to Turkey was the result of a long period of hard work that I had done in Iran, in the worst possible conditions, far away from home without friends and family. I thought of my past, of the culture of Afghanistan, and of my incompatibility to it. Reflection and brooding till dusk on that day made me completely confused, and I lost my appetite. Finally I asked myself, *How long will you think of your pain and suffering, and what will you gain from it?* This questioning reminded me of the words of Professor Sayyaf, an Afghanistani leader, and it somewhat calmed me down; I felt slightly better.

Professor Sayyaf and his allies in a war with the Taliban lost control of Kabul city in 1996. In an interview with BBC Radio, he said, "We have retreated from Kabul, but our retreat does not mean that we have accepted defeat. Because the outcome of Islam is never defeat, there is a weakness but no defeat. Ultimately we will succeed."

I said to myself, *I also think like Muslims. I will not be defeated. Defeat is not in my nature. I have retreated, but my retreat does not mean I have accepted defeat. I have weaknesses but no defeat. Ultimately I will succeed.* Then I gently hit my forehead with my fist to cast away my confusion; I rubbed my eyes with my hands. I decided that I would go to the traffic circle tomorrow and start working.

Early the next morning I went to the traffic circle, where they picked up laborers for work, and I started working from there. From that day onward I went there every morning. I was never jobless. Thus, I worked for six months in Tehran and saved enough money to give to a trafficker and go to Istanbul once again.

From Tehran I contacted Navid in London and my Marjan in Kabul several times, and I asked for their help to go to Turkey again. But they insisted that I should go back to Afghanistan, and that it was no good to go to Turkey or Europe. They did not agree to help me, and I had to pay the telephone bills, which were increasing, so I did not contact them anymore. I did not have a phone, but my cousin who was in Tehran had one. My

Marjan and Navid did not contact my cousin to inquire after my health. During those six months, I was completely uprooted and homeless; I had no room or place for myself. At night I shared the room of either one of my two cousins or one of my several friends, whom I had made acquaintance with in Iran. During those six months I paid them no money for food, but I shared food with them. Whatever I earned, I saved to go to Turkey once again.

I saved eight hundred and fifty dollars within six months. I spoke to the trafficker who had previously sent me to Turkey. He demanded nine hundred dollars. I told him that presently I would pay him whatever I had, and I'd get him the remaining fifty dollars later, when I arrived in Turkey. He accepted and he sent me to Turkey. No money was left for my basic needs. After twelve days of travelling in the back roads of Turkey in the cold winter days, without money, empty-handed, and without a room or place to live, I arrived in Istanbul.

* * *

January 2005, Istanbul, Turkey
I knew several people in Istanbul from before and phoned one of them named Navid, who was a close friend of mine. Navid was engaged in construction work in the Umraniye neighborhood in Istanbul, and his employer needed more laborers. Navid asked me to join him. I went there and worked for them for some time. There I had a place to sleep, and the employer gave us three meals a day. I worked there for over one month. It was a good life, and I had an adventurous time.

A few days after my arrival in Istanbul, I contacted my brother Navid in London and said to him, "I am back in Istanbul."

He said, "Now I know that you are not going to give up. Find a trafficker. I'll send you the money to come to Europe. But you should know that you will have no future here, even if you come to Europe."

* * *

February 2005, Marmaris, Turkey
Navid sent me the money for the trafficker, and I spoke to one to send me to Greece. I gave the money to the trafficker, and he sent me by bus, with a group of twenty individuals, to the coast of Marmaris in the southwest. From there we were to go to one of the Greek islands by ship. We got on the bus, and after about fifteen hours of driving we arrived at the Marmaris coast, where we waited until sunset for the ship to arrive. When it grew dark, the ship arrived and we embarked on it. The ship had not yet started when a high-speed Turkish coast guard boat came toward us and arrested us, and we were sent to prison again.

On the previous occasion, one of the Afghanistani passengers who was with us identified himself in the prison to the police not as an Afghanistani, but a Mauritanian. He was not deported to Iran but freed in Turkey. This time I and five other Afghanistanis identified ourselves as Mauritanians, not Afghanistanis. We remained in prison for one week, after which the Iranians and Afghanistanis were deported to Iran, but we were sent to Istanbul.

* * *

March 2005, Istanbul, Turkey
Before going to Greece, I settled my accounts with the employer for whom I worked. When I could not go to Greece, I did not go back to that employer but went to my previous friends, with whom I previously shared a house in the Zeytinburnu neighborhood in Istanbul. I lived with them again and worked in a shoe factory in the same neighborhood.

The trafficker could not send me to Greece, but the money I had paid him remained with him. I asked him to send me to Greece again. He replied, "Wait till I find more passengers. When I have a group of twenty passengers, I'll send you with that group."

I waited to go to Greece while working in the shoe factory. I worked there for more than one month. Meanwhile, I thought that if I went to Greece illegally and was caught and arrested by the police, they might deport me to Iran. So far I had attempted three times to go illegally. Before I tried the fourth time, wouldn't it be better to try the UNHCR in Turkey? The owner of the factory was a middle-aged Afghanistani named Qalandar; about fifteen individuals worked in the workshop. I made inquiries about the UNHCR to some workers. Four of them said that they also wanted to apply to the UN, but none of them knew anything about it. The owner of the factory, Qalandar, had some information about the UN. He had previously applied to the UN and was waiting for its reply—but he was doing it secretly, and nobody knew anything about it. When we spoke of the UN, Qalandar said, "I have no knowledge of the UN's conditions, but I know that its office is in Ankara. If you want its address, I'll give it to you. You go there and inquire what their conditions are."

* * *

11 April 2005, Ankara, Turkey
We took the address of the UN office in Ankara, and one day four workers and I approached that office to see what the conditions were. On the very first day they registered us in the office and conducted a brief interview with all of us. A summary of my interview is as follows.

"What problems are you facing in Afghanistan?"

"Ridicule, violence, and maltreatment by society against homosexuals."

"Are you a homosexual?"

"Yes, I am a homosexual."

"How did you enter Turkey?"

"Illegally."

"From which border did you enter Turkey?"

"From the Iranian border."

"Did you come to the city of Van in Turkey from the Iranian border?"

"Van was one of the cities through which I passed."

"If you go back to Afghanistan, what do you think will happen to you?"

I thought what I should say so that they would accept me. If I said that I could not bear their ridicule, it would not be a strong case, and they would say that everyone made fun of each other. If I said that I suffered from mental stress, they would say that everybody suffered from mental stress. I should say something to which they could not reply that it was not a problem. I said, "If I go back to Afghanistan, they would kill me."

"Who would kill you."

"People would kill me."

"Who are people? Can you say specifically who will kill you?"

"Specifically, my own family before everyone else."

My interview came to an end. They gave all of us a piece of paper (see Appendix 2) to which they pasted our pictures. Three of us, including myself, were told to go UN's office in the city of Van for a final interview. We were led to the city Van because we had entered illegally from that direction.

Prior to going to Van, I first went to Istanbul to prepare myself. When I arrived in Istanbul, the trafficker contacted me and told me that a group of passengers was ready to leave for Greece tomorrow and that I should get ready to go with this group. But I was afraid of getting arrested and deported to Iran, and I preferred to try the UN first. Two of my friends left with this group, and the next day they contacted me from Greece; they had made it. It was my bad luck that I did not leave with this group. I boarded a bus in Istanbul and came to Van, which was the easternmost city of Turkey, close to the Iranian border.

Part Eight

The Spider's Web

27 April 2005, Van, Turkey

I contacted the UN office in the city of Van on 27 April 2005, not knowing that contacting the UN would not only fail to bring me any support, but it would also waste my precious time. There they told me to first register myself with the security directorate of Van, and then I should come back to the UN, when they would set up an appointment for me. I contacted Van security for registration.

The Turkish police had a friendly attitude toward all refugees; it was very strange for me to see the police treating people in a friendly way, not in the usual fascist manner. On two previous occasions I had not seen any bad treatment from the police when I was arrested as an illegal traveler and was in prison, perhaps because I was not focused on police treatment and was enamored in my own plight. I had not seen the police treating people in a friendly manner in Afghanistan, Pakistan, and Iran, but in Turkey I never saw an unfriendly attitude, either from the police or from the people of Turkey.

The task of registration with the security directorate of the city took two weeks. Then I contacted the UN again, and they set up an appointment for me one week later.

***

18 May 2005, Van, Turkey

On the appointed day a lady named Bedia, who was the UN representative, interviewed me. The interview was long and lasted four or five hours. She asked me a lot of questions, most of which, in my view, were totally irrelevant. But I could not bring myself to ask her why she was asking me irrelevant questions. Moreover, I did not think that she would consider those questions at the time. The questions and answers that in my mind were important were as follows.

"Why did you leave Afghanistan?"

"I am a homosexual. I do not have sexual freedom in Afghanistan. Not only I do not have sexual freedom, but also I am subjected to ridicule and humiliation because it is a culturally backward society."

"When did you realize you were a homosexual?"

"Around the age of fourteen or fifteen," I replied.

"When did you leave Afghanistan?"

"Over four years ago, in 2001."

"What will happen to you if you go back to Afghanistan?"

"If I return, they would kill me."

"Who would kill you?"

"My own family. But I have problems not only with my family in Afghanistan but also with the entire society and the government too."

"In all those years when you knew that you were a homosexual, how were you able to live in Afghanistan?"

"I had no choice but to live there. As long as I was able to put up with the situation, I did so. When it became impossible, I left Afghanistan. I have a problem in Afghanistan with my own nature, not with my beliefs. If the problem was my beliefs, I could hide them. But how can I conceal my nature?"

* * *

According to the police laws in Van, I was required to stay there until I received a final reply from the UN. Bedia, who had interviewed me, was a small, thin woman with a pale and long face. Her eyes were deep set, and her neck and her hair were thin. She looked very meek, like the walking dead. When she spoke, her voice remained trapped in her throat. During the interview I noticed that her lips moved, but nothing came out of her mouth. My translator had the ears of a mouse who listened to her keenly and interpreted her words to me, and mine to her. With Bedia's oppressed face, I never thought that she would turn out to be an oppressor herself.

Three months after my interview, Bedia declined my refugee claim. I am not saying that she was cruel because she declined my claim. If she accepted the claims of those who were indeed genuine claimants, there would have been no room for bribe. A year later, I heard that Bedia was arrested by the police on charges of administrative corruption, and she was dismissed from the UN.

* * *

According to police regulations, refugees in the city of Van were required to go to the security directorate's foreigners department twice every week to sign. I rented a house in Van and started to live there. I did not work there, but my brother Navid sent me money from London. I spent the money thriftily so as not to put much pressure on my brother. After the interview I waited for three months, when the UN declined my appeal. But they had given me the right to object to their decision. (See the refusal letter in Appendix 3.)

I wrote my objections on the white sheet they had attached to their letter of rejection for writing my appeal, and I mailed it to the UN head office in Ankara, because letters of appeal were not accepted at the UN branch office in Van. In order to make sure that they had received it, I phoned the head office in Ankara one month after mailing it to them and made inquiries about it. They said that they had received my letter, and my file was assigned to another representative to review it. (See my letter of appeal in Appendix 4.)

The sign appearing underneath my appeal letter is the UNHCR's logo, showing a human being under the protection of its hands. I drew up this logo at the foot of my appeal letter and wrote the question on top of it, "Is it true?"

Qalandar's Lost Reputation

August 2005, Van, Turkey

When I arrived in the city of Van, I lived alone for three or four months, and then I shared a house with Qalandar. He was the guy who owned the shoe factory in Istanbul, and I worked for him there. He too left Istanbul and came to Van. About one month prior to his coming to Van, his wife eloped with another man, and he came to Van together with his two children to register himself with the UN.

Qalandar was sad because of his wife's elopement, and he said, "Because of my wife's elopement, I have been humiliated and have lost my honor; I can no longer look anyone in the eye."

In Afghanistani tradition a man whose wife elopes is ridiculed by the people and is taunted until the end of his life; after his death his children are also taunted. In such circumstances many people would pick a fight with him on any excuse, just to taunt him about his wife's elopement. Qalandar said, "I can no longer speak to people with honor because they would taunt me about my wife's elopement on the slightest pretext."

Qalandar had a ten-year-old son named Bahram. Qalandar was sad for his son and said, "I desired Bahram to be proud and courageous and honorable among the people; but his immoral mother, with the villainy she has done, has humiliated and damned him forever. He will always hang his head before the people, and he will always be a coward. People will call him names and will consider him of less noble birth."

Indeed, genealogy and family pride are first and foremost in Afghanistani ethics; they are more important than one's character. From my early youth, I was strongly opposed to those notions of parentage and family honor. If I saw anyone boasting about their lineage and family honor, I would think that they were comparing themselves to me and regarded themselves superior. In this situation I often could not control myself and would start an argument with them.

My maternal aunt was in the habit of boasting about her lineage. When I was thirteen or fourteen, I saw her boasting about those things. Although she was not talking to me, I said to her, "Very well, now that you have an excellent lineage, tell it to everyone every day, and boast. We who have no proper lineage should probably die!"

"Why are you so touchy feely?" she asked me. "If one says something, you take it upon yourself. You are not without a good lineage. All members of your father's family are great and honorable people."

"No, I don't like us to be of good parentage. You boast about your lineage every day. That's good enough for me."

We did not have an ill reputation, and yet if someone boasted of their lineage in front of me, I would think that they were comparing me to them. In such circumstances, what would happen to Qalandar's children if they wanted to live in Afghanistan? For such children in Afghanistan, it was not a question of a sense of inferiority; they had to drown in that inferiority. They would be ridiculed and reviled beyond measure. Because I was a homo, I knew how painful it was to be laughed at; I understood others' pain.

Qalandar did not smoke previously, but the pain of his wife's elopement turned him into a chain smoker. He lit a cigarette every few minutes. He had not been a habitual drinker, but now he drank every day to forget his wife. At the same time he cried every moment. In order to console him, I said to Qalandar, "If you pay too much attention to what people say, you will die. It's better to pay no attention to what people say." In order to make him realize that there were others who were less fortunate than him, I said, "No one is more reviled in the Afghanistani tradition than an *eezak* or a homosexual. I am one, and if I paid too much attention to what people said to me, I would have died a long time ago."

In those days, when I received a rejection letter from the UN, I wrote my appeal letter in Qalandar's presence and with his advice. When he saw that I wrote my appeal letter in that way, he did not believe me. He told me several times, "Don't tell those lies to the UN. No one believes those lies, let alone the UN. They won't accept you on the basis of those things."

I swore and said to him, "By God, I am telling the truth. I am what I am saying I am."

But he still wouldn't believe me and would say, "You are making a big mistake. You think the UN will accept you on the basis of those words?"

I said to him, "Then how do you think I can prove to the UN that I am a homosexual so that they would accept my petition?"

"I do not believe that you *are* a homosexual. First you have to prove to me."

"How do I prove it? I am what I say I am."

"You should prove to me in action; I should see you in action to believe that you are a homosexual."

"You want to see me in action?"

He laughed and said, "Yes, I want to see you in action."

Qalandar was an attractive man and was about forty years old. I was attracted to men in that age group. He had a large frame and was strong; I liked men like him. I told him, "It will be nice for me if you see me in action."

He said happily, "Very well, then come and show me."

In order to see his reaction, I put my hand behind his shoulder and bit his lips. His reaction was immediate, and we both started to kiss each other's lips. Right there I proved to him that I was a homosexual in all respects.

The next day Qalandar came to my house and said to me, "Why do you live here alone while I am lonely in my house? Come live with me. You'll be happy, and it will cut your costs, too."

Qalandar lived with two of his children, and I went to live with him in the same house.

* * *

Qalandar was rueful and regretted his past. He said, "I suffered pain for years and sacrificed my comfort so my wife and children would live comfortably. There was no shortage of anything in my house. That dishonorable woman lived in the best house, had the best furniture, wore the best clothes, and ate the best food. But ultimately she bit the hand that fed her and disgraced me before everyone. I did not expect her to live with me only for comforts. If she was unhappy with me in any respect, she should have told me that she was not happy with me. I would have divorced her, and she could have left the house honorably. But she humiliated me before everyone."

Why his wife eloped was a question for me. At first I thought that perhaps she ran away because he could not meet her sexual needs. Later, when I saw Qalandar in action, I knew that was not the case. He was the type of man who would satisfy anyone in the best possible manner; he would neither overdo nor underperform. In terms of attractiveness and manliness, most women fell for him.

Refugees went to the foreigners department in the city of Van twice a week to sign. At the foreigners department, several times I saw that Iranian women surrounded Qalandar and were anxious to establish a relationship with him. Normally it was improbable for Iranian women to look at an Afghanistani man. In terms of his attractiveness and manhood, I was surprised at why his wife eloped. His only weakness was that he was too proud; he never let anyone feel friendship and love on his part.

Overcoming

I finally asked him, "Why do you think your wife didn't want you?"

"Women who are not wise are easily deceived by the red and green market."

"What do you mean by 'red and green market'?"

"If a man looks in her eye with a smile and says, 'I love you, you are the best woman, I adore you,' and so on, the woman falls for appearances but does not think of the inner self."

The man with whom Qalandar's wife had eloped was very young, inexperienced, poor, and illiterate; Qalandar was an experienced man with a degree in veterinary medicine from Kabul University, which he obtained during the government of Dr. Najibullah. She left with the young man and went directly to Afghanistan. However, she repented pretty soon. When I lived with Qalandar at his house, his wife contacted him by phone several times and told him that she wanted to come back to him.

Qalandar replied to her, "When you left me you didn't want me. Now that you wish to return, I don't want you."

"Yes, I know I made a mistake," she'd say. "Please forgive me, and I promise never to make any mistake in the future."

"It is a mistake to try the one who has already been tried and tested. Even if I accept you, you are no longer what you used to be. You are a blot, you are a curse, and I don't want a curse."

"Please do not say those words. You and I cannot be separated."

"It's now too late for these things. You were not happy with me. I know everything about you. You have been unfaithful to me for a long time. I have suffered for your sake. I have been despised by others. I did everything for you that I could. Yet you were so ungrateful that you were fucking another man behind my back. If you were not happy with me, why didn't you ask for a divorce? I would have given you an honorable divorce, and you could have freely gone wherever you wanted to go. Now I cannot look anyone in the eye. Despite all that I suffered for you, that's how little you think of me? You still want to come back to me and expect me to accept you!"

"If you forget me, maybe I can forget you, too. But I cannot forget my children, not at all. I'll certainly come back because of my children. I want my children."

"Shut up, don't even talk of them. You are not their mother. They don't want a disreputable mother. My children have no mother at all. You always beat them up."

"You cannot take away my children from me."

"Get lost, you harlot! I told you not to even talk of the children. Don't phone me again. I don't want to talk to you anymore."

Finally, in order to stop his wife from contacting him again, he changed the SIM card of his mobile phone.

My Acquaintance with Manouchehr

December 2005, Van, Turkey

Since I'd come to the city of Van, I wanted to make friends with a couple of people like myself. I wanted us to wear special clothes, to look a special way that was neither male nor female. I wanted us to walk together so the people would realize that we were neither men nor women. I was thinking along those lines when I went to the foreigners department one day to sign. There I noticed an Iranian refugee who was my own age; his face and body looked half female and half male. With short hair and male dress, he looked like a man. But his makeup, trimmed eyebrows, shiny eye shadow, false eyelashes, lipstick, and painted fingernails made him look like a woman. He had arrived from Iran recently and had not yet the courage to use more advanced makeup. He had just begun to change his appearance but had not pierced his ears.

I felt happy when I saw him. I came close to him, said hello, and asked how he was doing. He replied to me and said, "I am fine, thank you."

"My name is Hamid."

"Thank you, Hamid."

"May I ask your name?"

"Sure. I am Manouchehr."

"How long have you been in Turkey?"

"Three, maybe four months," he replied.

"Excuse me, may I ask what kind of a case have you reported to the UN?"

"I have reported no case; I have social problems. I have reported my problems."

"Can you tell me more specifically what your social problems are?"

He became angry and, in a completely female voice, said to me, "Why are you asking me so many questions? I don't like people asking me many questions."

I tried to calm him down and said, "Because I am like you, and I want to know more about you."

"Because you are like me?"

"Yes."

"How are you like me?"

"I am the way you are."

"How do you think you are like me?"

"You are a homosexual, and I am a homosexual too."

He scrutinized me carefully and said, "You are not at all like me. You may be a gay, but you are not like me."

"Yes, you and I both are gay, and I am like you."

"Please don't talk like this. You are not like me. I am not a gay—I am a transvestite."

I did not know what transvestite meant, so I said, "It's not much different. Whatever you are, you and I are birds of the same feather."

He was a bit egotistic, and in order to pretend that he was superior to me, he said, "Please don't talk like that; it makes me unhappy. A transvestite has nothing to do with a gay, and you and I are not birds of the same feather."

As the saying goes, a guest doesn't like another guest, and the host doesn't like both. He did not like gays, and straight people didn't like either the gays or the transvestites.

I said, "In any event, I wanted very much to make friends with a couple of people like myself. Now I am pleased to meet you."

"Please don't talk like that. I am not like you."

I looked at his makeup and said, "I like to use makeup like you, and change my appearance."

"I am a transvestite and you are a gay. Makeup doesn't suit you at all. It's better for you to look the way you are."

"I have nothing to do either with the gays or transvestites; I like to change my appearance."

He was a monopolist; he wanted to be unique in every respect. He could not bear to see another person by his side looking like him. I soon came to know him better, and I realized that he could not bear to see even another transvestite by his side. He himself said that he was a jealous person, and his jealousy showed his feminine trait.

When I said that I wanted to change my appearance, he jealously replied, "You want to change your appearance? But you are a gay, and it doesn't suit you to change your appearance. I told you so, but if you wish to look like a clown, go ahead and do it."

In short, he did not receive me well and did not want to have anything to do with me. I told myself, *He is alone, he wears special makeup, he walks alone with his typical makeup, and does not want me to put on makeup like him so he won't be alone. So, why don't you dare put on makeup, and why do you seek someone's company?*

* * *

I went home and said to Qalandar, "From now on I am going to change my appearance. I will part my hair from the middle and dye one half ashen and the other half black. I will pierce my ears and will wear a gray-colored earring in one ear and a black one in the other. I will have a custom-made dress that is half gray and half black. I will buy a pair of gray shoes, and I'll paint one black and leave the other gray. I will put makeup on my face and paint my nails."

Qalandar replied, "Don't do this—if you do, people will know what relationship I have with you. Even if there was no relationship between you and me, they would think that there is one because we live in a house together."

"What difference does it make if they know? Let them know that you have a relationship with me."

"Well, people can't know this; no one should know this."

"I want people to know that you have a relationship with me."

"I know that you'd love people to know, but it will be bad for me."

Prior to this, I had told some of my friends there about my relationship with him. I said to Qalandar, "Certain persons know about it; I have told them about our relationship."

"If you told them, that was a mistake. No one must know about it. Especially if my children come to know of it, it will be very bad."

"Don't worry. It is unlikely that the children will know it or guess anything from my appearance."

"No. If you dress the way you wish, children will know that you are a catamite."

"For thirty years I have played a role and have concealed myself in a closet. I am now tired of playing that role, and from now on I want to be myself. People should know that this is how I am."

"You never tire of getting fucked. You want all the people to know and fuck you."

"No, by God; I do not think like that. I just want the people to know that this is how I am."

"If you like people to know, then first get out of this house, and then let the people know. If you wish to stay here, you can stay, but I will leave."

I had made my final decision to change my appearance. It was now very hard for me to postpone my decision, but I was not in a position to rent a house by myself. Thus, I remained there for some time and did not change my appearance.

*** * * ***

February 2006, Van, Turkey
Two months later I went to the UN office one day and saw Manouchehr there. This time Manouchehr happily came toward me and spoke to me sincerely. He apologized for the way he had treated me previously. Before leaving he invited me for lunch at his place. I accepted and accompanied him for lunch. He lived alone at his house and asked me to share it with him. I agreed. I had lived with Qalandar for six months, and now I decided to live with Manouchehr. The next day I picked up my belongings from Qalandar's house and came to live with Manouchehr.

There were three or four Iranian refugee families around the house where Manouchehr lived. All those houses were owned by one individual who was known as Haji. Haji had rented out his houses to Iranian refugees. When the neighbors saw that Manouchehr had brought me to his place, they reproached him for bringing an Afghanistani to his place. They said that the Afghanistanis were not good people, that none of them can be trusted. They insisted that Manouchehr kick me out of his place as soon as possible. They said that one day I would kill him and steal his belongings, and that my presence there posed a danger to them as well. Manouchehr regretted having invited me to his place, but because he had initiated it himself, he was not comfortable asking me to leave. But the neighbors constantly pressured him to kick me out.

Manouchehr started to test me, to see if I stole anything from the house. He would leave money all over the house and check if the money was lifted. The amount of money he left around was not much. But Manouchehr's fear was beyond stealing money; he was afraid of his own life, because the neighbors had told him that one day I would kill him and run away. During the one or two weeks I lived with him, we talked to each other, and I soon gained his trust. But the neighbors still insisted that he kick me out of his house. Gradually as his trust in me increased, he started to defend me against his neighbors. But he said nothing to me about how they thought of me, and I was not aware of the fact that the neighbors had taken a stand against me.

Manouchehr soon became more sincere to me, and one day said to me, "Hamid, the neighbors are pressuring me to kick you out from the house. They say that the Afghanistanis are not good people. I defend the Afghanistanis, but they don't believe me at all."

"Don't defend the Afghanistanis, but defend me."

"No, you are like them. I don't believe at all in what they say. All of them say that the Afghanistanis are bad people. I defend the Afghanistanis before anyone who says that the Afghanistanis are bad."

"No, not all of them are bad."

"All of them are good. None of them is bad."

"No, there are a lot of bad people among the Afghanistanis, too,"

"You are a selfish person. You say that only you are good, and the rest are bad."

"I didn't say that *all* of them are bad. There are good and bad people everywhere."

"Yes, I know that there are good and bad people everywhere. But these neighbors say that there are no good people among the Afghanistanis, not even one."

"No, that's not possible. There are lots of good people, and there are lots of bad people."

"There are more good, and fewer bad."

I conceded, "The long and short of it is that you can't trust everyone."

"Yes, I know that you can't trust everyone. You say that there are bad people among the Afghanistanis, and I agree with that. But these neighbors say that there is not even one good person among the Afghanistanis. At first I believed them and was afraid of you. But now when I see that you are a good person, I am sure that they are lying. Everything they said was a lie. If there is one good person among them, certainly there are many more. If there are bad people among the Afghanistanis, there are bad people among the Iranians, too. You cannot say that all people are bad because of a few."

Because I was still a newcomer there and they did not know me at all, the neighbors' opposition to me did not make me angry, and I showed no reaction to Manouchehr's words. I said to myself that if I stay here a little longer, they'd come to know me, and their qualms would go away.

In the following days Manouchehr told me a couple of times that the neighbors still insisted that he kick me out of his house. But these things were completely normal to me, because I grew up all my life among such criticism. *If I live there a few more days, everything will be all right,* I repeated to myself.

* * *

It was more than a month that I was with Manouchehr, when he said to me one day, "Hamid, these neighbors are not willing to give up on you. No matter how much I defend you and tell them that you are a good person, they still reproach me and tell me to kick you out."

"When was the last time they asked you to kick me out?"

"This very day they were angry and said, 'Why don't you kick him out?'"

"Which neighbor said this to you?"

"All of them say it."

"Specifically which neighbor said to you, today, to kick me out?"

"These selfsame neighbors in front of you. They all support each others' words."

Manouchehr refused to name the neighbor who had said those words today. I said to myself that so far they had not understood me, so the issue was not trust but stupidity. I had left Qalandar's house because of Manouchehr. If Manouchehr kicked me out, I could not go back to Qalandar's house, and I had no other place to go.

Manouchehr's Broken Tooth

Manouchehr told me about his past life, and in light of what he told me, it seemed that the situation of homosexual and transgender people was equally bad in Iran. When I was in Iran, I was not in close contact with the Iranian society so as to learn about their social behavior toward each other. As a laborer, I was at a distance from the society and was engaged in my construction work. In the past I used to think that the problems for homosexuals in Iran ware limited to the absence of sexual freedom and nothing more. I never thought that Iran may also have a culture of ridicule and revilement.

One day I said to Manouchehr, "Whether the UN accepts you or refuses you wouldn't make much of a difference for you, because returning to Iran is not such a big problem for you. Your problem is not having sexual freedom, and nothing else."

"So what problem do you have in Afghanistan?"

"I don't have sexual freedom in Afghanistan either, but my main problem is not sexual freedom. My problem is ridicule by the people. Perhaps I can put up with the absence of sex, but I cannot bear the ridicule and revilement by the people."

"What do you think happens in Iran?"

"Oh, they ridicule in Iran too?"

"Of course! Do you think that they pat you on the back? Do you think Iran is like Europe? Believe me, even if you go to

Europe, there will be people who ridicule you. Wherever you go, it's no different from Afghanistan."

"Maybe they ridicule in Iran, but in Afghanistan they ridicule you in a different way."

"It makes no difference. Ridicule is ridicule all the same."

"They ridicule savagely in Afghanistan. They don't simply laugh and talk. There are some who will attack you physically on one pretext or another."

Manouchehr was my age; we both were born in 1974. But some of the hairs in his beard and head had become gray, and he looked much older than me. He pointed to his gray hair in his beard and head and said, "Look, we are both thirty-one years old. But I don't look so old for no reason." Then he pointed to his broken tooth and said, "Look at this broken tooth. Kids made fun of me every day on my way to school. Ultimately I became angry one day and swore at them. They punched me with their fists and broke my tooth."

* * *

Manouchehr told me the story of his life; he had had a pitiful life, indeed. Both society as well as his family had treated him extremely badly, but not as badly as in the Afghanistani community. He told me how his family had treated him. "When I was eighteen years old, I decided to disclose my sexual orientation to my family. We were sitting around eating food. At that time I told my family that contrary to other boys, I had no interest in girls and was attracted to men. As soon as I finished my words, my father hit my face with his food bowl. After that, whenever my brother passed me by, he would punch me in the belly. The next day my father and brother went to the military draft department, and my older sister grabbed my hair and hit my head hard against the wall. In the entire family my mother was the only one who showed no reaction to this matter. After that they did not allow me to go to the school. They prohibited me from going to people's houses. They subjected me to hormone therapy and psychotherapy for a long period of time.

Because of the psychotherapy, they prohibited me from mixing with girls and women so as to stop their influence on me."

Like Manouchehr I also sometimes wanted to disclose my issues to my family in Afghanistan, but I dared not do it for fear of being called crazy and being ridiculed by the people. When Manouchehr described what happened to him, I said to him, "I used to think that perhaps I have made a mistake by not telling it to my family. But now when I see how much you have suffered at the hands of your family, I think I have done the right thing by not telling it to my family."

"Yes, you did the right thing. Had you told them, they would have expelled you from the school and caused you many more troubles."

"But I think that it would have been much worse than this. You, who are an Iranian, were treated this way in Iran. I can't begin to think of what they would have done to me in Afghanistan."

"There is no difference between Afghanistan and Iran. You would have suffered the same fate that I did."

"No, Afghanistan is much worse than Iran."

"What do you think of Iran? You think Iran is much better than Afghanistan?"

"However bad Iran may be, it can't be like Afghanistan, where they barbarously ridicule you."

"The way you talk of Iran, no society in the world has reached that humanitarian level. If you and I go to Europe, there are many people even there who would ridicule us. If Europe is like that, Iran has a long way to go to get to other nations' level!"

Reaction of People in Van

When Manouchehr and I lived together in the same house, because we both had spent all our live in constrains, we broke all limits in the relatively open environment of the city of Van. We pierced our ears and wore earrings. We dyed our hair, we wore ladies shoes, we applied makeup to our faces, and we walked outside on the streets. No one had ever done those things before us in the city of Van. In the early days no one got angry, but it was strange for them, and everyone looked at us. Sometimes we walked together down the sidewalk, on opposite sides of the street. The cars that frequented the road would be between the two of us, and we would laugh and talk to each other from the distance. The locals did not speak Persian, but we spoke Persian and laughed. There were many Iranian and Afghanistani refugees there, but we didn't care whether or not they understood our words. Some men followed us by car or on foot and suggested sex. Gradually a number of people became angry about what we did and swore at us, spat on us, threw rocks on us, and even attacked us.

When the people showed their reaction, it made Manouchehr sad, and he would simplify his appearance. But as far as I was concerned, the sharper people's reactions, the more excited I became, and I would make my appearance more feminine. When people cursed, laughed, and spat, it deeply hurt

Manouchehr, and he would become melancholy; he would lose his spirits and would complain about the reactions toward him.

I would say to him, "Why do you feel bad because of the people? Don't even think about the people!"

"How can I not feel it? I am a human being like the others. Why do they humiliate me so much?"

"They do it because of their stupidity. Whatever they do, it shows their foolishness, not your and my character."

"Hamid, lucky you that you think like this! I cannot think like you."

"It's simple. Just ignore them!"

"How can I ignore it? They curse me, they laugh at me, they spit on me," he complained.

"Those who curse you are the same as dogs that bark; those who laugh at you are the same as the monkeys that laugh; whatever else they do is the same as other animals."

"Hamid, good for you that you think like that! It's because of this that you haven't grown old. I cannot think like you. I wish I could."

When people cursed, it made me happy, and I would say, "Burn baby, burn; go on and curse." When they laughed and spat, I wore heavier makeup to burn them even more. When they attacked, I would run away. When they could not beat me up, I would say, "Damn you."

* * *

What Manouchehr and I did made our landlord angry, and he gave us a fifteen-day notice to vacate his house. But before that, Manouchehr asked me one day, "Do you know a bachelor man among your friends and acquaintances, and can you introduce me to him?"

"I know four or five young men, but I do not know any middle-aged man."

"The younger, the better!" Manouchehr said with a grin.

"I don't know whether or not they are interesting for you. They proposed sex to me, but I turned down their proposal because young men do not interest me."

"I like young men."

"Okay, I'll introduce you to one of your fellow countrymen. You could be friends to each other, if you want."

"What is his name?"

"Abolfazl."

"How old is he?"

"Twenty-seven, twenty-eight years old."

"Is he attractive or not?"

"Young men are not attractive to me. I don't know if you'll find him attractive."

"Then go and bring Abolfazl here tonight. But don't tell him that I have said these words to you."

I went to Abolfazl's house and said to him, "The effeminate with who I share the house has asked me to find a young man for him. Do you wish to be friends with him?"

"Hamid, why don't you become friends with me?"

"I don't have any interest in young men; I only like men who are at least eight or ten years older than me. You are younger."

"How is your friend? Is he handsome or not?"

"Haven't you seen him at the Foreign Nationals Bureau, where he had gone for signing?"

"I have seen him a number of times from a distance, but I haven't looked at him up close."

"If you look at him up close, you will find him more attractive than me."

"Okay, Hamid, I'll come with you tonight. But don't tell him that you have spoken to me in this respect."

"Interesting enough, he also told me to bring you here on some pretext, and he asked me to not let you know that he wanted to meet you."

"So I will come with you, and both of us will pretend that we saw each other by chance, and I came to see your house."

Thus I introduced Abolfazl to Manouchehr. They became friends with each other the very same night, and from then onward either Abolfazl came to our house or Manouchehr went to Abolfazl's place each night.

When our fifteen days' notice was up, Manouchehr and I went to Abolfazl's place to live with him. We shared our expenses and cooked together. I lived there for only about a month before Manouchehr and Abolfazl married each other, and they jokingly said that I was their daughter.

When we started to live together, Abolfazl stopped Manouchehr from putting on makeup and walking with me on the streets. Sometimes I put on makeup, changed my appearance, and went out to walk on the streets after sunset. Abolfazl would often reproach me for this, "Hamid, don't act like a whore, or they will beat you up one day in the street."

"So far no one has been able to beat me up; they tried a few times, but I ran away and burned them," I said.

"People are serious. I have seen that they don't like what you do. Ultimately they will beat you up pretty bad, or kill you."

"I am not afraid of dying, but I am afraid I might lose an eye or a tooth."

"Don't make fun of me! By God, they will beat you and kill you."

April 2006 Van, Turkey

One afternoon I went out to walk after sunset and entered an Internet café. I sat there behind a computer until 11:00 p.m. and then got up to go home. I was walking along the sidewalk when I saw an expensive red car with tinted glass windows stop close to me. The front-door window was opened, and I saw two young men sitting on the front seat. They asked me, "Where are you going?"

"I am going home," I replied.

"Come, get in; we'll take you home."

"No, I will walk."

"Why don't you get in? We'll take you home."

"What do you want from me?"

"We want to have fun with you."

"You are young. I don't like young people. I like only middle-aged men."

"Why do you like middle-aged men?"

"If you were forty-year-olds, I would have come with you. But not now."

"You want a forty-year-old"

"Yes."

"Then there is one in the rear seat."

One man was sitting in the rear. He himself opened the rear door and said, "Come to me. I am a forty-year-old." He was a big man and no more than thirty or thirty-two, but he introduced himself as forty.

I replied to him, "No, you are much younger. I cannot join you."

"If you don't want it, I don't want it either," he said. "Get in; I just want to talk to you."

I got in the car and sat beside the man who was sitting alone in the rear seat. When I sat, he brought himself close to me and put his hand on my shoulder. I said to him, "Remove your hand. I don't like to do this with you."

"I don't mean anything. I only put my hand on your shoulder as a friend, so that we could talk together. If you don't like me, I will withdraw my hand."

"It's okay if you don't mean anything."

"No, I told you that I mean nothing."

I asked them to take me to my home. They said, "Don't hurry. We'll take you home, but first we will drive around on the streets and talk. Then we'll take you to your home."

They drove around the street a couple of times. I thought that they wouldn't go far. The man who was sitting by my side put his hand on my shoulder. All of them were talking to me. Whatever they asked, I answered. They started to travel farther from the city. I thought that this time they wanted to take a longer route. The man who had put his hand on my shoulder put his hand inside my shirt and started to play with my chest. I tried to push his hand and said, "Don't do this to me. I don't like it."

But he did not let me remove his hand from my chest and said, "Just let me be happy; I don't expect anything more."

"I don't want this. Don't think that I like this, and that you can do anything you like. Do not expect to go any further."

"Okay, I'll be sure to not expect any more from you."

"I am warning you. You should know that."

"Rest assured. Only this much is good enough for me. If you don't want it, I don't expect it from you."

Overcoming

He was playing with my chest, but I had no interest in him. The car came to the farthest corner of the city and continued toward the outskirts of the city. I became alarmed and said, "I don't want to go farther than this. Go back. I want to go home."

"Don't be alarmed. We are with you."

We were four or five kilometers away from the city, and the man embraced me with his two hands and started to kiss my lips. This gave me a very bad feeling, and I pushed him away, but he was clinging to me and won't let go of me. The only thing that I could do was to press my lips together so he won't be able to suck my lips. But he continued to kiss my lips, face, and eyes. I felt extremely uncomfortable but had no choice. Ultimately we came about ten kilometers away from the city. They stopped the car in the countryside along the road. Two of them who were sitting on the front seat came out, and the one beside me told me to remove my pants.

"No, I don't like it," I said.

"You don't like it?" he said, and then he hit me in the face.

He wanted to have sex with me right there, but I said, "I am afraid that another car will come here and see us. Move the car and do whatever you like while the car is moving."

He called the other two and said, "Let's go." They got in the car and started it. The one sitting beside me sucked my lips and then my chest. He unzipped his pants, removed his organ, and asked me to suck it. He was completely aroused. I refused and said, "I don't want to do anything with you."

He insisted and pleaded, but I still refused. Finally he had had enough and shouted at me, "Why? Why not? You knave! I asked you politely..."

While he was shouting and yelling, he punched me hard in my face and head, and he squeezed my throat with his fingers and choked me completely. He kept choking me for about thirty seconds; I could not breathe at all. When he released my throat, his finger marks appeared on my throat and remained there for about ten days. He could have killed me with one hand. The punches that landed on my face and head made my entire face blue and black; those marks also remained for about ten days.

The man who was sitting by the driver's side took out a revolver from his pocket and pressed its barrel on my neck. He said, "Quickly, do whatever he wants you to do. Otherwise I'll kill you."

"Then what are you waiting for? Shoot. I am not afraid of dying."

The one who was sitting by my side hit me hard several times and said, "Shoot you? You want him to shoot you? You knave!" I saw his unzipped pants, and suddenly a strange idea entered my head. I brought my mouth close to his organ, as if I wanted to suck it. He said, "Now you are okay, aren't you? Now you want to have fun with me, right?"

"Right. Now it's okay."

In a gesture of thanks, he embraced me and patted me, and then in order to enjoy it better, he opened his belt, drew his pants below his knees, and leaned back on the seat with languid eyes so that I would make his day. This was the best opportunity for me to act on my plan. I took his penis in my mouth and pressed my teeth hard on it, but due to his erection it slipped out of my mouth. Luckily the soft tip of the penis got caught up between my teeth. Now I bit so hard on it that my lower teeth became crooked, which hurt my tongue for the next five or six months. When I bit hard on it, I expected him to cry and shout and the man in front to shoot me. But after about five seconds of biting, the remaining part of it also slipped out of my teeth, although I had no intention to let go. My purpose was to paralyze him, which I had achieved. In the meantime, I anticipated that the situation would worsen. The car was still moving, and we were getting farther from the city. Two other individuals were still waiting for me. There was no question of death anymore. Perhaps they would break my hands and legs, but they wouldn't kill me. The car was speeding.

I moved forward, grabbed the steering wheel, and tried to bring the car off-road. Now the only choice left for the driver was to apply the brake, which was what he did quickly. The car slowly veered off the road. There was a lot of empty and flat space on both sides of the road. The driver opened the door by my side, and the two of them pushed me out, which was exactly what I wanted. I relaxed myself so they could push me out. I fell out from the car and ran toward the farmlands. I thought that they would get out and beat me up, but they were trying to escape faster than me. They drove the car in reverse toward the road, changed their course back toward where they had come, and quickly sped away.

* * *

About a year had passed since my contacting the UN, but my case was still left undecided after the first rejection and my appeal against it. I wanted to raise that night's event before the UN as a security concern for me so they would decide my case quickly. Thus, the day after that, I contacted the UN, and they conducted an interview with me there. But the UN representatives paid no attention to this problem and left my case undecided.

Manouchehr's Nose Breaking

Four days after what had happened to me, Manouchehr had a second interview at the UN, eight months after his first interview. On the day of his second interview, Manouchehr left the house for the UN. On his way, five unidentified persons got out of their car and attacked him, punching him and kicking him so hard that his nose was fractured and his entire face became blue and black and swollen. He bled from his mouth and nose. At this same moment I came to the UN to talk about my security interview with the UN. I saw Manouchehr coming to the UN by taxi in his wounded state. His bleeding had not stopped yet, and he fell in front of the door, blood all around him.

The UN representative for Manouchehr came out with an interpreter, looked at him indifferently, and paid no attention. He looked at Manouchehr as if he were a sheep. Manouchehr, who had waited for eight months for an answer and yet another interview, said to the representative, "See what has happened to me?"

The representative said, "I am sorry."

"This has happened to me because of you," Manouchehr accused.

"Those who have beaten you up are animals."

I said to myself, *You utter the word "animal," but do you understand the meaning of it? What is the difference between you and the animals? Despite the obvious problems we have, you still do not wish to accept us.*

In response to what he said, I said to him in front of about fifteen people, "You are more animal than those animals. When you see it for yourself that we have such problems with people, why don't you accept us like human beings?" While Manouchehr was in a very bad condition and the UN representative looked at him indifferently, I shouted at the representative and said to him, "Animal! Why do you look at him like an animal? See what you have done to him?"

I humiliated him so much in front of the people that he became very angry, and he started to breathe heavily from his nose. A little later an ambulance arrived and transferred Manouchehr to a hospital. His interview was postponed for a few days and then held at last.

In the past I used to think that only intelligent and understanding people achieved high positions such as a judge or a UN representative, but the truth of the matter was that even dumb people could occupy such positions.

On the day of the interview, the UN representative asked Manouchehr, "Who were the people who beat you up?"

"I have never seen them before and do not recognize them," Manouchehr replied.

"Where were they from?"

"They were Turks."

"How do you know that they were Turks?"

"They talked to me in Turkish. As soon as I said that I didn't speak Turkish, they attacked me from all sides and kicked and punched me."

"Why did they beat you up?"

"Ask *them* why they did it."

"Why don't they beat me?"

"Are you a transvestite? Why would they beat you up?"

Twenty days later the UN representative gave Manouchehr a positive answer. Perhaps because of this beating, they did not reject his case. After his acceptance it was decided to send him to a country that accepted refugees, but the bureaucratic stages of this process would take one year before he could fly from Turkey to a refugee-accepting country. In the meantime they transferred him from Van to Sparta, in the west of Turkey, because of his security concerns. Both Manouchehr and Abolfazl went to Sparta, and I was left alone in the house.

Mehdi and Behroz

Almost a year had passed since I'd submitted my appeal letter to the UN, but my case still remained undecided. I used to visit the Human Rights Office every now and then in order to keep pressure on the UN to decide my case. During this period I saw no homosexual refugee other than Manouchehr in the city of Van. The refugees who were there before me told me that there were two Iranian homosexual refugees in Van prior to me: they'd filed appeals, waited for two years, and ultimately received the final rejection and left. At the Human Rights Office, they told me and Manouchehr that apart from us, there was another homosexual who had contacted them but didn't like to be recognized; he didn't want to come out of the closet. When Manouchehr went to Sparta, he became acquainted with eight or nine other homosexual refugees who had come from Iran and other Arabian countries; most of their cases remained undecided for a long period of time, or they were rejected. I spoke on the phone to two of them, Mehdi and Behroz. Mehdi had applied to the UN in 2004, he had filed his appeal in 2005, and his case remained undecided until 2006. Behroz had applied to UN in 2005 and had filed his appeal in 2006.

When I spoke on the phone to Mehdi in Sparta, he said to me, "There is no use for you and me to stay here. I have decided to go to Europe illegally. Come here if you like, and let us go together."

I said, "I have waited for one whole year. If I go illegally, what will happen to this one year of waiting?"

"Yes, you have wasted one whole year, but for no reason. Nothing can be done about it. It's better not to waste any further time."

"Are you sure that my waiting here is of no use?"

"Yes, I am positive. About a month ago three other homosexuals who had waited for two or three years ultimately went to Greece illegally."

"Is no homosexual accepted by the UN?"

"No, they have accepted two or three persons, but they do not accept all of us."

"Why don't they accept us? Don't they believe that we have problems in Afghanistan and Iran?"

"No, that's not the case. They know very well that we have problems. But they don't want to accept us."

"Why does the UN not want to accept us?"

"I don't know the reason. They accept someone if they want to; they don't accept someone if they don't want to."

"Are there a large number of homosexual refugees in Sparta?"

"There are about eight or nine of us here, but there are many in Kayseri and other cities."

"Has the UN rejected those who are in other cities?"

"It has accepted some of them, but it has either rejected most of them, or the cases are still pending."

"Is your decision to go illegally final?"

"Yes, because remaining here makes no sense."

"I'll not let go of it so easily, until I get the result of one more year's waiting."

"It's a mistake. You will waste your youth, and when you go, you will no longer be able to do anything for your future."

"Whether positive or negative, it doesn't matter, but I'll not waste my waiting time without getting a result."

Mehdi tried several ways of going to Europe illegally and suffered a lot by wandering from place to place. But like me, he never succeeded in going to Europe. I did not feel sorry for myself, but I felt sorry for those who, after years of waiting, abandoned their goal as if it were worthless. In the past I was very hopeful of being accepted by the UN, but now, when I heard that a lot of homosexuals received a final rejection, I gave up even that little hope that I had and waited only for my own final rejection. I now wanted to receive a final answer and then think about other options, so that I would not regret in the future why I had abandoned my cause halfway through.

Yilmaz, a Turkish Gay

When Manouchehr and Abolfazl went to Sparta and I remained alone in Van, I sometimes wore women's clothes, applied a little makeup, and went out on the streets to walk. Often I wore simple dresses—that is, only a pair of slacks and a rather feminine shirt. But for a few days I went crazy. I would wear a short, sleeveless, open-neck T-shirt and a miniskirt thirty centimeters long. My arms up to the shoulders, my chest, my abdomen, and my legs high up would be exposed. With this appearance I would walk on the streets at sunset, at a time of high traffic. People on all sides would look at me. In the past when I wore relatively simple dresses and makeup, those who didn't like it had showed their reaction, but now they were bewildered. The cars that passed through the street would slow down, and some would take my picture with their mobile phones. Van was a traditional city where even girls did not dare doing things like that.

My adventure lasted only three or four days. One day when I went out in a miniskirt and T-shirt, headed toward the photography studio to take my picture, a police car stopped in the middle of the road and forced me to get in the car. They brought me back home and said to me, "You are not allowed to wear a miniskirt."

I replied, "Turkey is a democratic country, and everyone is free to do what they like."

"Yes, Turkey is a democratic country, but our duty is people's security. If you wear skirts, one day they will take you to the mountains and kill you there."

* * *

There were over a thousand refugees in Van, but there were no homosexuals among them save me. At least, if there was one, he was not out of the closet. I made acquaintances with a few local homosexuals from Van, but because it was a small, orthodox, and traditional city, they concealed themselves and did not do anything to arouse people's suspicion. What I did there was dangerous.

One day one of the local homosexuals, Yilmaz, who worked at the Human Rights Office and defended the rights of homosexuals, said to me, "Hamid, what you do here is very dangerous. It is quite possible that they will kill you one day for what you do."

I said, "Your life and my life is over; this life is no good for you and me. We should pave the way for those who will come after us. We must make a bridge of ourselves so that the future generations can pass through us. We condemn our predecessors for leaving behind them this absurd culture; our future generations must not condemn us."

"Many have tried what you say, but it has cost them their lives."

"You think you are alive? How many years do you wish to live like this?"

Yilmaz was a male homosexual, but his face, the way he spoke, his actions and his habits were more of a woman than of a man. His body trembled, and he gesticulated with his arms and shoulders like a woman. "Wow, don't you know what kind of people live here. I grew up here, and I know that the people here are very dangerous. They *will* kill you one day."

When he trembled and gesticulated with his shoulders, I burst into laughter and could not speak for a moment. But I said to him in my head, *It's not your fault that you are terrified of death, because you have not seen death so as to know that there is nothing terrible about death. If you go to Afghanistan with this girly appearance, and you see the extent of ridicule and revilement by them, only then will you appreciate death.*

He asked me with surprise, "Why are you laughing? Don't you believe me?"

"Yes, I know that's how it is, and I believe you. But I am laughing because you don't know from where I come."

"I know you come from Afghanistan, and it is a dangerous place. But here too it is dangerous."

June 2006, Van, Turkey

In the twilight of the evening, while dressed somewhat like a woman, I was walking along the pavement beside a large parking lot. The parking was on my left, and on the right there was a deserted highway. A car with three young men in it followed me. It was dark, and the parking lot was completely empty and quiet. The car that followed me entered the parking lot and stopped close to me. Three young men told me to get in the car. I threw a quick glance and saw that they were young men. I said nothing and continued walking. They called me again, and I continued walking without replying. That was the right thing to do. I would not respond to men I didn't want, and I'd pretend as if I had not heard them.

They drove the car out of the parking and came to the highway. The road was one way; in order to get to me, they had to drive a long way and then turn back toward me. The car drove for a while and then came toward me and stopped close to me. One of them called out, "Come here."

This time I had no choice but to answer them, because I felt danger and thought that if they got angry, they would attack me in this deserted place. In order not to give them any opportunity, I did not stop, but while continuing to walk, I said calmly, "What do you want?"

"Get in and come with us."

"I don't go with anyone."

"What are you doing here at this time of the night?"

While I slowly distanced from them, I said, "I am just walking."

"Why don't you come with us?"

In order not to incite them, I preferred to remain quiet and continued walking. They called after me. "Are you a woman or a man? If you don't go out with anyone, why are you dressed like this? You son of a gun!"

By now I had gained a considerable distance from them, and they could not come to me because the road was one way. They drove away again and turned back toward me. I realized that my situation was precarious, and I maintained my composure so as not to incite them. I did not resort to any other trick and continued to walk calmly so as not to make them get out of the car and run after me. My heart throbbed with fright.

They moved toward the intersection, arrived at the point of the intersection, turned toward the return road, and started on the long road to get to me. In the meantime I quickly changed my course 180 degrees, because if I had continued on the earlier course, I would have reached the most secluded and quiet spot. As long as they were far away from me and I was hidden from them, I ran a long distance. But when they came close to the point on the other side of the road where they thought they would meet me, I started to walk again so as not to incite them.

When they came close, they noticed that I had changed my course on this side of both roads. This time they wanted to turn toward me from the intersection accessible to them, to trap me. The intersection was at a distance where I was not concealed from them. They came toward the intersection, and I immediately changed my course again, toward both roads. They noticed that I had changed my course once again. From the return road they came close at a slow speed and stopped. Suddenly three doors from both sides of the car flung open, and the three people ran toward me.

Before they could cross the width of the road, I started to run with all my might, not wasting a second. At a distance of about two hundred meters from here, there was a restaurant with some patrons inside. I ran this distance with speed that I had never used before. As long as I did not enter the restaurant, they were following me. But as soon as I entered the restaurant, where a number of people were sitting, they stopped at the door for a moment. They were shamefully defeated, so they did not wait for long. Had I fallen in their hands, I have no idea what they would have done to me!

* * *

More than a year had passed since I'd approached the UN, but my case was still undecided. I wanted to raise the last night's event as a security concern before the UN, so they would respond to my case sooner. Early the next morning I contacted the UN. An interpreter came to the door, and I explained to him what had happened. The interpreter went inside to his boss to explain my situation to him, and to report his decision back to me. I waited for a moment. The interpreter returned and said, "Whatever problem you have, write it down on a piece of paper and submit it to the UN."

I became extremely angry because the issues I had in Afghanistan were serious from my own perspective, and the UN paid no attention to me at all. They had paid no attention to my security problem on the previous occasion, either. At the height of my anger, I sat down and wrote a letter to the UN and submitted it to them (see Appendix 5).

My decision of Committing Suicide

July 2006, Van, Turkey

My newest complaint got nowhere, and my case remained undecided. During the period of my wait, I saw many people who, without any serious problems, approached the UN and were accepted quickly, even within one or two weeks. There were some like me who submitted an appeal, and they were quickly accepted. But despite the serious nature of my problem, which was more serious than others, no one paid any attention to my case in the UN. I waited there like secondhand furniture, to be thrown out one day. That was the UN's policy. If they considered someone important, they accepted him within the first few days. Those who were not important were kept in the dark for a very long time, their files to be thrown out in the garbage at the appropriate time.

    The experienced refugees there said that if a person had a strong chance of acceptance, he or she was accepted within the first twenty-four hours. The weaker the likelihood of acceptance, the longer the period of wait was. In fact there were people who were accepted within the first 24 hours of their approaching the UN, and there were many who received absolute rejection after six, seven, or even ten years of waiting.

    Meanwhile, the UN's treatment of homosexuals was not good. I had completely lost the hope of being accepted; I was only waiting for absolute rejection. I had made myself a captive of waiting. Time was passing to my detriment. I had no hope for my future and suffered from extreme depression.

About a month had passed since I'd sent my last letter, but they did not reply. I was so tired of my life in those days that one day I decided to commit suicide. I bought five liters of gasoline to douse my clothes and to set myself on fire in front of the UN office. I wanted to commit suicide, but in such a way that the UN representatives would be held responsible for my action. For that purpose I first went to the Human Rights Office and informed them that I had decided to commit suicide because of the UN's negligence toward me. They told me to refrain from it and that they would convince the UN to make an early decision on my case. I said no, they were stubborn and would never decide my case; I had bought the gasoline and would certainly set myself on fire in front of the office. When they saw my determination, the Human Rights Office phoned the UN and spoke to its representatives about my problems. But the UN representatives said that I had to wait until it was time to deal with my case.

The Human Rights Office sent a German correspondent, who was visiting their office, to interview me about my life. The correspondent came to my house and interviewed me, photographing my house and the gasoline container that I was holding. Then he contacted the UN office to plead on my behalf. The UN replied to him that he was only a correspondent and that they could not do anything about me outside of the UN regulations. The correspondent came with me to the UN office so as to interview me there. Outside the office, three security cameras were installed, and the guards watched from inside the office whatever went on outside. When the correspondent set up his filming camera in front of the UN office and started his interview with me, the office door was opened immediately, and the guards, who did not speak English, came out hurriedly, made noises and gestures, and stopped the correspondent from shooting the interview. They said that filming of the building was prohibited, and the correspondent could not shoot the interview.

* * *

I had made the decision to commit suicide, but on the day when I wanted to commit it, I said to myself, *For whom you want to kill yourself? For the UN representatives who are not worth a penny? If you kill yourself, what difference will it make to them? If they were decent people, if they had conscience and honor, they'd clearly understand that you cannot live in Afghanistan, and they should accept you like decent human beings. But if they are not worth a penny, why should you kill yourself for their sake? There are lots of malicious people among the public who see themselves as superior to you; you are a nobody to them. So you should stand up against the public and prove to them that superiority does not lie in large numbers.* It was this kind of thinking that made me change my mind, and I decided to stand up against the public and the UN representatives all by myself.

* * *

My decision changed, and I did something contrary to what I had intended to do. I took a long and hot bath, put on floral ladies slacks and a short floral ladies top, put on some makeup, and went outside at sunset to have a walk. I walked for a couple of hours along the sidewalk. A few people came close to me and proposed sex. Sometimes it was a lone individual, and sometimes two or three persons together. I did not count the number of individuals, but about a dozen times they proposed sex. I did not reply to any of them. When I did not reply, some insisted, and some went away without insisting.

Finally, the thirteenth time a man in a luxury car stopped close to me and gestured for me to get in the car. When I looked at him, I saw that he was the type that I liked. I got in the car,

Overcoming

and we said hello to each other. He asked me, "Where are you going?"

"Where would you like us to go?"

"How much will you charge?"

"I am not a prostitute and want no money; I want you. Let us go to our place. If you want to help me, I'll be thankful to you. If not, I want you, and I'll be thankful to you."

He came home with me and was my guest for a couple of hours. At the time of leaving, he gave me one hundred liras.

In the Middle of the Intersection

The next day I put on makeup and went outside around sunset to have a walk. While I was walking on the sidewalk, a man was following me and proposing sex. I looked at him and was undecided as to whether to say yes or no. While I was thinking, a car started following me and tried to take me on board. But I was not thinking about him because he did not interest me at all. He was in his late twenties, thin, and tall. I did not like young and thin men. He had followed me the day before and had insisted, but I had forgotten his face. This day he insisted several times, but I did not reply to him.

Finally he stopped his car close to me and got out of it. He came on the sidewalk, put one of his hands on my waist, and said, "I love you, my dear; come with me."

"Get your hand off my waist; people will see. It's indecent."

"Then let us go to a secluded place, so people won't see us."

"No, I am not in this business. Get your hand off my waist."

When I rejected him, he became angry. I was wearing a silver necklace. He seized my necklace and pulled at it. The necklace broke and bruised my neck. At the same time, while I was walking, he put one of his legs in front of my leg so as to throw me off balance, but I maintained my balance and did not fall on the ground. He started punching and kicking me. I continued walking, and he, while kicking and punching me, said, "You are not in this business! Then why have you put on makeup? You go with everyone else, but not with me? How much do they pay you? I'll pay you double."

"I have never gone out with anyone in my life and have never done this thing."

"You liar, damn you! I know someone with whom you have slept. I loved you. Yesterday I insisted so much, but you did not reply to me..."

He attacked me on the pavement right in front of the people. He threw a few punches and kicks and then let me go. He got in his car and drove away, but there were many people in the crowd who hated me and wanted to harm me; they simply did not have the courage to take the initiative and be the first to attack me. Now they had their chance. Two men from the crowd came and punched me a couple of times, and I started to run away from them while at the same time taking a mental note of the escaping car, so as to complain to the police. I thought that if I continued to run, those two individuals would stop following me, but no such luck. They were so mean that they continued to follow me. It was evening time, but it had started to grow darker. I was running on the pavement along the wide road, and many vehicles were coming and going at that time. There was no suitable place to take refuge, so I changed my course and ran from the pavement through the passing cars, to the traffic island in the middle of the road. But they were not to give up so easily.

First I continued to run on the traffic island, thinking that they would not follow me, but they too crossed the road through the passing cars and followed me quickly. Soon I arrived at the heavy traffic intersection, where traffic lights changed in quick succession. When I came to the middle of the intersection, many vehicles were crossing the road. I thought that if they got hold of me in a secluded place, they would beat the hell out of me. I decided to remain in the middle of the intersection and not move from there. Because the traffic was heavy at that place, they did not dare attack me. I remained there, and they went to the corner of the intersection and impatiently waited there for me to move. After a couple of minutes they lost their patience and started running in the middle of the intersection toward me.

I preferred to remain there and not move, because I thought that by running after me they only wanted to panic me and make me run—I never thought that they actually wanted to assault me there. But they came running and threw a few punches and kicks, so I deliberately ran toward the moving cars. They followed me for a while, and I stood right in front of the moving cars. They ran back to the corner of the intersection, feeling embarrassed in front of the drivers and thinking that they could be held responsible for the traffic jam. The intersection was in the shape of a simple square and had no roundabout or empty space in the middle. I was in the middle of the intersection, and the traffic lights continued to change every moment. Every time the light became orange, they would run toward me and kick and punch me. As soon as the other light became green, I would run toward the car that had started to move, and they would go back to the corner of the intersection and wait there for the light to become orange.

People all around the intersection realized that I was being assaulted. Gradually other passersby joined the attackers, and their number increased. I remained in the middle of the intersection for about eight minutes. At the beginning, when the number of attackers was small, they were afraid of being held responsible for the traffic jam and did not dare attack me in front of the moving cars. But there was strength in numbers. When their number reached about ten, they felt strong and no longer cared for the traffic jam or the red light, and they started moving slowly and purposefully toward me. When they came close, some threw punches at me, but some could not reach me due to overcrowding. In a situation like this, I became confused and did not realize from where the punches were coming. Blows were striking all parts of my body, and I barely noticed when I fell on the ground.

While I was on the ground, and kicks were landing on my body from every direction, I saw a police car that wanted to turn at the corner of the intersection and run away from the scene of assault. I immediately got up from the ground, blew a strong whistle from my mouth, and ran toward the police car. The attackers also looked toward the police car and immediately ran in the opposite direction. At the same time the police car also wanted to leave me there, but before it could do so, I blocked its way. Now they had no choice but to let me in the car.

At first I thought that the police wanted to run away from me because they too hated me, but later I learned that this intersection and this wide road separated two different jurisdictions from each other, which belonged to two separate police stations. The point where I was assaulted in the middle of the intersection did not fall under their jurisdiction. I had noted the license plate number of the first attacker and wanted to lodge a complaint against him then and there, but the police did not listen to my complaint. After some distance they made me get out of the car. I didn't want to get out and asked them to take me directly to the police station so I could lodge my complaint against the first attacker. The police told me to go there on my own. I learned later that the police made me get out of their car because they didn't want any trouble for themselves. In most cases they tried to avoid involvement and headache.

I was bleeding from my nose and mouth and my clothes were also bloodied, but I walked to the police station and explained to them what had happened. They asked me where the assault had occurred, and I replied, "The intersection along the Eki Nissan Jaddesi."

They said, "That point does not fall under the jurisdiction of this police station."

They phoned the other police station and asked them to come and take charge of me. Two police officers from the other station came by car and asked me about the place of assault. When I told them, they said that that place did not fall under their jurisdiction. While the police officers from both stations were there, they talked to each other so that one of them would take charge of me. Ultimately it was decided that one police officer from each station would come with me, and I would show them exactly where the assault had occurred.

When I showed them the precise point of assault, each of them told the other that that place did not fall under their jurisdiction but was the other's responsibility. Finally, in order to make them arrive at a decision quickly, I said, "I had nothing to do with the center of the intersection where I was assaulted. Initially I was walking along the sidewalk where they attacked me first, and then they dragged me to the middle of the intersection."

It was here that the main place of assault on the sidewalk had to be determined. One of the officers asked me quickly, "On which sidewalk were you attacked, on this side of the street or on that side?"

When I showed them, one of the officers became happy and handed me over to the other with a sigh of relief; the other reluctantly took charge of me. The sidewalk fell under the jurisdiction of the police officer who had originally wanted to run away from me.

* * *

I had written a letter to the UN office relating the attempt on my life, but my file was *still* on hold. This time I wanted to raise this recent assault on me as a security concern before the UN, to encourage them to decide my case at the earliest possible moment. My neck had been injured and my forehead had been wounded, I had bled from my mouth and nose, and my clothes were all bloodied. The next day I visited the UN office with my injured neck, broken forehead, and the bloodied clothes, believing they would accept my security concerns.

This time they agreed to conduct an interview with me because of the fact that I had been assaulted, and its signs could be seen on my body.

I entered the office with an interpreter, and then a middle-aged, aggressive woman said to be a British citizen and the head of the local UN office entered the room. First I thought that she might be a woman of character and personality, but she sat down in front of me, grumbled, and said, "Why do you fabricate a lie every now and then and come to us and waste our time?"

I also grumbled and said, "What lies have I told you? For everything I said, I have a solid proof and living witnesses."

She became a little softer and said, "What happened? What do you want to say?"

I remained stern as before and said to her, "Whatever happened to me before has happened yet again. If it was not repeated, I would not have to contact you."

Apparently she became soft and said, "Well, tell us what happened."

"I was walking on the sidewalk yesterday at sunset when a man asked me for sex. I declined his proposal. He became angry and physically assaulted me. When others saw him assaulting me, they also joined in." I explained everything from the beginning of the attack until the lodging of complaint with the police.

At the end she asked me, perhaps to make fun of me, "Why didn't you go to the police station before the attack? That's what the police are for."

"The police station is several kilometers from there. The only refuge that came to my mind was the intersection full of traffic, and I took refuge there."

"When you saw him coming toward you, why didn't you go to the police station?"

She repeated the same stupid question three or four times. Whatever answer I gave her, she would repeat the same question. Finally I said to her, "I am not as experienced as you are." Hearing the sarcastic reply, she smiled weakly and shut her mouth. When I saw that she was lost for words, I decided to overpower her in achieving my main objective of acceptance as soon as possible, which I thought was my absolute right. Thus, I said to her, "Of course you have the right to uncover the truth in whatever way you like, but as far as I am concerned, everything is absolutely clear. You can see that I have many problems here, let alone in Afghanistan, which is the center of all ignorance. You rejected me once, and I filed an appeal against your decision. Now a year has passed since then, but you still have not given me any reply."

She replied in a ridiculing way, "I am sorry for you. From our perspective you are rejected, and we can no longer do anything for you. You are now in Turkey, which is not a mean achievement. It is because of us that the Turkish police have not deported you yet."

In order to make her understand that I was not a small and hapless person, I replied, "Isn't it regrettable that you feel sorry for me? Whatever happened to me in the past was my fate; whatever will happen to me in the future is also my fate. Whatever happens to me has become normal to me, and nothing makes any difference to me anymore, because one might as well be hanged for a sheep as for a lamb."

My interpreter could not translate this expression, and she said, "You are rejected as far as we are concerned, and we can't do anything for you anymore." Then she added, "Your security concerns in Turkey have no bearing on your file with the UN office. If you have any security problems here, it is related to the Turkish police, not to the UN."

"The same security problems that I have here are related to my sexual orientation and are far worse in Afghanistan."

"You may request the police to transfer you from Van to another city. If you have indeed a problem, they certainly will transfer you."

I had no intention of going to another city because the UN had only two offices throughout Turkey, one in Van and the other in Ankara, and the police did not transfer refugees to Ankara. I intended to remain in Van as long as my case was open, in order to put pressure on the UN office.

My interview came to an end, and she said, "We cannot do anything at all. But if you still want to add something to your file, write a letter and deliver it to us."

Overcoming

I thought that despite what she said, she may not have any bad intentions in her heart. I said to her, "I don't see it necessary to write any further. Whatever I told you should suffice."

A faint smile appeared on her lips, and she got up without saying anything.

* * *

I left the UN office and started toward my house. I regretted having said what I did to her. I told myself that from the way this woman handled last night's incident, it was foolish to expect any humanity from her. I should not leave my file unchanged because of my expectations from this woman. I decided to write a letter to the UN office and submit it to them. I went home, wrote a letter, and delivered it to the office (see Appendix 6).

A few days passed after I dispatched that letter. So far, about sixteen months total had passed since I'd first contacted the UN, and it was about one year since the initial rejection and the submission of my appeal letter. I thought to myself that I had treated the UN office a bit harshly, and that with this attitude I would never get any result. Thus, I decided to change and soften my attitude so that they would at least give me a reply. I wrote a soft letter, and faxed it and mailed it as well (see Appendix 7).

One month passed since the dispatch of that letter. I wrote five letters to the UN, written in a soft tone, during the next five months. I faxed them to its office and also mailed the originals, but my soft approach was also to no avail.

Losing My Self-Confidence

During the period of my waiting, I saw a large number of new arrivals who would approach the UN office in front of my eyes, receive a positive answer, and be sent to refugee-accepting countries. But I, who had waited for almost two years, would receive no attention whatsoever. Those whom I saw having been accepted quickly were the ones who had political, ideological, or ethnic problems. When I compared my problem with theirs, I noticed that they had ten times better opportunities to live a natural life in their respective countries than I had. I saw many of them arrive in Turkey with a passport, being treated like a guest by the UN office and being flown to the refuge-accepting countries. But they did not treat me like a human being, although they knew my circumstances in Afghanistan, the conditions of my travel from Afghanistan to Turkey, and all the hardships I had endured.

Even I sometimes thought that perhaps I was not born with the same level of human evolution as others, and that's why the UN office did not treat me like a fully-evolved human being. I told myself that perhaps my brain, in terms of its structure, did not function like the brain of a fully developed human being, who displayed human behavior and reciprocally was treated like a human being. I did not consider myself corrigible since my brain, I thought, did not have the quality of corrigibility. I told myself that the reason the UN office initially accepted me and

Overcoming

people like me as asylum seekers was certainly our outward appearance. We had the outward appearance of human beings. But later the UN decided who was a real human being and who was not. When their humanity was determined first, their main problems and concerns were evaluated.

In fact anyone else who was bullied all his life like me would completely lose his self-confidence and would not consider himself as a human being. I was indeed bullied all my life. The culture of Afghanistan was the culture of bullying. I believed that anyone who had lived in Afghanistan had occasionally been bullied or had himself bullied others. If unfortunate people like me, who were born in the hell of ignorance and bullying, went to the heaven of wisdom, wise angels would turn into Azazel[3] for them.

There was one Afghanistani refugee there from the Hazara ethnic group named Dariush. Like me, his case had been undecided for about two years. Dariush used to tell me, "There are many like you and me who have actual problems and cannot return to their countries but are not accepted here. Then there are those who do not have real problems but are accepted quickly. The reason we are not accepted is our own fault, because we do know that we have problems but are not so logical as to make our UN representative understand that we indeed have those problems. People who are accepted quickly have a glib tongue; they know what to say to their advantage. We don't know at all what to say to our advantage."

---

[3] Azazel, name of the prince of Angels who later turned into the Devil

My decision of Returning to Afghanistan

I had lost all hope in my life, and there was no morale left in me to fight. I told myself that wherever I went, it would be the same for me; no place will be better. I finally decided to return to Afghanistan, and to maintain my feminine appearance to let people know that I was a homosexual. I also knew that if I did it in Afghanistan, I would be subjected to horrid violence. But I told myself that it would be better to be subjected to violence rather than ridicule and revilement.

Dariush, the Hazara refugee, was a very close and sincere friend. He was a Shiite and I was a Sunni-born, nonreligious person. We were two close comrades-in-arms.

When I was thinking of going back to Afghanistan, I said to Dariush one day, "I have made a firm decision to return to Afghanistan."

"It will be a mistake to do so," he said.

"I have no choice but to make this mistake. It was also a mistake to come over here, because the UN office has treated me so badly."

"The UN office's treatment of you is very different from that of Afghanistan. If you return to Afghanistan, and if they come to know what you have done here, they will kill you."

"Even if they do not come to know what I have done here, I will do the same again there."

"What will you do? Will you put on makeup and dress like a woman the way you do it here?"

"Yes, exactly the same. I'll put on makeup and dress like a woman and look at men whom I like so that they know what I want from them."

"When you go out here, how many people look at you and swear at you?"

"A lot of them. Why?"

"Well, think about it. The same number of people who swear at you here will attack you there with knives."

"So be it; I am not afraid of knives."

"They will hit you, kill you, and throw away your dead body."

"I am not afraid of dying, either."

Dariush smiled and said, "Before attacking you with knives, they would first arrest you and put you in prison."

"I am not afraid of going to prison."

Dariush was a happy man and always smiled. He often spoke excitedly and with laughter. He laughed and said, "When they arrest you, they will not put you in prison. In Afghanistan no one knows why you do what you do. They will think that you are insane. They will take you to a lunatic asylum and leave you among crazy men."

"Let them take me there. I am not afraid of mad men."

Dariush laughed excitedly and said, "How crazy are you! If they say nothing and do not take you to a lunatic asylum, children will follow you and shout at you, 'Hamid nadare.' What will you do then?"

Whatever Dariush said did not scare me, but when he suggested children following me and shouting at me, that frightened the hell out of me. I imagined at that very moment that children were standing behind me and shouting, "Hamid nadare." I said to myself: *Babeh nadareh freaked the shit out of* me, let alone Hamid nadare!* I said to Dariush, "I am not afraid of anything in this world, but I am afraid of people's ridicule."

"You wish to go back to Afghanistan and think that you have thought of everything, but there are certain things of which you have not thought."

Dariush told me a story. "Once upon a time there was a king. He had a servant who fell in love with his daughter. It was simply not possible for the servant to ask the king for his daughter's hand in marriage. Every time he saw her, it was hard for him not to have her. One day he was alone at home with the king's daughter. He thought to himself, *What would happen if I made love with her? The king would know and dismiss me from my job. It's worth it. But what if he ordered to break my hands and legs? It's worth it too. No, but what if he imprisons me? Still it's worth it. But perhaps he would hang me to death. Well, still it's worth it.* So the servant made love with the girl. When the matter was reported to the king, he ordered his soldiers to kick him out of the house. The servant said it was worth it. The king ordered them to break his hands and legs, and the servant said it was worth it. The king told the soldiers to imprison him, and the servant said it was worth it. The king ordered them to hang him to death, and the servant said it was still worth it. Then the king ordered the soldiers to shove the handle of a spade up his ass. The servant replied, 'I had thought of everything, except this one.'"

Dariush then said to me, "You want to go back to Afghanistan, and you say you have thought about everything. But you have not thought about children following you and shouting after you, 'Hamid nadare.'"

"I just won't let this happen. Before the children start to follow me, I will force their elders to kill me with their knives."

"You are stupid. No one has attacked you here with a knife. They won't do it there, either. The elders will have nothing to do with you. Only the children will follow you everywhere and shout, 'Hamid has no penis.'"

"Then why do the children not follow me here?"

"Here the children have not yet learned to follow you and shout after you."

"So the elders also have not yet learned to attack with knives," I said.

Although it was a children's habit in Afghanistan to shout "Babeh nadareh" and persecute, elders also had joined them indirectly. In societies where social upbringing was of a higher quality, elders of families controlled the upbringing of their children to some extent. But in culturally backward societies, the upbringing of elders themselves required improvement. The bigger problem was that where a pattern hardened in a different mold, it was difficult to reshape it to one's liking.

* * *

January 2007, Van, Turkey

I had decided to return to Afghanistan, but since I had wasted almost two years waiting to receive a reply from the UN office, I did not want to simply lose those two years without a result. Even in the case of my return to Afghanistan, I wanted the UN to remain involved. One day I contacted the UN to deport me to Afghanistan. They scheduled a date for an interview in this respect.

On the date of the interview, I came to the UN office in makeup and dressed like a woman. This time instead of the chief, a lady came to interview me and asked, "Do you wish to return to Afghanistan?"

"Yes. I want to go back to Afghanistan."

"If you return, the cost of your trip will not be paid by the UN. You will have to pay the costs yourself."

"I do not want you to pay the costs of my trip. I only want you to pave the way for my lawful deportation."

"If you pay the cost of your return, we will close your file here and will report to the police to deport you to Afghanistan at your own expense."

"You must tell the Afghanistani government to have nothing to do with me upon my return."

"If you have problems with the government of your country, we can't do anything. We do not interfere with the policies of governments."

"Yes, I do have problems with the government of Afghanistan and its society—and with my own family."

"Then if you return, you will return at your own request. If something happens to you, the UN will have no liability."

So far I did not know that UN representatives were responsible for refugees. I thought that if they liked someone, they accepted them; if they didn't like someone, even if he did have a problem, they didn't accept him. If something happened upon their return, they bore no responsibility for it.

I asked, "If I do not return of my own free will, and you deport me and something happens to me, will you be responsible for it?"

"Yes, in that case the UN bears responsibility. But the UN does not deport any refugee without his consent."

"It is almost two years that I contacted you, and you rejected me once already. If you reject me once again, and I return to Afghanistan and something happens to me, will you be held responsible?"

"If the UN deports you and something happens to you, the UN will be responsible; otherwise the UN has no responsibility. But the UN never deports anyone."

"If you ultimately reject me, then will you be responsible?"

"No, the UN never deports a refugee."

"Even if the UN absolutely rejects me, still it does not deport?"

"No, it will not deport you."

I said to myself, *Well, you are secondhand furniture that they have hauled from the street and stored in a corner for two years; when they find it useless, they'll throw it again on the street.* I said to her, "You are an intelligent person, and every reasonable person knows that in backward societies like Afghanistan, people like me have problems with their government, with their society, and with their family because of their sexual orientation. I will go back to Afghanistan with this makeup and in these clothes—I can no longer remain in the closet and conceal the pain in my heart. I only want you to convince the government of Afghanistan to have nothing to do with me. I do not ask you to do anything about the way society and my family will treat me." I said this so the government would not send me to a prison or a lunatic asylum.

She replied, "I already told you that the UN does not interfere with government policies. If you feel endangered by returning to Afghanistan, you do not have to return."

"I do not wish to go back as my choice; I want you to deport me forcibly."

She laughed and said, "The UN will never do this. If you do not want to return, you may wait until the UN office gives you a reply."

"If you do not wish to accept me or to deport me, then why have you wasted so much of my time here?"

She said politely and courteously, "Excuse me; my apologies. Can I do anything else for you?" She stood up respectfully and continued. "Before it gets too late, you may go and attend to your business. We'll talk about this matter later."

This display of courtesy and respect made me mad. I said to her in my head, *If you are indeed so ladylike, show your humanity in your acts and deeds; do not put on such a show of politeness. You dandies think that you are better than the vagabonds whose words and deeds are one and the same!* In order to put her in her place, I said angrily, "I am not talking about these five minutes that I spent here with you; I am talking about my two years that you have wasted here."

With the same courtesy and politeness, she sat down again and said, "Yes, I am sorry. I know that you have waited a long time here. If you have patience and wait a little longer, you'll get a reply from this office."

"Why should I wait when it is clear that I do have a problem, and when it is not certain whether or not you will accept me? Why should I wait? Do you promise that you will certainly accept me? If that is the case, I will wait."

"The UN office never promises anyone that he or she will certainly be accepted. The UN may accept or reject you. The reason that you waited a long time is the heavy workload. We have too many files and too few representatives. Our representatives continuously work on files and deal with them in turn."

"Which turn? I have seen more than a hundred persons who came one year after me, and they were accepted within one or two months. But I have been waiting for two years, and you tell me I should continue to wait?"

"Because you were rejected once, the stages of your file have become complicated and will take more time until a decision is made."

"I have seen several people who filed an appeal and received a reply one month after filing their appeal letter."

"The problem of each individual differs; some files are clear whereas some are more complicated."

"If the problem of each individual is different, why do you talk of turns? Where is my turn?" She found herself at a loss for words despite her smooth tongue and cleverness. I continued. "If my problem is not important from your perspective, why don't you reject me sooner? Why do you waste so much of my time?"

"You have waited so far; if you wait a little more, you'll get your reply."

Whether they accepted or rejected me was not important anymore. They had treated many homosexual refugees the same way they had treated me, and ultimately they had rejected them. The interview ended without a conclusion, and I left the office.

I Discovered the Secret of Asylum

When that lady told me at my interview that if the UN deported someone and something happened to him, the UN was responsible, but that the UN never deported anyone, I discovered the secret of asylum. I realized that even if the UN representatives were lions, I had to snatch my right from the lion's mouth. I said to myself, *If I leave a decision to the honor of the UN's representatives, they will continue to mistreat me the way they have mistreated me so far, and at the end of the day will reject me dishonorably and with humiliation.* For that reason I started to find a way to force them to either accept me or to deport me to Afghanistan as soon as possible, before they could reject me absolutely.

If a person is constantly bullied, he loses his self-confidence. In the past I used to think that the UN representatives could do whatever they wanted. I suffered from an inferiority complex in the extreme—even I didn't consider myself as somebody. But now that I realized they could not bully me here, I thought to myself that either I was not a human being, or the UN representatives were not. If I was somebody, I would teach those dandies a lesson.

Prior to this meeting, they didn't want to accept me and rejected me without any excuse; they kept me waiting without any excuse. This time I wanted to do something so that they would not be able to reject me or keep me waiting without excuse. For this purpose I first wanted to find a strong reason for them and then to go after my objective. I thought and pondered a lot, but to no avail.

At Kabul University we had a professor named Dr. Mohammad Usman Baburi, and he taught pharmacognosy, the study of medicines derived from natural sources. Professor Baburi was a very logical person, and all his speech was based on knowledge and logic. He lectured in literary language with a sweet Herati accent. During lectures he would place his right hand under his jaw, hold his right wrist with his left hand, tilt his head slightly to the right, and rest it on the palm of his right hand before he began his lecture. Whenever he gave us a lecture, I would enjoy it immensely.

When I wanted to find a strong reason to stop the UN representatives from making excuses and harassing me, nothing came to my mind. Then I thought of Professor Baburi and said to myself, *I wish Professor Baburi were here to write a beautiful text with a strong argument for me; I would give it to the UN representatives and to all the people so that the representatives could not mess up my file.* While I was thinking of those things, suddenly I imagined myself as Professor Baburi. I placed my right hand under my jaw, held my right wrist with my left hand, tilted my head slightly toward the right, rested my head on my right hand, and began to think. No more than twenty seconds had passed when an idea struck my mind: *The true host and the true home of every human and every living being is nature, and every living being in nature has equal right to live naturally.*

As soon as this thought struck me, I awoke from my fantasy of being Professor Baburi and started to write a letter to give to the UN office. I composed the letter (see Appendix 8), faxed the letter to the UN offices in Ankara and Van, and mailed copies of the letter itself.

I hand-delivered the original letter to the Van office and said to the interpreter, "Give this letter to the person in charge. I will wait here until the responsible official gives a reply to me."

Overcoming

The interpreter took the letter to the official and translated it for him. He returned with the letter, gave it back to me, and said, "The chief says that this letter does not relate to us. Send it to the UN office in Ankara."

I said, "I have sent one to Ankara as well. If it does not relate to you, keep it on my file. Tell the chief that I'll wait one month. If I don't receive any reply by then, I will show my reaction to you right here. I'll have nothing to do with Ankara."

The interpreter said nothing and took the letter inside again.

* * *

I made forty copies of the letter. When I delivered it to the UN office, I stood in front of the office and gave one copy each to all refugees that came there. I said to them in front of the interpreter and the guard, "I have written this letter to the UN representatives. You see how characterless they are! You will see how I would discipline them, in a way that they would not dare treat anyone in the future the same way they have treated me."

After writing this letter, I waited for one month. During this period I repeatedly contacted the Human Rights Organization, Amnesty International, and the police and said to them, "The UN representatives do not give me a reply. This is a rude act. If they do not reply within one month, I will discipline them." During this one month the employees of the Human Rights Organization contacted the UN representatives several times to get a reply for me, but they said that I had to wait. I had previously contacted the Human Rights Organization several times over the last year, but the mediation by the Human Rights Organization came to no conclusion. I said to them, "The UN representatives will not understand logic. I am forced to pay them back in their own coin."

They said, "But what you want to do is not the solution; the only solution is dialogue, and we will help you so that they give you a reply soon."

"If your help was any good, it would have done its job by now. So far it has been to no avail, and it will be fruitless even in the future."

I spoke to the police chief as well and told him, "If the UN representatives do not reply within one month, I will certainly discipline them. I am telling you in advance so that you don't ask me later why I did what I did."

He said, "Don't behave like an animal, or else we will deport you."

"If you wish to deport me, why don't you do it right now? I will certainly discipline them."

"You have a quarrel with the UN, not us. Why do you come here every day and speak to us? Go and tell them whatever you wish to say."

"I told you so you know in advance what I am going to do."

I informed Amnesty International of the matter as well, and I said to them. "If I do something against the UN office, do not let the police deport me."

I had been in contact with Amnesty International for over a year, and they replied to me, "It is your right to defend yourself. Rest assured that the police will not deport you, because the police do not deport any refugee. We will also intervene and would not let the police deport you."

The Police Officer's Crying Face

February 2007, Van, Turkey

When one month passed since the dispatch of my previous letter, I wrote another letter (see Appendix 9). First I faxed it to them, and then I carried it with me to hand-deliver it. UN employees regularly parked three or four cars behind the UN building. I bought an axe from the market, wrapped it in a newspaper and put it in a plastic bag, and carried it with me when I went to deliver the letter. When I came close to the door, I saw three cars parked there.

Before attacking the cars, I wanted to give the letter to the security guard. But because my fax had already been received by the office, the guard refused to take the letter from me and said, "I have been instructed not to accept letters from anyone."

While he was talking to me through a small window, I threw the letter inside the window and said to him, "You may take it or not; it was my job to bring the letter, and it is your job to accept it. Go and tell your dumb boss that I want a reply to this letter right away."

As soon as I threw the letter inside, two police officers responsible for the security of the UN office came out and took me under their surveillance. They looked at my hands and saw that I was holding a bag, from which the newspaper was popping out. But the axe that I had hidden in it was not in sight. One of the officers asked, "What do you want?"

"I have handed in a letter. I am waiting for a reply."

"Go; they'll reply later. They won't do it now."

"As long as they do not bring a reply, I'll wait here."

"What will you do if they don't bring it?"

"If they don't, I'll throw rocks and break the glass."

The police officers had known me for a long time and had seen that I was always at loggerheads with the UN. They knew that I was in the right, and for that reason they did not take the matter seriously and said to me, "It is our duty here to see that you do not throw rocks."

"If they do not bring the reply to my letter, you will see how I will throw rocks."

The police officers waited outside for a couple of hours to prevent me from doing something. I said, "How long will you wait here?"

"As long as you stay here."

"I'll not go."

"As long as you don't go, we'll stay here."

"At last you'll run out of patience."

"Our patience has no limits," they replied.

It was lunch time, and the police officers went inside to have their lunch. Outside the door, three cars were parked, one after the other. First there was a high-end white Benz without any luxury, which reflected its owner's personality. The next two were also high-end, expensive luxury cars. First I wanted to hit and destroy all three cars. But I said to myself, *No, this time it would be enough to show my reaction only; I'll save brouhaha for the next time. Perhaps only one violent reaction won't be enough; perhaps it would be better to repeat this violent act several times, to force them to make a decision about me.* Thus, I decided to hit only the white Benz. I unwrapped the axe from the newspaper, hit the car, and damaged the glass and its frame.

When the guards heard the sound of the axe and the breaking of the glass, one of the police officers quickly opened the door and saw me attacking the car. Suddenly fear appeared on his face. He was afraid that if he came close to me—as it was his responsibility to stop me from hitting the car—I would attack him. With his scared and pale face, he tried to come close to me. When I saw him in that condition, I felt sorry for him and said to him in my head, *You think I'll attack you? Who wants to attack poor you?*

In order to dispel his fear, I threw the axe on the ground. Even then, when he came close to me, he quickly grabbed my hands and forcibly twisted them behind the back of my head, holding me securely from behind to prevent me from attacking him with my bare hands. I showed no physical reaction, to assure him that I did not intend to attack him. I said to him, "This time I have shown you only my reaction; from now on I'll do it every day."

Following him, another older and senior police officer came out and saw that I had targeted his car. I saw his face suddenly change from normal to meek. He did not cry, but he looked as if he was crying. He did not shout and did not shed any tears, but he looked exactly as if he was crying. He came and looked at the car up close. I was standing by his side. He turned toward me and looked at me with his crying face. Suddenly he grabbed my hair with his two hands and shook my head. Then he grabbed my collar with his two hands and shook me forward and backward, shouting, "Why did you destroy my car? Why?"

I was extremely excited. I looked at my hands and saw that they were pale with excitement, and I said to myself, *If my hands are so pale, God knows how pale my face looks.* I replied to the police officer, "I have showed my reaction. From now on I'll do it every single day."

He was extremely angry and shouted at me, "Why did you destroy my car?"

"If it is your car or anyone else's, it doesn't matter to me. Whatever car is there, I'll destroy it."

"This is my car, don't you know? Why did you destroy it?"

"It doesn't matter if it is your car."

"You destroyed my car!"

"If it was God's car, I'd still destroy it."

He grabbed me from my collar again, shaking me and saying that I had destroyed his car.

* * *

The police officer whose car I had destroyed contacted the police station from there and asked them to come and see what I had done. He took a few pictures of his car to use as evidence of the extent of damage. The police came and took me to the station along with the officer whose car I had destroyed. There he explained what had happened, and they opened a file of his complaint. The police officer said to one of the other officers, "He came here and went on strike outside the door, and he attacked my car."

In order to frighten me, an officer said, "This is a terrorist act. Now I am going to open a file for it, and you will be sent to jail."

I said to myself, *They are trying to frighten me with these words! How simple they are. They have no idea who the devil I am.*

He asked me, "Why did you destroy the car?"

"Because I was on strike."

"Why are you on strike?"

"Because it is two years that I am waiting for a reply from the UN, but the office refuses to answer."

"If the UN doesn't give you a reply, it has nothing to do with the police. Why did you destroy the car?"

"This will not be the only time. From now on I'll destroy cars every day. As long as the UN office does not give me a reply, I'll attack the office every day."

The police officer phoned the UN's head office in Ankara and said, "A refugee has destroyed the car of a police officer. He says that as long as the UN does not give him a reply, he'll attack the UN office every day. When will you give him a reply?"

They asked, "What is the file number of that refugee?" The office gave them my file number, and they replied, "He has to wait until his turn. He will get his reply when it is his turn."

When the complaint file was opened at the police station, they asked for explanations both from the officer and myself. Then they took me from the police station to the hospital for physical examination, to determine if the police had physically attacked me at the time of arrest, and whether or not there were marks of assault on my body. Turkish law prohibited the police to torture and assault in such cases. Then both of us were taken to the public prosecutor's office.

There the prosecutor asked for explanations from the officer, and from me. The prosecutor asked me, "Why did you destroy the car?"

"Why? Because the UN office does not give me an answer. Two years have passed since I approached them. My problem is clear: I am a homosexual and cannot live in Afghanistan. Nevertheless, they don't give me an answer. They accept people who have no specific problem within a month or two. They have caused me loss; they have wasted two years of my life. Because of the UN's mistreatment, I have suffered in terms of my health as well. I have developed nervous problems, and there is nothing more valuable than one's health. I cannot take it anymore, and now every day I'll attack the UN office until they give me an answer."

"Did you know that the car belonged to an officer?"

"No, I didn't know that. But it is not important to me. I'll attack every car that is outside the UN door, whether I know its owner or not."

The prosecutor asked the police officer, "Isn't your car insured?"

"No, I have not insured the car."

"Then the payment of damages for your car is the UN's responsibility. Tell them to pay the damages for your car. Write a letter in this respect to the UN office here, as well as in Ankara, and request payment of damages."

One-Week Protest

The next day I went again to the UN office to see what their reaction to yesterday's action would be. The only change that I noticed was that no cars were parked there. It was 9:00 a.m. The interpreter talked to refugees through the hole in the window. I expected that the interpreter would tell me about the UN's decision. But when I came close to him, it appeared as if nothing had happened, as if the interpreter did not know me at all. He did not even look at me. I became extremely angry and said to myself, *They have not noticed what I have done, as if a fly sat on the cow's butt and the cow whisked it away with its tail, and now the cow is sitting contentedly. Perhaps the UN representatives are the cow, but I am not the fly. I will certainly make them talk.*

Without saying a word, I picked up some rocks right in front of the interpreter and hit the glass of the building. My throwing of stones was also girlish; I could not throw them forcefully enough to break glass. The rocks reached the glass several times, but because they were thrown from a distance, they did not gather speed and only the corner of a window cracked.

When I threw a few rocks, the police came down quickly and stopped me from throwing any more. They grabbed my hands forcefully, preventing any movement, and they contacted the police station to come and take me away. The police came and took me to the police station. On the second day they asked me at the police station, "Why do you make trouble?"

"Why ask me why? As I told you yesterday, you will see me there every day until the UN office gives me a reply. I don't think it is necessary for you to ask me for explanations every day as to why I make trouble. If you don't want to send a police car after me every day, tell the UN to give me a reply soon."

The police again contacted the UN officials in Ankara and asked, "When are you going to give him a reply?"

The reply was the same. "He must wait until his turn. We cannot do anything out of turn."

"He says that he will attack the UN office every day until it gives him a reply."

"We are sorry. We have no choice."

They kept me at the police station until sunset and they released me. I came to the conclusion that it was difficult to put the UN office under pressure because the police intervened. I said to myself, *It's a mistake on the part of the police to intervene; I must create so much trouble to tire the police and force them to put pressure on the UN to give me a reply.*

During the week I went to the UN office every single day and hit the glass with rocks, but I could never break the glass. Mostly the rocks fell in the yard before reaching the windows. Every time the police guarding the UN would call the police station, and the police station would send a car to take me to the station and hold me there until sunset. Every time the police station would phone the UN officials in Ankara and would tell them that I had created trouble again; they asked when they would give me a reply so that I would no longer create problems for them. The UN official would say that he was sorry and that he could not do anything for me.

* * *

I went to the UN office on the second week to continue my troublemaking. This time when I came close to the office, I saw the police guard had changed his tactics. He stopped me from coming close to the office, and tactfully tried to keep me away from that point, probably assuming that I would be afraid of his tactics and would refrain from getting closer. I said to him in my head, *You are such a fool. You think I would be afraid of you? I'll show you right away how I can make a fool of you.*

There was a large, empty space the size of a football field right in front of the UN building. When the police stopped me from coming close to the office, I walked toward the middle of the field so as to get close to the office from another angle. The police also started to walk along with me to stop me from getting closer to the office. It looked exactly like a game of football, as if I wanted to shoot at the goalpost, and the police wanted to prevent me from shooting at the goal. When I was treating the police guard like this, I remembered the memory of *Babeh nadareh* and that the children treated him the same way and threw stones toward him.

There were a few other refugees standing there watching us. The policeman was a few years older than me. This game looked foolish for him rather than me. When the policeman noticed that he was acting like a fool and was being laughed at, he got angry and ran toward me. I also ran a little bit and tried to get closer to the office from another angle. He ran several more times toward me, and I ran away from him and approached the office from another angle. Finally he thought that he looked like a buffoon and that enough was enough. He phoned the police station, and soon a car came after me. They had tired of taking me to the police station every day. This time they took me to a place far away from the city—behind the Van castle, close to the lake. They dropped me off so I could not get back to the UN office. There was no bus or minibus route to the UN office from this location. If I walked, it would tire me, and it would be late and the UN office would close before I could get back. I decided to go home that day, but I would still go to the UN office the next day to continue my troublemaking. I started walking toward my home.

Overcoming

I had hardly walked a hundred meters when I saw a car passing by. When the driver saw me, he stopped and called after me. He was a middle-aged man. He said, "Get in. Be my guest today."

I got in the car and said to him, "I am busy right now. Take me to the UN office; I'll be your guest another day." I gave him my phone number, and he quickly took me to the UN office.

Again I reached the UN door, picked up a few rocks, and hit the glass. One window pane finally broke. The police came out quickly. I threw a few more rocks right in front of the police. The policeman had pepper spray in his hand. He came close to me, showed the spray, and said, "I'll spray your eyes."

I opened my eyes wide toward him and said, "Spray."

He did not spray and brought his hand down. There were three other Iranian refugees there who had gone on a hunger strike, and they were standing there and watching us. When the policeman did not spray and brought his hand down, I said to him in front of the three Iranians, "You thought you would frighten me? I am not afraid of anything."

He said, "I'll hit you."

I put my hands over my kidney areas, brought my chest close to him, and said, "Hit me! You think I am afraid of being beaten up?"

He put his hands on my chest and pushed me. I lost my balance and easily fell on the ground. It was winter time, and I was wearing winter clothing. I got up from the ground, took off my windbreaker, and threw it on the ground. I placed my hands again as before, brought my chest closer to him, and repeated, "Hit me! I am not afraid of you."

This time the policeman looked at me with surprise and showed no reaction. I took off my sweater as well, repeated my motions, and yelled, "Hit me!"

He did not say anything. I took off my shirt and undershirt one by one and threw them on the ground. I took off my pants and threw them on the ground. The policeman gathered my clothes, brought them to me, and said, "Put on your clothes."

I took my clothes from him and threw them one by one in all directions. Then I quickly collected my clothes. The policeman thought that I wanted to put them on. I threw all my clothes one by one inside the UN building's fence. The UN office employees brought them out from inside. I threw them inside again.

It was a residential area. I looked at both sides of the street. I saw that all neighbors had come out and were looking at me. Those days when I made trouble for the UN office for several days consecutively, many people had taken notice of me and now were waiting see who would win the game at the end of the day, me or the UN representatives. The police, the Human Rights Organization, Amnesty International, and the townspeople had all taken notice of me and wanted to see what the UN office would do to me, or what I would do to it.

When I threw my clothes inside the second time, all office employees, both male and female, came out and brought my clothes with them. At that moment the police car arrived. I put on my clothes and went to the police station with them. This time the station phoned the UN office and asked them to give me a final answer at the earliest moment. I had put the UN under pressure from all sides. The Human Rights Organization phoned them every day, as well as the police.

When the UN officials treated me with such obstinacy, I came to the conclusion that all human beings are first born as children, and Thus, no matter how much they grow up and educate, they always maintain their childish nature and obstinacy.

* * *

My house key was in one of the pockets of my clothes, and it got lost when I was throwing them here and there. Because my house was locked and I could not go home, that night I went to the house of one of my friends, Kourosh. He was an Iranian Kurd and was a refugee in Van. He shared his house with another Iranian Kurd named Jalal, also a refugee. I saw Jalal for the first time and asked him, "What is your name?"

"Jalal."

"I am pleased to meet you, Jalal. You have a beautiful name. I forget some of the Iranian names quickly, but I will remember your name because it is beautiful."

"It may be beautiful, but I don't like it because it is an Arabic name."

"I am strongly opposed to this view. Some people don't like Arabic words in Farsi, but if we take out the Farsi words based on Arabic, nothing would be left. Right now when we are talking to each other, at least one out of every two or three words used is Arabic."

"Yes, indeed. Language is actually a means of communication, and the roots of words are not important at all. It doesn't matter from which language they came."

I often went out in the city of Van in makeup and ladies clothes. Because of this there were many people who talked behind my back. I didn't like people talking behind my back. I was thinking of doing something to stop them from talking behind my back. I said to Jalal, "There are many people who talk behind my back. I do not know what to do to stop them from doing this."

"You should be happy even when they talk behind your back."

"They don't say anything good about me—they say only bad things."

"Good or bad doesn't make any difference. The fact that they talk behind your back means that you exist and are in the limelight. That's why they talk about you. If they don't, that means you don't exist, that you are nothing. So even if they say bad things about you, it means that you are very much alive, and that's why they are talking about you. You are doing things here that no one else has done before. Whether they say good or bad, I believe that you are doing the best because whatever you do is original. There are lots of people among us who follow others, but those who do their own thing are few. Those who follow others are exactly like sheep because they have no independent ideas of their own; they merely follow the herd in front of them, like sheep."

Those words of Jalal put me at ease. It doesn't hurt me any more when people talk behind my back. Jalal convinced me to stop my violence against the UN. Instead he recommended discussion for the solution of my problems.

* * *

The next morning I got up and went again to the UN office. When the police saw me there, he thought that I wanted to throw rocks. He said, "What are you doing here?"

I said to the guard, "It has nothing to do with you. Go tell the official to come here. I want to talk to him."

"The UN does not have an interpreter to translate your words to the official."

"It's okay. Bring the official here. I speak the Turkish language."

"Okay. I will tell him right away."

"Tell him that if he doesn't come quickly, I'll break all the glass."

The UN office did not have an interpreter during that period; it was said that the interpreter was arrested by the police on charges of bribery and administrative corruption, and he was in jail.

Soon a representative came out named Deniz. He said to me, "Do you have a problem?"

"I have told you of my problems several times in the past, and I'll tell you again."

"I am a newcomer. I was not here before. Actually, I am not from Van."

"You may come from any country of the world or any city of Turkey; it is not important to me where you come from. Suffice for me that you are a human being." Deniz smiled but said nothing. I asked him, "What have you decided about me? Do you want me to continue my strike?"

"Now we have come to the conclusion that whatever you say, you actually do; we have decided to reply to you at the earliest."

"When do you wish to reply me?"

"At the earliest possible opportunity."

"Specifically when?"

"I cannot give you any specific date."

"I am giving you one week's time. If you don't respond within one week, I will continue my strike."

"No, one week's time is not enough. Please be a bit more patient."

"I am giving you only one week's time, and that's it. Don't haggle with me." Deniz said nothing. "I know that in the past you have given a final, negative answer to some homosexuals."

He said, "Yes, that's right. A final answer may be positive or negative."

"Why do you give a negative answer to homosexuals? You should accept the homosexuals."

"No. In our eyes no one has preference over another group. We may accept or reject anyone."

"Do you not accept that I am a homosexual?"

"We do accept that you are a homosexual."

"Then why do you reject me?"

"Being a homosexual does not mean that you may be considered a refugee. We accept that you are a homosexual. If you have a problem in your country, you have to prove it."

"You know that being a homosexual is a problem in itself in Afghanistan. I do not have sexual freedom in Afghanistan. If being a homosexual is not reason enough to be considered a refugee, do you think I should give up my sexual instincts?"

"We don't say that."

"Then why do you think that being a homosexual is not reason enough to be considered a refugee?"

"Your past is important to us; whether anything has happened to you in the past or not is important."

"You mean my future is not important to you? It is not important whether or not I will have sexual needs in the future, whether or not it will be dangerous for me?" I shot back.

"It is important for us to know about your past."

"If I go back to Afghanistan, do you think that I should conceal my sexual orientation from the people? Should no one know that I am a homosexual?"

"No, we do not say that."

"You do not say that, but that's exactly what you mean. If you do not mean this, then why should a homosexual be rejected?"

Deniz thought for a moment and then said, "I do not mean you specifically; we accept that you are a homosexual. But there are others who are actually not homosexuals and lie about it so that they can immigrate to foreign countries."

"If you doubt someone, you may refer him to a physician."

"Referring people to physicians is not a part of our work agenda."

"Then you may test him in action."

"How in action?"

"Do female representatives work here or not?" I asked.

"Yes, female representatives also work here."

"Do they work for refugees or not?"

"Yes, they do."

"Do they receive their salaries because of refugees or not?"

"Yes, they do," he repeated.

"Why then are the female representatives here?"

"I do not get what you are trying to say."

"For instance, that woman who worked on my file here, did she work for me or not?"

"Yes, she worked for you."

"Did she receive her salary because of me or not?"

"Yes, she did."

"Then she could sleep with a homosexual and find out if he is telling the truth or not."

He looked with astonishment at me and then assumed an angry manner. "What nonsense are you talking? You make me nervous." He turned his face in anger, as if he had nothing else to say and wanted to leave.

I said curtly in front of others, "I am naturally nervous."

He was afraid that I might start making mischief again. He returned and said, "Why did you use those words?"

"If you doubt that someone is not telling you the truth, test him with the help of a female representative. You will see whether he is telling the truth."

"I told you that I do not mean you."

"I am saying that if you doubt a person is telling the truth, test him with the help of female representatives."

"There are certain people who are homosexuals, and the tests show that they are indeed homosexuals. But they abuse their sexual orientation and go to overseas countries on this pretext."

"What do you mean when you say that they abuse their sexual orientation? They don't use your sexual orientation, so you may call it abuse? If they use their sexual orientation, you cannot call it abuse."

"Yes, their sexual orientation is their own, but it is called abuse because they do not want to live like a homosexual despite being a homosexual. They use their sexual orientation as a pretense to immigrate to foreign countries. Once they are there, they do not continue to live like a homosexual. If they do not live like a homosexual, they should not use their homosexuality as an excuse to consider themselves as homosexuals."

"It is their right to obtain their freedom; whether they live this way or that way has nothing to do with you. Abuse is the reason you cite to reject their applications."

Some people may not believe my statements, but I give you my word that this is the exact conversation I had with Deniz! God only knows how many people they have rejected on the basis of these foolish reasons, in addition to wasting much of these people's time. The problem is that at the time of the decision the refugee himself is not present to defend his rights against the reasons cited by the representatives. Only the representatives sit with each other; one makes a proposal, others second it, and a final decision of acceptance or rejection of the refugee is made on the basis of this copycat attitude. I am surprised how this competence is given to the representatives, to sit with each other and judge in the absence of the refugees.

* * *

I claimed I'd give them one week's time, but I did not want to go to the UN office for another two months. I wanted to go there when my reply was ready. Hardly three weeks had passed when I changed my mind thinking - if I don't go there for another two months, this entire ruckus that I've raised will be to no avail, and they will reject me in silence and ask the Turkish police to deport me from Turkey. In that case no one would ever know what became of me. Thus, it would be better not to remain silent but to continue this troublemaking.

Again, I went to the UN office and saw that nothing had happened. The file numbers of cases that they had decided would be typed on a sheet of paper, and the paper would be pasted on the exterior wall of the office. The refugees could read the results of their cases on the paper, and no one needed to knock at the door separately to ask the result of a case. When I did not see the number of my case on that paper, I felt nothing but angry. Clenching my fist I hit the door so hard that I thought it would fall down. A few refugees were standing there and laughed when they saw me hitting the door. They said to me, "No one knocks on the door of even a stable the way you knock on the door of the UN office."

Soon the policeman, breathing heavily and with a flushed face, opened the door and said, "What do you want? Why are you knocking on the door this way?"

"Call the representative!"

"Why can't you knock softly? Why do you have to hit so hard?"

"I have no patience for you. Go and tell the representative to come quickly."

A little later they called me in, and I went inside the office. A female representative was sitting there to interview me. When I went inside, she said to me, "Please have patience! Soon you'll get a reply."

"No, I have no patience. I want a reply right now."

I talked with her for an hour. We said a lot of things, and then I lost my patience. I was sitting beside a window. I hit the window glass with the back of my hand and broke the glass. My hand bled a little. The policeman came inside and threw me out. I wanted to throw rocks at the building from outside, but the policeman grabbed my hand tightly and did not let me throw the rocks. Again the policeman called the police station, and a police car was dispatched to take me to the station. I had made trouble for the police station many times previously, so this time they sent me to the foreign nationals branch. The chief of the branch called the UN head office in Ankara and asked them what decision they had made on my file.

Now the UN officials were forced to make a decision on my file at the earliest possible moment. They had to reject me so the police could deport me, or they had to accept me so I could be sent to a new country.

**

March 2007, Van, Turkey
I did not go the UN office for one week. When I went there after a week, they scheduled a new interview ten days after that date. Many of the appeal cases that were considered acceptable after studying the appeal letter were accepted without a repeat interview. But in my case, which was not important to them, they scheduled a repeat interview.

**

19 March 2007

I went to the UN for the interview on the appointed day, and a male representative named Deniz interviewed me. The interview lasted a couple of hours, and he asked me a lot of questions. I'll not describe all the questions. However, at the end of the interview he asked me, "In your view, if you return to Afghanistan, what will happen to you?"

"My view is not important; it is your opinion that is important."

"No, here your view is important."

"If my view was important for you, you would have respected my view from the very beginning, like a human being."

"It is important that you tell us what you think."

"If you have honor, you should know what will happen to me upon my return."

"Well, then tell us what will happen."

"I am a homosexual, and homosexuality is a crime in Afghanistan, punishable by death. If you ask me to forget my sexual instincts and return home, and you think that nothing will happen to me, then you are wrong to ask me about my sexual orientation. You are also wrong again about my sexual instincts, because your parents did not forgo their sexual instincts to bring the likes of you into this world." Whatever I said, Deniz noted it in the file. I asked Deniz, "Are you acting as the UN representative on my case?"

"No, the representative is someone else, but I have been charged with the duty to interview you."

"Who is the representative acting on my case?"

"The representative's name will not be told to you."

"Why not? I should know who is acting on my case."

"I have not been permitted to disclose the representative's name to you."

Since I had sent in my appeal letter and my file was picked up by a second representative, his or her name was never disclosed to me. I saw all the appeal refugees who, after the filing of their appeal, were told the name of their second representative. But they never told me the name of my UN representative.

*　*　*

12 April 2007, Van, Turkey
On 12 April 2007, exactly two years after I had contacted the UN office, they accepted me as a refugee. Was it really so difficult for them to accept me as a refugee? Was all that long, drawn-out tug of war necessary? You see, this is the plight of Afghanistani homosexuals! The UN representatives who have been appointed at the international level as the saviors of humanity treated me like this. As the saying goes, a knot that can be opened by hand needs no teeth. But the UN representatives tied a knot that was not a knot in the first place; they tied it with their tails and then opened it with their horns. I could speak for myself and was treated like this. What about a totally illiterate refugee from a remote village of Afghanistan, unable to defend his right by argument, yet he seeks asylum with the UN? How will he be treated? How many obstacles would the poor devil have to pass to attain his right?

Using the little education and a lot of boldness and audacity, I was finally able to achieve my right of freedom after two years. There are a lot of institutions in the world that engage in sloganeering, saying that freedom is the right of every individual, but in practice they do not grant that same right of freedom to anyone so easily. Over 60 percent of Afghanistan's population is absolutely illiterate. So how much can an illiterate Afghanistani homosexual have to convince the UN representatives with arguments, to obtain his right of freedom? It may be inferred from the UN office's treatment of me that those who cannot prove their claim with convincing arguments and actions do not have the right to claim refugee status. But if the UN representatives themselves engage in this mistreatment, it will be really hard for anyone to convince them. Thus, this is the logic of the world: Those who have always been deprived of human rights and the right of education, and who cannot provide supporting evidence, shall remain deprived of even the most basic right to live!

Undoubtedly those who read my memoirs will feel sorry for me. But at least I have been able to not surrender to oppression and ignorance. I have been able to unveil the faces of stupid and cruel people who nurtured the idea of superiority in their heads. Thus, one must feel sorry more for the innumerable oppressed people who have no legs to escape and no voice to shout.

I owe my UN acceptance to my older brother Navid, who, during my waiting period, always helped me financially. If he had not helped me, I would have had no financial support and certainly could not have defended my right against the UN representatives with peace of mind; I could not have been able to tear down their demonic wall of silence with my sharp arguments.

The UN and immigrant-accepting countries extensively accept their favorite groups which are relatively discriminated against as decided by these countries as well as immigrants related to certain jobs, specializations, or investments, directly from the countries of their origin. But they do not generously accept Afghanistani homosexuals even in the far-off countries, despite the discrimination against them and the violation of their human rights. *Will they have the honesty, notwithstanding their discretionary views, to accept the Afghanistani homosexuals from within Afghanistan as refugees?*

Part Nine

Ashakan Had Psychological Problems

May 2007, Van, Turkey

Last year when Manouchehr was attacked by unidentified persons in Van, the police transferred him to Sparta for security reasons. Then he married Abolfazl, and both of them went to Canada. When he left for Sparta, I was the only public homosexual left in the city. One year after he left, I was accepted by the UN office, and then I met an Iranian boy in his early twenties. Although he was wearing simple male dress and was without any makeup, it was completely clear from the way he walked and acted that he was effeminate.

When I saw him, I went to him and said hello. He looked at me like a girl and said in a soft voice, "Hello."

I asked, "Are you an Iranian?"

"Yes."

"How long are you here?"

"It's about two month's time."

"Are you a refugee? Have you approached the UN?"

"Yes."

"Your case is similar to mine."

"What? My case is similar to yours?"

"Yes, your case is similar to mine."

"Have you been accepted or not?" he asked.

"Yes, I have been accepted."

"For which country you have been accepted?"

"The country is not clear yet."

"Will you marry me? Will you take me with you?"

"No, I do not want to marry you. I am interested in older men only."

"Marry me only to take me with you, not for sex."

"Do not worry about going overseas. You will be accepted."

He said sadly, "I don't know—they have not interviewed me yet. I don't think the UN office will accept me."

"On what date has your interview been scheduled?"

"It is scheduled after a week."

"I know what you should say in your interview so that they accept you quickly. If you have time, come with me so that I can coach you about your interview."

"Okay, let us go. Tell me what questions they will ask me at the interview, and what should I say to them."

The name of this boy was Ashkan. He agreed to come with me so I could coach him about his pending interview. We were downtown and started walking toward my house, which was about half an hour away. During this half hour I realized that Ashakan had psychological problems. Whenever we came close to a group of people, Ashkan would think that they wanted to make fun of him. The poor boy had a strange appearance. He had a man's face complete with a beard, but the way he walked, talked, and acted was completely feminine.

During that week before his interview, I prepared him, and it went very well. Three months later, he was accepted by the UN office.

* * *

Ashkan later told me the story of his life. He had spent all his life in such a wretched way that, compared to him, I had lived like a prince. In Iran he was ridiculed by his neighbors, friends, and family as well as his classmates. Ashkan told me that his teachers and the school principal made fun of him. He was the only child of the family, and his life was so miserable that his father suffered heart trouble because of him.

When Ashkan was in Iran, his parents wanted him to marry early so they could see their daughter-in-law. Ashkan married early and lived with his wife for three years. During this time he never had sexual intercourse with her. His father was proud of his taking a wife and would say that no matter what the people said about his son, he was a man and had a wife. Everyone knew that it was impossible for a woman to never have sexual relations with her husband.

Later, when his wife saw that he was sexually dead, she made friends with other men. Ashkan did not oppose her but told her that the men who would sleep with her should also sleep with him. His wife accepted this condition, and both of them found a way to live their lives.

The woman whom Ashkan had married was eight years older than him and had been divorced by her previous husband. Ashkan told me that when he reached agreement with the woman and they decided to marry, he told his father, "She is eight years older than me, but I want to marry her. Is it okay for you if I marry a woman eight years older?"

His father, who doubted his son's manliness, said to him, "No, my dear, even if she is fifty years older than you, still she would be our loved daughter-in-law. She is most welcome." The only thing important for his father was to make sure that his son was a man; whom he married was not important at all.

When all the secrets between Ashkan and his wife were suddenly divulged, he separated from his wife at his family's insistence and then set out to Turkey. This was how the secret between them was divulged: One day two men who had a sexual relationship with Ashkan and his wife came together to Ashkan's house and went in the bedroom with Ashkan and his wife. None of them remembered to lock the door from inside. Meanwhile six guests arrived at home. The door bell rang, and Ashkan's mother opened the door to them. Ashkan's father had sold out his old house and purchased a new apartment unit in one of the towers in the north of Tehran; they had moved to this new place recently.

When the guests entered the apartment, they wished to see all the rooms. Ashkan's mother opened all rooms one by one and showed it to them. Then it was time for Ashkan's room. She told her guests that this was Ashkan's room, and she opened the door for them to see it. In the meantime the four people inside the room had taken off their clothes, and one man was lying on top of Ashkan's wife with another man on top of him. All of them froze in front of the guests and couldn't move. Ashkan's mother also froze and was humiliated in front of her guests. Ashkan admitted the real issue to his parents and told them that he never had any sexual relations with his wife. His father threw Ashkan's wife out of his house, and Ashkan himself left Iran for Turkey.

* * *

After Ashkan, I made acquaintance with a number of other Iranian homosexuals and transsexuals who were once married but later separated from their wives. Most homosexuals and transsexuals are able to establish sexual relationship with the opposite sex; however, they not only do not enjoy this relationship, but it is also unpleasant to them. It is estimated that every society has 3–6 percent homosexuals among its population. In countries like Afghanistan and Iran, homosexuality is one of the main causes of divorce.

* * *

Ashkan and I lived in Van for six months, and we became close friends. I have many beautiful and unforgettable memories from this period. Ashkan's file at the UN office was also referred to Canada. During the last days when I was in Van, Ashakan married a male Iranian refugee named Sajjad who was an active homosexual, but Ashkan was a passive one. Ashkan and Sajjad celebrated their marriage, which was videotaped. A correspondent from the Turkish TV channel NTV came to film their marriage ceremony, which was broadcast by NTV.

Haider Was University Educated

There were many Afghanistani refugees in the city of Van, and they could have been potentially dangerous to me because of their Afghanistani sense of honor.

One day I went to the Foreign Citizens Bureau for signing, and when I was returning, two Afghanistani men said hello to me. "Hello, fellow-citizen."

"Hello," I replied.

"Where are you going?"

"I am going home."

"You are an Afghanistani?"

"Yes, I am an Afghanistani."

"You are a fellow-citizen! Why didn't you introduce yourself to us?"

"I have had no chance so far to introduce myself to you."

"We want to get to know you better," they said to me.

"Thank you very much. It's a pleasure to make acquaintance with you."

"Are you going home now?"

"Yes, I came here for signing, and now I am returning home."

"Where is your house? We may come sometime to talk and get to know each other better."

"If you have time now, you may come, and we will talk to each other."

"Yes, we do have time. We are unemployed; we have nothing to do here but to wait."

"Yes, of course. I'll be pleased if you come with me and see my house. If we have each other to talk to, this waiting time will not be that hard."

Thus the two persons came with me to my house. When we arrived there, we started talking. Hardly five minutes had passed when one of them said to me, "What do they say about you? Have you a sex problem?"

"Yes, I have a sex problem."

"What sex problems have you?"

"I cannot marry a woman."

"What about outward appearance? Are you like others outwardly, or different from others?"

"I am like others outwardly, but my feelings are different from others."

"You mean you are not different from others in terms of your sex organ?"

"No, I am exactly like others in this respect."

"Can you show us once how you are similar to others?" He asked.

"No, I cannot show you."

"But it is important for us to see you."

I asked suspiciously, "Why do you want to see me?"

"Because that's why we are here, to see you."

"Forget about it. It's not possible."

"It is not at all possible for us not to see you."

He insisted vehemently that I remove my pants and shorts, but no matter how much he insisted, I did not agree to do this. Ultimately it came to a point where he started making advances beyond my limits, and he wanted to remove my pants and shorts by force. I resisted. At first I thought that he was not serious, but he was using full force to remove my clothes. In terms of age he was about ten years older than me; he was thin and small like myself, but he was much stronger than me, and my resistance to him was nothing.

I was wearing tight pants and a tight belt. He pulled my pants down to remove it, and I held it tightly with my two hands to stop him. In this struggle the seat of my pants was torn, and he quickly grabbed my pants again to pull them down. I thought that if I continued resisting him, he would not only remove my pants but also would tear them to pieces. So I opened my belt, and he angrily removed my pants. I was wearing brief women's shorts; he removed them.

He carefully looked at my penis and testicles up close, and when he saw that I was no different than others, he became very angry. He spit on my penis and said, "Goddamn you! You have no sexual problem. Why then are you giving a bad name to Afghanistanis all over?" He raised his fist in anger as if to hit me.

I quickly said, "You know it very well that if you touch me, the police will tear you harshly. I will complain to the police. Here it is not Afghanistan, and you can't do whatever you want."

When he heard the word police, his expression changed, and he opened his fist. He looked a little at me and said, "We only wanted to know whether or not you have a sexual problem. Now we have seen that you have no sex problem. When you have no sex problem, why do you defame Afghanistanis all over only to get accepted as a refugee by the UN?"

"All right, you have seen what you wanted to see. I will not complain to the police against you for this, and you can also forget about the why. If you would like a cup of tea, I'll make it for you. If not, it's time to leave."

The other man who made no interference and only watched as a bystander said, "If you make tea for us, that'll be really good. Let's forget about all this and sit down and talk."

They stayed for one hour, sipped their tea, and left. I assured him that I would not lodge a complaint with the police. I forgot all about this, but the man later tried to incite other Afghanistanis against me. He particularly tried to incite two persons from Parwan who were my fellow citizens. Those two from Parwan were Suroush and Fariburz, and both were my close friends; we saw them both frequently.

* * *

Several days had passed since the incident. I was at home when someone knocked at the door. I opened the door, and Suroush and Fariburz angrily entered my house. I said hello to them. Fariburz replied softy, but Suroush did not respond. I said hello to him again, but he kept quiet. I said, "Looks like you are unhappy."

"You are cheeky to say that I am unhappy."

"What happened? Who are you unhappy with?"

"Who should I be unhappy with?"

"Is it me?"

"Who else?"

"Why me? I haven't done anything wrong."

"You commit a sin, and you don't even realize that you have committed a sin!"

"What sin?"

The man who had pulled down my pants was called Haider. Suroush said, "A few days ago, Haider and Nawab were here."

"Yes, two persons were here, and one was Haider."

Suroush said to Fariburz, "See, they haven't lied! If they were here, then everything they said was true."

I was afraid that they might have said something to Suroush and Fariburz about me. "What did they say? I haven't said anything to them about you."

"I didn't say that you have said something to them about us. Were they here or not?"

"Yes, they were here."

"They pulled down your shorts?"

"Yes, they did."

"See how shameless he is! He simply says that they pulled down his pants! When they removed your pants, did they fuck you or not?"

"No, they removed my pants, but they did not fuck me."

"Then, at the end, did you serve them tea or not?"

"Yes, I served them tea as well."

"Well, well; quite interesting that you admit everything. You served them tea as well!"

"Why? Was it wrong to serve them tea?" I asked.

Suroush was very angry and replied, "They pulled down your pants, and you served them tea! You think that you have done a good deed by serving them tea? If you had honor, you would not have allowed them to walk out alive."

"What difference does it make if they pulled down my pants?"

"Now they will go and tell everybody that they pulled down your pants."

"So what if they say that?"

"Yes, we know it makes no difference to you. If a tree grows in your ass, you'll be happy to sit in its shadow. But it does make a difference for us."

"What difference does it make for you?"

"They won't name the name everywhere; they won't say that they pulled down the pants of Hamid. Nobody knows you, so they will tell everyone that they pulled down the pants of a northerner. Today we were sitting with fifteen other Afghanistanis. They came and said in front of everyone else that they had pulled down the pants of a northern kid. They did not know your name. They pointed to us and said that he was our fellow citizen. You dishonored us before fifteen people."

"But I am not a northerner; I come from Ghorband."

"Whether you are a northerner or not, they said in front of fifteen persons that they pulled down the pants of a northerner, and they pointed to us and said that he was our fellow citizen."

"Why didn't you say that he was not a northerner, he was from Ghorband?"

"People think that Ghorband is a part of the north, and we cannot argue with them."

There are limitless ethnic and regional conflicts in Afghanistan. Because of those conflicts the people of different ethnic groups and regions try to find weaknesses in each other so they can taunt them. The northern part is one of the geographical regions of Afghanistan, and the flatlands in the north of Kabul are known as the north. The region of Ghorband from where I come is a mountainous region located adjacent to the northern territory. In relation to regional differences and conflicts, people of other regions would consider Ghorband as a part of the north if there is something bad that can be associated with it. If there is something good about it, they will associate Ghorband with a region other than the north.

Suroush and Fariburz were both from the flatlands of the north, and the honor of this region was important to them. Because they were thinking of honor of the north, I said to them, "Haider is an ignorant man. You should pay no heed to what he says."

Suroush replied, "How can we not pay heed to what he says? We were humiliated in front of fifteen people—all of them looked at us."

I laughed and said, "What's done is done. There is no use thinking about it. Nothing will change."

Suroush said angrily, "No, you have to take revenge from them. We have to humiliate them and make them regret what they did. If you do not seek revenge, I'll break their hands and feet—as well as yours."

"If I pick up a fight with them, people will say that the Afghanistanis are unforgiving and constantly fight with each other."

"If they keep telling everyone that they pulled down the pants of a northerner, then it doesn't matter! But if people say that the Afghanistanis constantly fight with each other, then it's important, right?" I laughed but said nothing. Suroush said, "Don't laugh—I am not joking with you. I am talking to you seriously, and you have to take revenge on them."

Fariburz nodded and confirmed Suroush's words, saying, "Yes, we are not joking with you. Now we are talking to you seriously."

Overcoming

I was not afraid of Suroush and Fariburz, and I did not consider them dangerous to me because they were not the quarrelsome type. I wanted to put them at ease and did not want to offend them, because they were close friends. So I asked them, "What do you think I should do to take revenge from Haider?"

Suroush said, "You should make them say in front of us that they are sorry about what they did, and that they will never do it again."

"Both of them did not remove my pants; only Haider did. So I will take revenge on Haider alone and will have nothing to do with his friend, right?"

"Okay, Haider must say to our face that he is sorry about what he did, and that he will never do it again."

"All right, rest assured and leave it to me. I'll make Haider say so to your face."

* * *

It was decided that on the day of signing, Suroush and Fariburz would come to the Foreign Citizens Bureau, and I would make Haider repent about what he had done to me. On that day Haider came with three of his friends for signing. He walked slowly toward the building. I called to him from a distance in order to draw people's attention to him. "You idiot, come here; I need to talk to you." Haider immediately realized that he was in trouble and was about to lose face. In order to avoid this, he acted as if he heard nothing and did not reply. I called him again, "I am talking you, wimp! You pull down people's pants—now answer to police." Some people heard me and looked at me to see to whom I was talking. Haider bowed his head down and pretended not to see me at all. When people paid close attention, I came near to Haider and shouted at him, "You came to my house in the name of being a fellow citizen and pulled down my pants! Had you thought about the police? Now come and answer to the police."

While his head was lowered, he saw me from the corner of his eye and whispered, "Keep quiet—it is indecent. Stop talking like this."

I had caught the attention of some people around me. I looked at them and said, "You see this idiot who presents himself as a man of character and personality? He came to my house in the name of being my fellow citizen and tore my pants, removing them from my body. Now I will discipline him so he will not repeat it ever again in his life." Now I pestered him in front of the people. "Hey, I am talking to you! Do you understand it or not? Come and answer to the police. You do not know me yet. I am the one who has disciplined the likes of you. Now when the police will discipline you, you will realize what it means to pull someone's pants down. Idiot, come and answer the police!"

All people around us became aware of our fighting. The matter was very strange for them because Haider was a married man in his early forties. It was especially strange for him to forcefully tear and remove the pants from the body of another man. People thought that he did it with the intention of rape. Haider said nothing out of shame, and I deliberately kept quiet so they would think he intended to assault and rape me.

People said to me, "If he indeed has done so, it's a very shameful act. But you should not complain to the police."

I said, "I will not complain to the police on one condition: he must apologize to me and say that he made a mistake."

Suroush and Fariburz were standing there watching, but they said nothing. Haider said to me, "Forgive me, I made a mistake."

"Say you are ashamed of what you did."

"Yes, I am sorry."

"Say that you will not repeat it in the future."

"I'll not repeat it in the future."

"Say that you made a gross mistake." Haider did not reply. If we were alone, perhaps he would have beaten me up, but he said nothing in front of the people. "Say that you made a gross mistake," I repeated.

Again he kept quiet. I repeated it three times. Finally Suroush said, "Enough, Hamid. He says he made a mistake and will not repeat it. He has asked your forgiveness. Now there is no need to further disgrace him."

When Suroush said those words, it made me happy because I knew that his grudge was gone. I said good-bye to them. When I left, Suroush said to Haider, "I am glad that he let you go. If he had lodged a complaint with the police, you would have been extremely humiliated and ashamed. Now that he has not complained and you have escaped, you must give alms. Kill a sheep, arrange a feast, and invite friends."

Haider indeed killed a sheep, arranged a feast, and invited his friends. Haider had university education and was a member of the Peoples Democratic Party in Afghanistan. This party was the largest party at the national level, and its members boasted intellectualism and democracy.

The UN Representatives Creating Openings in the Schedule

October 2007, Van, Turkey

After I was accepted by the UN office, within the month I made acquaintance with four newly arrived homosexuals other than Ashkan. All of them were Iranians. Only Ashkan was treated well by the UN office; the others were ill treated. One of them was quickly rejected, and two of them were interviewed too late and received no reply. One of them was granted no interview for six months; they scheduled an interview for him but delayed it two times.

During the same period I saw some political and religious refugees who were interviewed and accepted within one month of their approaching the UN office. The UN representatives delayed the scheduled interview dates for those who were not important from their perspective, and they created openings in their schedule for those who they felt were important. When I saw this discriminatory treatment against the homosexual refugees, I became extremely angry.

My file, after acceptance by the UN office, was referred to Canada for placement. Six months after my acceptance I was supposed to contact the Canadian embassy in Ankara with my medical record, and the UN office was supposed to give me my bus ticket. When I went to the office to collect my ticket, I saw that the interpreter was writing the file numbers of persons contacting the office on a piece of paper, indicating their sex by the letters "F" and "M." He also noted the subject for which they had contacted the office. When I saw this, I became angry and asked the interpreter, "Is sex so important that it should be mentioned here, too?"

"Yes, it should be mentioned here."

"In that case the UN representatives are making a gross mistake by not respecting our sex. When it is clear that homosexuals are seeking refugee status due to their sexual problems, the representatives make a mistake by not accepting them and by making trouble for them. I have seen a homosexual refugee here who was not interviewed in six months, while political and religious refugees were interviewed within one month and accepted. Why do the representatives do this? Why do they disrespect us?"

"Here no one disrespects anyone; it is you who is disrespectful."

"It is reciprocal respect. If someone respects someone, he is respected too. If he disrespects, he is also disrespected. Swearing at us is not the only disrespect; the very fact that they pretend to be dumb, as if they understand nothing, is also disrespect. They understand that we do not have sexual freedom, and yet they evade issues—that is disrespect."

"If you have a complaint against someone, write it on a piece of paper and bring it here. Do not shout and yell."

I collected my ticket to Ankara and went there for my medical examination. When I returned, I wrote a letter and delivered it to the UN office (see Appendix 10).

After I delivered the letter to the UN office, those four homosexual refugees were quickly accepted. In the course of the next few months, I made acquaintance with three other newly arrived homosexuals. Apart from them, I heard that there were some more new arrivals. Luckily the UN office did not treat the new arrivals the same way it had previously treated me and others, and they were accepted relatively easily. I did not see two of them, Mehdi and Behroz, face-to-face because they were in Sparta, but I talked to them on the phone.

Mehdi had approached the UN in 2004 and Behroz in 2005. Ultimately, both were accepted in 2008. Later I learned, regretfully, that because the UN does not send any Afghanistani refugees to any refugee-accepting country, the Afghanistani homosexuals are also not accepted. In the past, when there was no national discrimination against the Afghanistanis, the Afghanistani homosexuals were subjected to sexual discrimination. Now that there is no sexual discrimination against the homosexuals, they are subjected to national discrimination.

When I see the human trait of avoiding logic at various levels that despite raising very strong arguments, they still trickily evade the rights of each other, I draw the conclusion that: We humans are still an inseparable part of the wildlife that some of us have to scrimmage with a savage and unfair competition of life with the others to survive. One Afghanistani homosexual, from his childhood, must struggle alone against the societies of millions of population of all ages, all together, already alert, and fully trained. In certain places certain laws and regulations have evolved that give us the opportunity to argue. Without law, even the selfsame UN officials who speak of humanity are quite likely to respond to people's arguments with fists and slaps.

In October 2012, a gay Afghanistani man from Norway, despite being prosecuted and facing the risk of certain death, and despite passing through all the obstacles and border restrictions in many countries, was deported back to Afghanistan by the government of Norway—then with the help of the NATO soldiers and the UNHCR he was immediately diverted to Pakistan where he went into hiding.

My Journey from Van to Eskişehir

November 2007

I was waiting for the day of my flight to Canada; it was late fall and the beginning of winter. The Turkish police transferred me from the city of Van to Eskişehir. I was afraid of going to Eskişehir in light of the coming winter because I was in bad financial condition and did not know anyone in Eskişehir who would help me out. I was between a rock and a hard place: I could not refuse to go because I was obliged to go due to police rules. If I refused, I would have problems at the time of my flight out of Turkey; if I went, I didn't have even ten days' rent, let alone other living expenses. My brother Navid, who was in London, always sent money for me, but lately he had become tired of sending money for me because there were persons other than me whom he always helped, and he was under financial pressure. For that reason I could not ask him for money.

    I told myself that these hardships had become normal for me. I had experienced everything in my life: comfort and discomfort, having and not having, heat and cold, home and homelessness, clothes and nakedness, hunger and satiety, good and bad. No circumstances were different for me from the other. So - what the heck, I'll go to Eskişehir and start a new life, a new chapter. Thus, at the beginning of winter I boarded a bus, and after twenty hours it arrived in Eskişehir.

I was required to report to the Foreign Citizens Bureau in Eskişehir, which I did immediately upon my arrival. The police at the bureau asked me, "Do you have a place to live in Eskişehir?"

"No, I do not."

"Do you know anyone here?"

"No, I do not," I said again.

"What was your problem in Afghanistan?"

"I have told everything in the interview. I see no need to repeat it again."

"Are you gay?"

"Yes."

"Then why don't you say that you have this problem in Afghanistan?"

"I have said everything at the time of my interview."

"Do you know that Eskişehir is expensive and that life is hard here?"

"Yes, I know that rent is high and everything is expensive."

The interviewer said, "I will introduce to you another refugee who is gay like you; he might help you."

The police gave me the telephone number of a Palestinian gay named Hasib. I contacted Hasib by phone, and he asked me my situation and told me to stay where I was until he came to see me. Hasib came, and we introduced ourselves. I sought help from him about housing, and he asked me, "What type of men do you like?"

"Men over forty, large and hairy, not thin."

"You are exactly opposite of me. I know a couple of them and might find you a place to share with one of them. Presently I will show you a hotel where you may spend the night. First I need to talk to them about you. If one of them is prepared to share his house with you, I will take you to him. If none agrees to do so, I will find another solution for you."

Hasib showed me a cheap hotel that looked like a soldier dormitory. Two long rows of double-deck beds were laid in a long hall. There was a large coal heater burning in the middle of the hall, with a large tea samovar boiling on top of it. The poorest travelers were the customers of this hotel.

I spent the night in that hotel. The next afternoon Hasib came and said, "Leave your suitcase here. Right now I have to see someone. You come with me, and then we will go to a place where I'll talk about you."

Hasib had not told me the truth. He had nothing to do with the one he said he had to see first; he had already talked to him about me. I went with Hasib to the house of an Iraqi man named Ibrahim, who was in his midforties. His wife and children were in Iraq, and he lived alone in Eskişehir. When I arrived at Ibrahim's house, Hasib spoke to him in Arabic. Ibrahim was happy to see me. At first he looked tired, and then a smile appeared on his face. Hasib told me, "Ibrahim lives alone in this house and wants to share it with you. Do you have any problem sharing it with him?"

"No, I have no problem. The important thing is that Ibrahim should have no problem."

Hasib asked Ibrahim something in Arabic and then translated his reply to me. "Ibrahim says that he has no problem with you. Do you have any problem with Ibrahim?"

"No, I have no problem with Ibrahim."

"Are you sure that you have no problem? If you share the house with him, he might ask you something in return."

"Yes, it's okay. I am sure that I have no problem with Ibrahim."

I agreed to share the house with Ibrahim. He did not speak the Turkish language and said to me in English, "Hamid, welcome to this house. I have no problem with you, and you may live here with me."

That was how I shared the house with Ibrahim. I lived in Eskişehir for four months, and I shared the house with Ibrahim until my last day there.

* * *

March 2008, Eskişehir, Turkey

All my memories and writings are based on one interesting coincidence. Among the refugees in Eskişehir, I met with a Sudanese man named Usman who was very sincere and kind. In the last days before I was supposed to fly from Turkey to Canada, Usman said to me, "You who are a displaced Afghanistani must certainly have suffered a lot in life like me. Now that you are going to Canada and are about to be saved from the hassles and hardships of life, you will have the opportunity to write your memoirs. I recommend to you that when you arrive in Canada, write about what happened to you in life, right from the beginning to the end. If I were in your place and I had this opportunity, I certainly would do so."

Usman was a man who had suffered a lot in his life. He had lived for years in the country of his birth as well as overseas as a miserable, displaced person. Regretfully the UN office, after two years of his waiting in Turkey, had finally rejected him as a refugee.

In response to his recommendation to write my memoirs, I said to him, "What is the use of writing my memoirs?"

"If you write your memoirs, it would show in which culture you have lived. It would be interesting to read for those who are not familiar with this culture and want to understand it. You are going to a first-world country, and it would be interesting for its people to know how third-world people live and what their culture is."

"I do not have such command of the English language, to be able to write everything in English so that the people of Canada can read it."

"If you do not have command of the English language, then write it in the Turkish language."

"I do not have a command of the Turkish language, either."

"Write in whichever language you can; write in the language you speak, the language of Afghanistan."

"If I write in the language of Afghanistan, no one would ever read it."

Overcoming

"You just write—forget if someone reads it or not. Ultimately someone will read it."

Usman did not know anything about me, and yet he asked me to write my memoirs. Because I was never in the business of writing or reading stories, it was unlikely that I would think of writing something. But this recommendation by Usman, a Sudanese refugee, prompted me to think about his suggestion and write my memoirs. Previously I had a vague feeling of wanting to do something to make Afghanistani society aware of what they did not know. But it had never occurred to me how to do it; at least, I had never thought of writing my memoirs. At the beginning I only thought of starting a TV channel in order to increase awareness and to nurture ideas, so that society's knowledge could be increased through this medium by means of educational programs designed with a view to all issues of the country. But this was an idea that could not be implemented without extensive experience and big money.

In the summer of 2007, when I was in Van, Mr. X, the director of the Human Rights Organization for LGBTs, with its headquarters in New York, travelled to Van. In the course of his trip, he interviewed me as an LGBT refugee. I said to Mr. X in that interview that the best oath in the area of human rights was to increase social awareness. I suggested that the easiest way to do so was to start a TV channel for the purpose of nurturing ideas. I said that if the Human Rights Organization started such a TV channel at the national level in Afghanistan, there would be no need to collect the cases of human rights violations from the streets and bazaars. But Mr. X threw an ambiguous glance at me and said nothing about my proposal.

When Usman suggested the memoir to me, I suddenly felt that I had found what I had been looking for. I immediately decided to start writing my memoirs so it would serve as the first brick of the building of social education and reciprocal respect in the depth of Afghanistani society. I always considered education as the key to unlocking social injustice. But, regretfully during the past three decades in Afghanistan, along with poverty acting as a great impediment to acceptance of this view, the imposition of war on this country has also made education harder.

* * *

During my stay in Turkey, I did not have the opportunity to learn the Turkish language because there was no Turkish school for us. Nevertheless, I learned Turkish to some extent and was able to get along with the locals. I even wrote letters. During the last days, when the Canadian embassy issued me a visa, the Turkish government was also supposed to issue an exit visa for me. To do this, the Turkish government initially asked me to pay a fee. I wrote a letter in Turkish to the governor's office in Eskişehir (see Appendix 11, and the translation of the letter in Appendix 12).

The government of Turkey rejected my application. I asked my brother Navid in London to give me this money. He sent it for me from London, and after I paid the government, it issued me an exit visa.

Part Ten

Arrival in Canada

18 March 2008

My gratitude and thanks are due to the Canadian government and society for accepting and protecting me, as a refugee and for their ending to restricting me from this section lands of my own nature, as an immigrant. I had a flight from Istanbul to Toronto in 18 March 2008. I took some Turkish coins as a souvenir and set out from Eskişehir toward Istanbul. I had been in Istanbul three years ago, and I missed it very much; when I saw it again, I wanted to cry. My eyes became filled with tears. When it was time for my flight, I went inside the airport and boarded a plane for the first time in my life. Our first stop was Frankfurt. I sat beside the window. I wanted to watch the land below during our flight. The weather was cloudy and rainy. When the airplane took off, I saw only a small part of the Marmara Sea and the city of Istanbul. Soon the aircraft ascended over the clouds. Up to Frankfurt the weather was mostly cloudy; only at certain points did green mountains appear from the cracks in the clouds. When we came close to Frankfurt, it became completely sunny, and the land mass appeared. Small and large cities surrounded green land, and the city of Frankfurt was one of them.

After a four-hour layover, we boarded a second aircraft, which took off for Toronto in Canada. At first I thought that the aircraft would fly directly in a straight line to Toronto, and we would go over Belgium and Britain. But the TV screen inside the aircraft showed the flight path, and the aircraft was flying along the northwestern coast of Germany in a curved line over the Atlantic Ocean, and then it flew over the territory of Labrador and Quebec as it headed toward Toronto. I sat by the window this time as well. At the coastal regions and parts of the ocean, the weather was sunny, but then thick clouds covered the ocean again. After several hours the weather became clear and sunny, and the land below was covered by snow. That day became about six hours longer for me because of the difference in time zones, the aircraft was moving toward the west. It was evening when the aircraft landed in Toronto and we disembarked.

About fourteen other refugees flew from Turkey with me on the same flight. One of them remained in Toronto like me, and the rest went to other cities in Canada. It was March 18, and three days remained before the Nowroz. The weather was still cold, and the winter of 2008 was said to be the coldest winter in Canada during the last forty years. At the airport the Canadian immigration department gave us shoes, gloves, and a winter jacket. One of the officials of Immigration Canada met us at the airport and took us to the welcome center. We were supposed to stay at the welcome center for a few days until we found housing. I did not know anyone in Toronto, so I decided to first see the various parts of the city and then choose a place to live.

Rahman Was a Lunatic

When I was at the welcome center, there were new refugees there coming from various countries of the world. Among them were some other Afghanistanis. There were a number of chairs at the end of the hall on the second floor of the building. One day I was sitting there on a chair, and another young Afghanistani man was also sitting beside me. In those days when I was new in Toronto, I had many thoughts in my head and was totally confused. I was sitting on the chair and thinking about God knows what. The Afghanistani man noticed me and started to talk about religion, the Day of Judgment, prophets, and so on. Although I came from a religious family, I was not interested in talking about religion because of my own confrontation with ideologies and philosophical beliefs. At first I thought that he would stop soon, so I listened to him for a few minutes. But he was one of those who, once he started talking about religion, would go on for hours. I finally interrupted him and said, "Excuse me, are you a religious person?"

"Yes."

"Good for you!"

"Why, aren't you a religious person?"

"No, I am not."

"Then what is your ideology?"

"I do not accept anything that I do not understand logically."

"What is your religion?"

"I have no religion."

"You abandoned your religion so you could come overseas?"

"No, I did not renounce my religion so I could come overseas. I had sexual problems in Afghanistan."

"What sexual problems did you have?"

"I am a homosexual, and I had problems in Afghanistan."

"Are you really a homosexual, or did you just say that to be accepted as a refugee?"

"I am actually a homosexual."

"Damn! How much do the Afghanistanis dishonor themselves, just for coming to a foreign country! I never thought that an Afghanistani would want to disgrace himself so much."

The next day he talked about my homosexuality to five other Afghanistanis at the welcome center. Two of them were sensitive to this issue, but the others showed no prejudice. One of the sensitive ones had a friend named Rahman who had come to Toronto six years ago. Rahman came to see him at the welcome center. Rahman was both a homophobe and completely empty-headed. People who met him often felt that he was a thick, impregnable wall of ignorance.

Rahman started to talk to me and tried to convince me to accept his proposal to never talk about my homosexuality to anyone in the future. He said, "I have been living in Toronto for the last six years. You talk nonsense, and Toronto is the center of nonsense; it is the world capital of homos. Please save the pride and honor of Afghan, because you are an Afghanistani. Homosexuals are the dirtiest, vilest, cheapest, characterless, and the most laughable people on earth. Too much of this dirt and filth has been exposed in every nation. So far no Afghanistani has said that he is a homosexual. Do not say those words anywhere else. I am telling you this as a brother. Please choose the right path. If you do not think much of your own character, at least do not try to play with the pride and honor and prestige of the Afghanistanis. I am saying this for your own sake. Of course you cannot harm Afghan. Rest assured that if you try to do something to harm the reputation of the Afghanistanis, I'll be the first to kill you. But I won't have to do that, because there are thousands of proud and conscientious Afghanistanis who will destroy you."

Thus on the very first day, Rahman talked to me and argued with me for a couple of hours. I was not used to remaining silent against anyone. I spoke to him with reason, as far as it was possible, in order not to hurt his feelings and not to leave any misunderstanding. But no argument could convince him. He left only two choices before me: either change my ways and be friends with him so he could help and guide me; or disregard the pride and honor of Afghanistanis and continue to be a homosexual, and he would eliminate me from this world.

At thirty-eight or thirty-nine years old, Rahman was tall and well built, unlike most Afghanistanis. He displayed his physical strength and talked a lot about his past, especially about his wrath and fury and manliness. There were many people in this world who were showy, self-centered daydreamers and who lived in a fantasy world.

Out of the two choices he had offered me, I made the choice of reform and friendship with him. A tentative fear of him overcame me because of his ignorance; I feared that he may actually make an attempt on my life one day. But my real reason for choosing friendship with him was because I wanted to encourage him to open his mind and become more social. He seemed to me like a child who needed a little guidance. During the next few days, Rahman and I walked and sat together many times, and we talked. Rahman was a few years older than me in terms of age, but in terms of intellect he was simple and childish. Whatever he said, I listened to him without paying any serious attention to his ideas. As far as his shortsightedness was concerned, it was not his fault; he was not exposed to conditions where his intellect could grow. I liked him both as a child and a man.

* * *

My friendship with Rahman lasted only a few days. I put up with all his stupid ideas. He cursed many times at all the homosexuals of the world, especially me and my family. Calmly and without any irritation, I agreed with his cursing. No matter how harshly Rahman spoke to me, I responded to him softly. Ultimately he was forced to soften his attitude toward me.

Rahman told me several times, "My dear, you are a dirtbag, and you grew up in a dirtbag family."

I used to listen to him as if he was talking about everyday matters. Once I replied to him, "Yes, my dear, my family is a dirtbag. That's why I gave them a dose of their own medicine. That's why I exposed my family and shamed them before everyone."

"You are proud of shaming your family?"

"Didn't you say that they are dirtbags?'

"Yes, your family is a dirtbag, and that's why they have raised you like this."

"Well! That's why I should have taken my revenge and shamed them."

* * *

Rahman wanted to encourage me to become a womanizer. Whenever we went out together, he would show me young and sexy girls and say, "Look at her—what a beauty!"

Every time he showed me a girl, I would point to a man and say, "No, not that girl, but this one is for me." This would drive him crazy, and he would curse at me.

He once took me to a girl to make me get used to female company. The girl embraced me and said, "You are very handsome."

I suddenly shivered and said to her, "No, I am not the one for you."

Several times Rahman talked of women's beauty on the streets, and I would talk back about men's attractiveness. He would go crazy and curse at my mother and sister. Once he said, "I am sure your mother and sister are dirtbags."

I said, "My mother became a widow in her youth. She was deprived of sex for years but never established a relationship with another man. My sister is very beautiful and young, but she is faithful to her husband and never looks at another man."

"If you defend them, then you certainly love them. Why did you lie to me when you said that you were pleased to shame them?"

"I said so in order to appease you. In truth they are not dirtbags, nor am I. They have an Eastern upbringing."

"No, I am sure that your family members are very uneducated and low."

"Everyone's definition of education reflects their own education."

"What do you think? Are they mean or not?"

"God knows I have no idea."

"You don't believe in God. Why do you swear in God's name?"

"No, I believe in God, and I believe in all gods. I believe in your god and in the god of others as well."

During the early days of my acquaintance with Rahman, he intended to kill me one night. I was still at the welcome center when he came at 11:00 p.m. one night and asked me and two of his friends there to go with him for a walk. His eyes were bloodshot, and his face was manic and excited. I understood from his red eyes and flushed face that he probably intended to kill me. Nevertheless, I went out with him so he would not think I considered him my enemy. If those two friends of his were not with him, I would not have gone out with Rahman alone; I thought that he would not dare kill me in their presence. Of course I did not know that he had already told those two about killing me, and they had consented to it by their silence.

We got on the Bloor subway train and got off at the Yonge Station. We boarded another train at Yonge and got off at Sheppard Station, and then we took another train there and got off at Don Mills. We got on a bus and got off at a secluded street. We walked a little bit while Rahman seemed very excited; he said it was Victoria Park. There we boarded another bus and got off at an unknown station. It was a cold night. We started walking aimlessly along the wide and empty road in the dark of the night. We walked quite a long distance and were cold. The two other Afghanistanis were also prejudiced and backward.

While we were walking, they gradually separated from Rahman and me and remained far behind us. Certainly they were waiting for Rahman to make his move. Rahman was restless and looked like a maniac. At that point I understood what was going on between them and Rahman. I knew that he intended to make an attempt on my life. However, I was sure that he had no guts to do it. It was clear from the turmoil on his face that his heart was full of apprehension and hesitation. I was very calm and surprised at myself. I knew that if there was someone else in my place, he would not have come out and would not have walked calmly with Rahman.

We kept walking for some time. Ultimately Rahman could not bring himself up to kill me, and he changed his mind. We boarded a bus again and arrived at Don Mills. We took the subway, and Rahman separated from us in the middle of our destination. The three of us returned to the welcome center.

Rahman was a lunatic and threatened me with death every day. A few days after that night's episode, without my asking, he himself admitted his intention. He said, "My dear, I wanted to kill you that night. I would be dishonorable if I tell you a lie. But those two did not allow me to kill you. They said, 'Forget about killing him. When he says he will be reformed, he certainly will be reformed. There is no reason for him to tell a lie.' But I see that you are never going to be reformed. You are telling a lie when you say that you will be reformed."

"No, rest assured that I will be reformed. Actually, I am already reformed. From the very first day when I became friends with you, I became a reformed man."

"My dear, if you tell a lie, I swear upon my religion and faith that I will kill you. If I don't kill you, I am not the son of a man; I am the son of a donkey."

Overcoming

"No, why would I tell you a lie? If I didn't want to be reformed, I wouldn't be friends with you, I wouldn't want to walk with you. Do you think that I made friends with you because I am afraid of you? No, I know that you are a dangerous man, but I am not afraid of people even more dangerous than you."

Rahman replied, "If you lie to me, I'll not walk along with you. If I learn that you have not changed, I'll be a dishonorable person if I walk even one step with you. I hate buggers. Buggers are the dirtiest and the lowliest people on the face of this earth. I am not a worthless person who would walk and talk to a bugger."

* * *

A few days passed. Rahman and I were continually in contact. I left the welcome center and rented a house. I needed household furniture and things, and Rahman told me that he knew a place where they sold cheap stuff. I phoned him and asked him to give me the address of that store. He said, "I also need to do some shopping, so let us go together."

I went to Rahman's place to go with him to the store. While we were walking, he pointed to a girl and said, "See, what a lovely thing!"

I did not look at the girl but pointed to a man and said, "No, that's not a lovely thing, but this one is!"

Rahman became angry, cursed me, and said, "I knew that you will not give up fucking your ass."

"No, don't take it seriously. Sometimes I like to say stupid things."

After this we kept quiet and said nothing to each other. Rahman was hungry and said, "Let us go eat first in a restaurant." We went to a restaurant, sat down, and ordered our meal. There he pointed to a girl and said, "What a beauty!"

I looked around, spotted an attractive man who was a server at the restaurant, and said, "This man is very attractive." After that I looked at the server several times and said to Rahman,

"When I see that type of man, my eyes follow him whether I want it or not, and I just become motionless."

I eyed him several more times. Rahman was aware that I was eying him. He became furious and said, "You'd love this server to fuck you. You are lying when you say that you have changed! I hate both a bugger and a liar. My father told me not to walk along with a bugger. Because you lied to me, I wasted my time for your friendship. I walked with you, I took you to my house, and I sat with you at the same table to eat. Although I hate buggers, I disregarded your past buggery in order to change you. But you lied to me!"

While he was talking, we came out of the restaurant and continued to argue with each other for perhaps another ten minutes. But when I saw that he was not going to give up, I stopped and said to him, "I didn't want to be friends with you—it was you who wanted to be friends with me. Don't think that I am afraid of you. You know it very well that I came from Afghanistan, which is the center of people like you. When no one could hurt me there, be sure that you can't do me any harm here. I accepted your friendship because I wanted to save you from your ignorance. A bugger is better than an ignorant. Come to your senses and do not expect stupid things from me. You have threatened me several times, but I ignored you every time. Perhaps I will have a relationship with a man one day in your presence, and it will have nothing to do with you."

As Rahman carefully listened to everything I said, his face became flushed with rage. His red eyes were redder, and he started to talk in a loud and shaky voice. He shouted continuously for five minutes, using the ugliest words against me and threatening me with death. His cigarette was lit, and he pointed to his cigarette and said, "You see this?" Then he dropped his cigarette on the ground, crushed it with his foot, and said, "Killing a man is that simple for me. Go away and never look at me." I left him and never talked to him again.

* * *

Rahman knew the neighborhood where I had rented the house but not my precise address. One of his two homophobic Afghanistani friends knew the street on which I had rented the house. I was afraid that Rahman might get to know my street through his friend, and he might come after me one day and knife me. I reported the matter to the police, so that they might give him a warning about killing me. The police asked for details, and I told them everything. They said, "Do you want him to be punished, or only warned?"

"A warning will be enough."

The police summoned Rahman in my absence and interrogated him. Then they summoned me and asked, "Do you want charge the person against whom you have lodged your complaint, or are you sure that only a warning will be enough?"

"A warning will suffice," I repeated.

"We summoned him and reviewed your complaint. The way you have informed us about him, he could be a dangerous man. We recommend that he be charged."

"I have no enmity with him, to want him to be charged."

The officer said, "Yes, we know that you have no enmity with him. But the offense he has committed must be charged. It is a crime in Canada to threaten someone with death, whether he actually intended to kill or not. But the crime he has committed is more severe than the threat to kill. If he has threatened you with death because of your sexual orientation, he has shown his hatred of not only you but all humans. He may be dangerous not only to you but also to many more. Thus, it would be better if you demand he be charged."

"No, I do not want him to be charged, because if he has committed an offense, he did so because of his ignorance. If he were not ignorant, he would not hate human beings."

"Yes, we know that it is based on ignorance, but we cannot ignore people's safety because of his ignorance. This man should be charged, and it is up to you whether to charge him or not. It would be better that you demand that he be charged rather than warned."

I thought that - if I want an ignorant man to be charged here, what about the thousands of other ignorant men who wield power in countries like Afghanistan, and who shape the culture of those countries? What can I do with them? Charging one individual will certainly not address this issue. I said again to the police, "No, I don't want you to charge him. A warning will suffice."

"Why not? We have summoned you here so you would demand that we charge that man. If we give him only a warning, he may prove to be dangerous for you."

"If you warn him and he understands that you know what has been going on, he will do nothing."

"He might do something in spite of this."

"If he were in Afghanistan, it is quite likely that he would do something, but not here in Canada. If he knows that the police have knowledge of his threats to me and will interrogate him, he will do nothing."

"Are you sure that if we issue a warning to him, he will not do anything?"

"Yes, I am sure he will do nothing."

I did not want Rahman to be charged, yet the case was referred to the crown prosecutor, and a court hearing was held in this respect. Rahman denied the charge and accused me of lying. He brought one of his two fanatic Afghanistani friends as witness in support of his denial of the charge. Despite witnesses supporting his claim, he lost his case. He was recognized as an offender and was reprimanded. Rahman had said to me that he hated all homosexuals and liars, but he wanted to deceive a Canadian court by lying. Luckily there was no Taliban or religious court here; if there was one, Rahman might have won his case and sued me for defamation. Rahman denied having threatened me with death, but he was so naïve that he expressed his hatred of homosexuals before the court. For that reason the court recognized him as guilty; otherwise it would not have been easy for me to prove my claim of having been threatened to death by him without strong evidence.

Toronto's Gay Parade

In the city of Toronto, Parade Day is held on the last Sunday of June every year. Homosexuals celebrate their homosexuality with the parade downtown. I went to downtown on Parade Day and saw hundreds of thousands of homosexuals, bisexuals, and transsexuals participating in the celebrations. The street was filled with people coming from all nations of the world, and they were celebrating this special day in full glory. I had previously heard that the homosexuals constituted about 3–6 percent or more of all humanity, but I had never believed it. On Parade Day, I believed for the first time that homosexuals are indeed a large part of the human population. Yet the people of Afghanistan still do not understand the meaning of homosexuality; they basically think that a homosexual is a pedophile or a person who rapes boys that have not reached the age of maturity.

Afghanistan's Gay Closet

I had not known anyone in Afghanistan who had admitted to his homosexuality. However, I had made acquaintance with four Afghanistanis through the Internet, three of who were in Afghanistan; the other was in Saudi Arabia. They told me that they were homosexuals. Three of them had taken wives and were extremely unhappy in having sexual relations with women. However, they said they were forced to live this kind of life and had no other choice.

When I came to Canada, I started writing my memoirs. One day, when a draft of my memoirs was complete, I made acquaintance with a midforties Afghanistani man in Kabul through the Internet. He was a highly cultured, knowledgeable, and courteous person. With my street culture and habits, I felt ashamed of myself when talking to him. He worked for a foreign-aid agency in Kabul. I told him the story of my life and also about my sexual orientation, and I sent him the file of my memoir. He also told me about his life but said nothing about his sexual orientation; he said that he was married and had four children, two sons and two daughters.

Some homosexual men look rather feminine compared to the average person in terms of their physique and the way they talk and act. But most homosexual men are not at all different in appearance. Not only that, but some of them are even manlier than the average man. My contact was this type of man: his outward appearance was manlier than most. When I sent the draft of my memoir to him, I never thought that he would spend time reading it.

But a few days later he contacted me and said that he had carefully read my entire manuscript. This surprised me. How could he give it so much importance and read it carefully? He praised my memoir and my past efforts, especially my tireless struggle and my refusal to submit to hardship. He said that he fully comprehended my pain and asked me to sit down whenever I had time and listen to him pouring out his heart. He said, "I have a lot of grievances against this primitive culture of Afghanistan, which always pains me. So far I have never been able to pour my heart out to someone and to soothe my heart. You are the only one to whom I can talk to and comfort myself."

I said, "Go ahead, my dear. Tell me whatever you want. I will listen to you and will completely understand your pain."

He said, "No, I cannot tell you everything at the spur of the moment. Tell me whenever you have time and patience. Then I will talk to you at length and tell you everything, and take comfort from it."

I said, "Whenever you have time, I am available. Right now I am doing nothing. Whenever you need to talk to me, I'll be there for you. If you have time right now, I'll be pleased to talk to you."

He started telling me about his life and spoke to me for almost half an hour; he even cried. He said, "I too am attracted to only people of my own sex, with the difference that unlike you, I prefer to act as the alpha in my sexual relations with other men. I feel myself completely as a man and am attracted to other men, and I want to be active toward them. I do not like female sex; I have never liked it. I was forced to marry a woman because of the primitive culture we have in Afghanistan. When I was newly married, I occasionally had sex with my wife, but day by day my feelings toward her became worse. For the last four years I have not been able to touch her; now I simply share the house with her. I am no longer willing to live one day with her, or be happy that I have a wife and children. I have never lived my life the way I wanted to live it—I always lived according to the whims of others..."

He talked, unburdened himself, and cried. At the end he said, "This is the pain I have kept in my heart all my life. Now that I have spoken to you, I feel better."

I said, "Yes, I understand that you really had a bitter and painful life. But at least people so far have not ridiculed you. You can be thankful for it. The most painful life in Afghanistani society is that of homosexual and transgender people whose outward appearance is feminine, for which they are extremely reviled and ridiculed by society."

He said, "Yes, indeed, theirs is the most painful life. But if one has a desire in one's heart and never achieves it, this also is painful."

This poor chap was a man who was attracted to other men but had never achieved his desires in life. I have seen a lot of men like him among the Turkish who, by marrying a woman, made another person of the opposite sex miserable along with them. Based on the 3–6 percent concept, out of a population of thirty-three million in Afghanistan, that means between one and two million people are homosexuals. One may imagine the number of members of the opposite sex who, because of their marriage, have become miserable along with these homosexuals!

*　*　*

When I came to Canada, I made acquaintance with a transgender Afghanistani who had left Afghanistan in his childhood with his family. He lived in Russia for a number of years and then came alone to Canada. He grew up in Russia and had even changed his sex. This person knows another gay and a lesbian who also come from his village, and they too lived and grew up in Russia. On the first day of my introduction to him, when I told him the name of my village, he burst in laughter and said, "Wow, what a scandal! If people knew that all of us came from the same village, they would think how infertile the soil of this village is—its men and women are all *eezak*!"

Among the Afghanistanis who live overseas, he knew only three or four other homosexuals. This being the case, one may infer that the culture of Afghanistan has suppressed homosexuals so much that at the world level, only a few Afghanistani homosexuals have dared to come out of the closet, whereas a large number of homosexuals from other nations can be openly seen all over.

* * *

During the last days of the writing this book, I contacted an Afghanistani publisher whose address I had found through Google. This publisher lived in Toronto and had several years' experience at the international level in the field of publishing Afghanistani books. In order to encourage him to publish my book, I pointed out the subject of the book and wrote to him in my e-mail, "The point that I must mention is the unique subject of the book. I have written this book about the circumstances of homosexuals in Afghanistan and believe that no book has been written so far on this subject in Afghanistan. For that reason I hope that its publication would be to your advantage."

He wrote back to me with complete disinterest. "Addressing the issue of homosexuality in Afghanistan is nothing new. *The Kite Runner* and parts of Zaryab's writings have already addressed this issue. Nevertheless, send parts of your book to me. If it is possible to publish it, I would publish it for you."

First I sent Part Three of my book and then the complete manuscript for him, but he showed no interest.

This great Afghanistani publisher thought that homosexuality meant pedophilia or the rape of young boys due to ethnic conflicts, to which a reference has been made in *The Kite Runner*. When a large Afghanistani publisher who has been engaged in cultural activities for years interprets homosexuality in this way, then what about the poor and illiterate majority of society, who never had the opportunity of education?

My Acquaintance with Hussain Zahedi

When I arrived in Canada, for the first couple of months I looked for odd jobs and postponed writing my memoir. Finally I decided I had to do it instead of wasting my time.

In the past I was not a reader of books or newspapers, and I had no experience with story writing. Thus, even without high-quality prose, the memoir was a tough nut to crack because of my inexperience. I remembered certain things from my schooling, and I had read some short stories. In order to better learn the English and Turkish languages, I sometimes read pages of newspapers and remembered certain things from them. I made a sample from whatever was in my mind and started to write. Because I had not read novels and stories in the past, I did not know which type of book would be more interesting for the reader: a short and concise book, or a voluminous book with detailed accounts of events. I was not an avid book reader, so even if I wanted to read a book, I would choose a short and concise book because I had no patience to read a voluminous book. I decided to write my memoir consisting of no more than fifty or sixty pages, believing that it would attract more readers.

I had written about ten pages when one day my cousin's friend, named Hussain Zahedi, came to Toronto from Hamilton. My cousin had given him my phone number to contact me in

Toronto, and this was the first time I saw him. I asked him, "When you were in Afghanistan, what did you do for a living?"

"I was a newspaper reporter," he said.

"If you were a reporter, you certainly can appraise the importance of a book. I have started writing a book that is based on my life, but in general it reflects the circumstances of all homosexuals in Afghanistan. So far I have written only a few pages. Please have a look at those pages and tell me what you think of it."

Hussain Zahedi read my pages and said, "The subject you are writing about is interesting. So far no one has written on this topic in Afghanistan. If you complete this book, I am sure that it will have a big response... but I cannot anticipate whether this response will be positive or negative. I have no idea whether the Afghanistanis' cultural and intellectual level has improved and whether they can take such a subject easily."

"You say that it will have a response?"

"Yes, I am sure that it will have a response—but I cannot say whether it will be positive or negative. Certainly there will be a response."

"It is important for me that it have a response; positive or negative doesn't matter to me."

"If a response of any kind is important for you, then rest assured that you'll have one, because among the Afghanistanis no one has written on this subject so far. Your style of writing is not bad, either. Try to write at least two hundred pages."

"With a volume like this, no one would want to read it!"

Hussain Zahedi smiled and said, "No, your thinking is not correct. The more pages in a book, the more it will be read."

"Wow, really? If I see a voluminous book, I am afraid to touch it, let alone read it."

"I know that large books have more fans," he reassured me.

"It is important for me to write about many things, but in order to keep the volume small, I have tried to disregard those things."

"No, just write whatever you want to write, and try to make the book at least two hundred pages long."

At the prompting of Hussain Zahedi, I decided to write a two-hundred-page book. I started to include more material.

My Family's Reaction

In the previous Persian edition of this book, I did not write about my family's reaction because I felt it shouldn't be solely a personal story. Subsequently, many readers asked me about their reaction. Therefore, in this edition, I wish to address this question in the text. It may also reflect the possible reaction of all Afghanistani families who would have the same issue.

Let me start with the story from my acquaintance with Hussain Zahedi. When at first I showed him my draft writings, and when he noticed that I was exposing myself as a homosexual, he was shell-shocked: how could I expose myself as a homosexual? He had never seen any Afghanistani individual who would admit that he was a homosexual, though he had seen many from other nations. He asked me, "When you are writing such a book, did you ever think of your family's reputation?"

I said to him, "I will lose my own reputation before my family's."

He pushed the point. "When you write this book, certainly you don't care about yourself, but what about your family?"

"In the backward society of Afghanistan, if one does not first sacrifice the reputation of oneself, of one's family, and the extended family, how can one change the way of thinking of the whole society?"

"It doesn't matter to you if your family notices that you have written such a book, after its publication?"

I replied, "Even before its publication, they should know that I am writing this book. I've already told them that I am writing a book."

"What if they notice that you are writing on such a taboo subject?"

"That's the point—they should know it and accept it."

"Have you told them that you are writing on this subject?"

"No, I haven't told them. But they would know after its publication, if they care to read it."

Hussain Zahedi was surprised and said, "Wow! Do you want them to read it?"

"Yes, of course I want them to read it. When I write a book, certainly I want everyone to read it. But I will not send it to my family myself. If they get a copy from someone else, they can read it."

"Won't they be angry with you?"

"It doesn't matter if they are angry with me, despite the loss of my own reputation."

"What about the shame and disrepute supposedly brought on them before other people?"

"When I am sacrificing my own prestige and reputation for the enlightenment of society at large, it doesn't matter if the prestige of others is lost as a result."

"Then you don't care if your family notices that you are writing on this subject?"

"They will finally notice it. It doesn't matter."

My cousin Kave was friends with Hussain Zahedi. Hussain asked me, "What about Kave? Does he know that you are writing on this subject?"

"Certainly Kave must know it first. Charity begins at home. I should start changing hearts and minds, starting with my relatives. If they realize that people like me exist among them, they would no longer try to find faults in others. When you go back to Hamilton, be sure to tell everything to Kave."

Hussain Zahedi was a member of a political and cultural publication. He asked me, "Then are you prepared for an interview with me on this subject that will be posted on our website?"

"Of course I am ready. It's my pleasure, if you wish to do something for the enlightenment of society."

Hussain conducted an interview with me in this regard and posted it on the website Kabul Press. This interview was a first for raising awareness of the issue of homosexuality at the national level in Afghanistan.[4]

* * *

When Hussain went back to Hamilton and met with Kave, he narrated our entire conversation to Kave. Hearing my story, Kave suddenly started crying, because he was extremely embarrassed before Hussain Zahedi.

The story of my acquaintance with Hussain was also interesting, because before meeting with him, I had problems getting in contact with Kave. The problem arose because of the disagreement in my family. Kave had lived most of his life outside of Afghanistan and was about eight years older than me; I had met him only one time in my entire life, several years ago, while he traveled from Russia to Afghanistan. He did not remember seeing me even once. He had married a Russian woman in Russia and had two children with her. Then he had left Russia for Canada, together with his wife and children, and had lived in Canada for several years. I had no contact with him before coming to Canada. When I was supposed to come to Canada from Turkey, I asked Navid and my Marjan to give me his telephone number so that I could meet him. But they refused

---

[4] The interview can be found at:
http://kabulpress.org/my/spip.php?article1793.

to give me his telephone number, because they didn't want me to be in contact with Kave or anyone else from the family. Since I had told them about my sexual orientation, they didn't want anyone else to know about me.

When I came to Canada, one day I met an Afghanistani man who by chance knew both Kave and my younger brother Valid. He had been acquainted with both of them in Russia, but he was no longer in contact with either of them. I gave him the telephone number of Valid, and he got the telephone number of Kave from him. Thus, I contacted Kave, and through him I became acquainted with Hussain Zahedi. If I had not met with Hussain Zahedi, my book would be no more than sixty or seventy pages long.

Because of my sexual orientation, I already had problems with Navid, and I had many arguments with him on this matter. A few days after I met Hussain Zahedi, Navid called me from London. He was very angry and said to me, "What the heck have you told Kave's friend?"

I had already told Navid that I was writing a book about the social and cultural conditions of Afghanistan, so I said to him, "I told Kave's friend that I was writing a book, the same book I have already told you about, and I showed him the pages that I have written so far."

"What did you show him? What are you writing about?"

"I am writing about the social and cultural conditions of Afghanistan, specifically about the circumstances of the gay and lesbian population."

"Didn't I tell you not to talk about this matter to anyone? You made up those stories so you could leave Afghanistan and go overseas, which is what you have achieved. Now, what else do you wish to accomplish from this idle talk? You embarrassed us before Kave."

"You mean Kave is such a characterless person that he instantly called you to taunt you about my sexuality?"

"No, he didn't taunt me. He himself had been ashamed before his friend."

"So, what was the need for him to call you and report this matter to you?"

"He was complaining about you."

"If he had a complaint, why did he not say it to me instead?"

"Because you had said to his friend that you intentionally wanted to sacrifice the reputation of the family and relatives, so he knew it was no use to complain to you."

I asked, "If it was not hypocrisy, what was the need to complain to you about this matter?"

"While complaining, he was crying because he was extremely ashamed before his friend. He called me after his friend had just told him your story. He had even cried in front of his friend."

"Surprise, surprise! Although he has lived for so many years outside of Afghanistan, he is still so sissy that he would cry because of the supposed shame involved in it! Well, what can one expect from those who have never been outside of Afghanistan and are still living in the utter ignorance and backwardness of Afghanistani society?"

"You see? This matter is so shameful. Don't talk about it anymore, and stop writing about it!"

"When you see this matter as shameful, think of those gay and lesbian people who are living in the heart of Afghanistani society. Imagine how difficult life is for those people: how can they tolerate the pressures of this culture? The culture of shame must come to end one day."

"Why does no one else talk about this issue? Why does it have to be you?"

"That's the point. When nobody raises the red flag, everyone says, 'Why should I?' Well, there is always a first for everything—someone has to start talking. Finally, the insanity of primitiveness in society must be challenged. How long will the world use us as an example of a primitive and backward nation?"

Navid said, "I am talking about the dignity and reputation of our family, but you are circumventing the subject. I say stop talking about this shameful matter, and don't bring disrepute and disgrace on the family…"

I already had arguments with Navid on this matter and my disagreement with him increased. Eventually, the writing of this book and the matter of me became the biggest shame and defamation even for all of my extended families and most of them did not speak to me anymore.

Before Kave cried in shame, my younger brother Valid had also cried for the shame I had brought on the family. While I lived in Turkey, he never talked to me because he was angry with me for leaving Afghanistan and not wanting to live there. I was in contact with his wife through e-mail and telephone, though I did not say to his wife verbally that I was gay. Once I sent her some of my pictures in which I looked rather feminine. Seeing those pictures, she had immediately realized that I was gay. She then had shown those pictures to Valid. Valid, seeing my pictures in the presence of his wife, became extremely embarrassed and suddenly went outside and started crying. He never talked to me at that time, but one day he called me from Netherlands and complained to me about e-mailing my pictures to his wife. He explained to me sheepishly that he had been extremely embarrassed in front of his wife.

Valid was well-known for his courage and pride; nothing seemed to worry or bother him. He was not a crybaby; tears were just not meant for him. It is not an exaggeration to say that hundreds of people, both in Kabul and in our village, knew him as a courageous soul. Yet the shame of my sexuality shook him to the core, and he cried because of that shame.

When Kave in Canada and Valid in Netherlands can cry because of the intense shame they felt, then think of this stigma among the traditional society in Afghanistan, especially the uneducated masses.

* * *

Let us turn back to the previous subject, which was about starting my writing. I had not read any novels or stories in the past, so I did not know how to write a story. In spite of that I started writing. Without the experience of having read at least one major writer, I wrote about 150 pages. I did not know how to use quotations. I wrote quotations as simple narratives: I said, he said...

There were other weaknesses in my writing. Finally I thought that I should not write without reading a book. Initially I should read at least a couple of famous books and try to copy their style. As the saying goes in Afghanistan, without reading, no one can become a mullah. I told myself that if I continued writing without first reading, my efforts would be futile.

I bought two books from a store in North York Center, Toronto. In the past I was not familiar with the name of even one famous writer or book, other than *The Kite Runner* by Khaled Hosseini, an Afghanistani American whose name I had seen on the BBC website. I picked up one copy of *The Kite Runner* and asked the bookseller to give me another famous book. He gave me a copy of *Blindness* by Jose Saramago, the winner of 1998 Nobel Prize for literature. I read those two books and tried my best to copy their style and taste in my writing—for instance, quoting other people and giving minute details in describing events.

Previously I paid no attention, while describing events, to the details that followed from those events. By reading those two books, I concluded that in order to better depict an event, importance should be attached not only to the description of the event but also to other surrounding circumstances and finer details such as the direction of light, shade, and more, as when painting a picture. In the past I used to think that readers read a book only to increase their general knowledge; I never thought that a book could serve as entertainment. When I read those two books, I realized that entertainment was also an important part of a book. For that reason I decided to include in my book certain matters that had entertainment value, and the volume of the book increased.

Perhaps for a professional writer the writing of this book may not be difficult, but for me it was. During the last seven months of 2008, I started writing my book and completed a major part of it by early 2009. The only thing that remained after seven or eight months was its correction and editing. Those months were the busiest and hardest working days of my life. I often worked in the construction industry during the daytime and wrote my book at night, and while I was unemployed. I was writing, but working to make money was more important to me because I was indebted to my sister, aunt, and two uncles. Before the arrival of winter, I needed to help them, which I did from my labor work. Had I not helped them, my conscience would be uneasy and would not let me continue with my writing.

   When we were in Afghanistan together as children, and my father was executed by the government, we lived for ten years with my aunt and two uncles at their house. There were in fact three uncles at that time, one of who regretfully died a few years ago as a result of a kidney disease. During those ten years, they also helped us in building our house, and we became a homeowner with their help. When we went to our own house, we were in bad economic condition. They tirelessly gave their support to us under all circumstances. My Marjan was a completely uneducated woman, but my maternal aunts and uncles were all educated. We grew up under their protection and received proper education; otherwise it was impossible for children without guardians in Afghanistan, in the absence of any support, to even think of a bright future. Now the fortunes had reversed. My uncles and aunts stayed in Afghanistan and raised their children and family there.

Conclusion

Usman had told me in Turkey that if I wrote my memoirs, it would reflect what kind of culture I lived in and what were the people's customs and their way of life. Although it is my memoir, it does not deal exclusively with my life; my life serves only as an example. In fact, it is the first description of the lives of thousands of people like me, who lived in a society and died with a cry concealed in their hearts. The world may simply ignore me, but they may not ignore thousands of people.

If I am not able to demonstrate with this book the significance of the lives of thousands of people and draw attention to their plight, I must admit that I have to surrender myself first to fortune and then to art. First to fortune, because if someone is born fortunate, he is important from the outset, with or without art. Then to art, because if someone is an artist, he may portray and conjure up an imaginary character, with the power of his art, as important. But if neither good fortune nor art is in the works, millions of real people will be no match for an imaginary character.

One is born with the potential of power, or wealth, or being a beauty queen; to the other, God does not have the courage of empowering, the generosity of good fortune, or the art of charm.

A prince in the womb of his mother is expected by a nation to lead them in the future, and all kinds of art will be in his service; the other is condemned even before he is born, and the world's eyes are blind to him. A sigh of the Prophet, prompted by his ridicule, reaches God's ears (Quran, verse of Al Kawthar); but the thousands of cries for justice go unheard and unheeded. A momentary, sudden sigh becomes eternal and remains fresh and pleasant forever; while thousands of concealed cries die down and sound repetitive and boring even before being uttered.

I would be thankful to those who would read my book. *Overcoming* is an outcome of confronting antagonisms and certainly it will face more antagonisms than welcomes—maybe some cold criticisms in lower levels and silence in higher levels. In any event, my message of this book is to challenge the humanity claims and human consciences; however I wish there were something between conscientious and conscienceless, that there isn't.

For those who are pessimistic, it would be very easy to coldly criticize the art and literature work of me or of those who die of hunger in Africa or to compare it from the angle of their own sight with the works of their same level or beyond. But they should consider that any government, society, or system which fed and trained them and their privileged ones, set up barricades against me.

Starting from the absolute zero and despite the inhibitive frictions, I could eventually overcome all those hostilities, prejudices, and obstacles against me in the world—by simply enjoying my recently found right to live natural in nature. However, in doing so, I would be in a way allowing the silent wall of indifference against every single Afghanistani homosexual left behind, to grow brick by brick. With no resources, they confront as I did, all those pertinacities of the world. Can *the Overcoming* be a catalyst for a happy ending to the ongoing vexatious and tragic history of Afghanistani homosexuals? "If you are optimistic and believe that it can be so and if you are pro-equality, then, please share your idea on this book with other people so as to support the cause. I will be grateful to you."

Hamid Zaher

More Things to Say

I didn't let Afghanistan be a lame donkey to drop behind the world caravan[5]

Eventually after several years of the gay struggle for freedom in the US, gay marriage became legalized in all of the fifty states on the 26th of June 2015. However, their struggle in the US and totally in the West has a long history, but in respect to Afghanistan and what I could do, I didn't let Afghanistan be a lame donkey to drop behind the world caravan. I introduced the existence of homosexuals in the Afghanistani society for the first time and I made their struggle for freedom simultaneous with the rest of the world. And if not at the top, at least I did place them at the bottom of caravan before the caravan reached its destination.

Western gays started up and carried on their struggle in large groups with full stomachs, and the support of several billion dollars, but I started alone, in hunger, with empty-hands while encountering my worldwide bread and fame enemies. All the East and West were my bread and fame enemies who restricted my nature to a limited, landlocked, dry, and desert area and counted a million of my people as nothing to a single individual of their own. They appropriated the immensity and prosperity of the nature to themselves. In addition to denying my natural right of immigration, they also ignored me from their boasting slogan of grandstanding, exhibitory asylum granting.

---

[5] caravan: a group of travelers on a journey through desert or hostile regions

Do as you would be done by.

If my sister and her husband were not the toughest opponents of my immigration to the West, since they themselves had already come and did not want their place to be tight, I would reckon that immigrant-bashing and usurpation of the nature might have been based only on racist motives.

Not only my sister and her husband but I also know someone who disclosed a fake refugee status claim of his sister by showing authentic documents to the refugee office of Netherlands. It happened without the existence of any previous hostility between them and within intimacy in a very cultured and educated family.

His sister said to the refugee office in Netherlands that she had married another man before, and then she escaped with this man from her ex-husband. So, if they returned to Afghanistan, they would be stoned to death.

Then, her elder brother who was in Netherlands before, delivered the video and pictures of her wedding party with this man to the refugee office to prove that she had lied—which means everyone stabs the poor in the back for one reason or another—the racist for their racist reasons and the jealous for their jealousy reasons.

Most of the selfsame newcomer immigrants of color to the West become extremist immigration opponents right after their arrival that some of them even oppose the immigration of their siblings. Before their arrival to their intended destination, while in hardships on the way, they expect other people to sympathize and support them. As soon as they get their wishes, they don't want anyone else to come to share in their fortune. While expecting exclusive privileges for themselves, they are afraid of cosmopolitanism and the formation of an equal and fair world for all humans.

Detained Afghanistani migrants were exhibited in cages by Iranian police—September 9, 2016. *But the real catastrophe is that if one day they become citizens of a rich country, most of them will most likely become anti-immigrants themselves.*

Sympathy for humans is sympathy for wolves.

My Japanese roommate, who was visiting Canada, was fighting hard with the toughest obstacles existing against the greatest wishes of his life: getting Canadian residence, citizenship, and a permanent job in Canada. I always felt pity for him why should there be such tough obstacles against him to kill his wishes.

One day I asked him an assumptive question: "Now, there are such obstacles against your wishes to get Canadian citizenship. Assuming, in the future you became a Canadian citizen and here you became a legislator, would you remove the immigration interdictions from the way of others?"

Even in the case of an assumptive condition, he could not give a positive answer but a negative one. Why then should one feel pity for those hungry, thirsty, naked, homeless, and helpless people from Afghanistan and other deprived nations? If they had the upper hand, they would have been insolently and discourteously standing against people with the lower hand.

The matter of the Japanese man was only achieving his wishes, but for many others from starving nations, it's a matter of life and death. I was feeling pity for him, but if he were in the judging authority, he would have been ready to starve me to death—which means *'to uncage the wolf.'*

When I see humans injustice to other humans, it makes me nervous. But when I see the level of their wisdom and honor, most of them are neither wise enough to know their own rights nor honorable to respect the rights of others. Then, I say to myself that *getting nervous for the injustice of humans to humans is like getting nervous for the injustice of animals to animals.* Regretfully, there is at least one person wise and honorable out of one-hundred who is victimized for the fatuity and effrontery of the rest.

The rest belong to them. But even if there would be one person honorable and conscientious in the world who may have been deprived of their rights, I know it as my duty to defend their rights.

Safe that the human-beings would be able to increase their lifespan by ten times!

Then all the races and ethnicities would start to exterminate generations of each other; but in pre-emption, the whites would exterminate generations of all of them.

I had a discussion with a Canadian, elderly, white millionaire who had lost his eyesight due to senility and was breathing the last years of his life. Nevertheless, he was still against the arrival of newcomer immigrants, especially people of color. He was extremely alarmed and prejudiced—while, their own arrival to North America was performed together with the target of massacring and making doomsday of the aboriginals.

When all the lives and all the generations of others is not worth the latest period of their senility, what a doomsday then will they launch to other people in all over the world if they can increase their lifespan by ten times?

Now they possess almost all the farmlands of the American continent. Yet, they are not satisfied only with the possession of farmlands. They don't want anyone else to come, even without having property. In their slavish acceptance or temporary permission of others as labour forces and tax payers, they take action with extreme consideration and very warily.

My application for Canadian citizenship was rejected for refusing to say the oath of citizenship.

> ***The oath of citizenship:*** *I swear (or affirm) that I will be faithful and bear true allegiance to Her Majesty Queen Elizabeth the Second Queen of Canada, Her Heirs and Successors, and that I will faithfully observe the laws of Canada and fulfill my duties as a Canadian citizen.*

On the day of my citizenship ceremony which was initiated with the citizenship oath, I delivered a letter (see below) to the Canadian Citizenship and Immigration office. In the meantime, I also expressed to them verbally that I cannot say your citizenship oath for two reasons. First, I do not believe in the heritage of kingdom and beggary that you would impose on me. Second, when the laws of Canada are for deprivation of the starving people of world from their 'natural' right of immigration, from my point of view, it is indecent to say an oath to those extortion and bullying laws."

Why did I refuse to say the oath of citizenship?

If I were to say the oath of faithfulness and allegiance to the Queen Elizabeth II and her heirs and successors and to the Canadian laws, I would be admitting their superiority. Then with superiority had hierarchy, I would have to admit the superiority of many other peoples too gradually. I had to acknowledge the rightfulness of the most superior to the most inferior people in world.

Why, then, would I have to struggle for a better condition? Everything was in the right order as required. I didn't have to try to come out of a land of poverty to a better part of the world where the superior people were not contented with my coming. I didn't have to become an activist and write a book for justice.

My letter:

To Citizenship and Immigration Canada
My immigration on the earth was my bread and my citizenship where I am living is my shoes. For 33 years of my life you stole my bread by preventing me from my natural right of immigration. Now please do not steel my shoes.

I object to two parts of your citizenship oath.

One: your condition for Canadian citizenship is, to say the oath of faithfulness and allegiance to Queen Elizabeth II and her heirs and successors, which means the descendants of a king should be always kings and the descendants of a beggar should be always beggars. But I do not believe in the heritage of kingdom and beggary. I want change in the world.

Second: if the laws of Canada are for deprivation of the starving people of the world from their natural right of immigration, I cannot say the oath of faithfulness and observance to those extortion and bullying *laws."*

Immigration is a natural right and at the same time, you yourselves immigrated to the American and Australian continents as aggressors, usurpers, criminals, and murderers and annihilated more than 95% of native peoples of these lands by types of biological, chemical, and destructive weapons. How then can you give yourselves the right to prevent the peaceful immigration of the starving people in the world and appropriate the vast and rich parts of nature to yourselves?

I am addressing you not as a government or a nation but as a unit of the tyranny and arrogance pole of the world. For making a stronger tyranny and arrogance you need for a larger, younger, and more active population. But in accepting your population, you are acting extremely selective and profiteering. If no one accompanies you in your goal, your oppression would last no longer. More than 99% of the people who with their aim of getting to a better life are allowed to this land get in collusion with you against the rest of the world's starving people and say the oath of indecency for you. I, as an individual, do what I can by expressing my objection and I will not say the oath of indecency for you.

Your condition for Canadian citizenship is saying the oath of faithfulness and allegiance to the inheritors of the ringleaders of criminals. That is the oath of indecency.

Sometimes you win, sometimes you learn.

When I was a child, while playing with other children of another family, I was discriminated against because I was not a part of their family. They didn't want me to enjoy the play as they did or even to join the play. I thought that their thinking ill of me was due to their childish immaturity.

Later, when I grew up, I experienced the same behavior from many elders of another ethnicity or nation inside Afghanistan and Iran. Then, I thought it was due to them being from primitive societies and stuck to tribal way of thinking.

Now, when I am facing the same behavior from all the Western elites and dignitaries, I have come to the conclusion that all humans are still not mentally developed to the extent that that one can expect them as humans. Many unimportant books of the Western authors, especially of their noble class, are considered and evaluated in all aspects by all western literary sources, just by noticing a hint from them; while this book is not paid a glance, even by a hundred of appeals.

I see no difference between the primitive tribal children and the Western elites and dignitaries.

They want to thwart me and make me fail by ignoring me, but I see it even as my bigger, real success when I see behind those unreal successful men are standing 'massive nations' who in fact, just act as symbols for the massive nations. If they had paid attention to my work and supported my stand, certainly, on that case, my success would have been theirs, not mine. Now, I know what a massive, multi-national, union of people I have been facing in my life that despite being hundreds of millions cannot see and tolerate the rising of even one person out of them.

Despite your massive union, when I have been able to get my bread out of you, let my fame be yours!

Are they really not ashamed when they acknowledge the importance and rights of gay people in their own societies and the celebration of Gay Pride with such glory, but for another society of the same

population as them, when only one person comes to ask them for their help and care for the same group of people, they ignore with such an effrontery?

The Westerners, or the white peoples' secret of hegemony is this that they count the small jobs of their insiders as great but the great jobs of the outsiders as nothing.

You may know by a handful the whole sack.

Very recently (May 10th, 2016), the observation of a corn field in the map of Mexico, by the name of *Discovery of the Lost Mayan City* by a Canadian, white teenager became newsmaker and came to the headlines of the media. He mistook a corn field in the map of Mexico to his imaginary *Lost Mayan City*. His discovery was achieved by the prior support and encouragement of the Canadian Space Agency. (Link of the news)[6]

While acting so hastily in reporting such unreliable news regarding him, the writing of my book is worth nothing to them.

Of course, his discovery must have been important for them because it was achieved by a government-supported, Western, white teenager, not by me or by a Black African, deprived teenager.

The fact is that neither the Mayans nor their lost city was important, but the child of a white, rich man was important to become a hero.

Certainly, if the writer of the first Afghanistani gay story and their safety-seeker were a white, rich man, they would also become important as a result, but not really to be accepted as refugees in their own nature's lands without jealousy.

I faced many of those who, while noticing my background, appeared to be even envious of my living in Canada. Will they come to value and welcome my literary work of justice?

---

[6] http://www.cbc.ca/news/canada/montreal/william-gadoury-quebec-teen-mayan-lost-city-csa-1.3575416

Okay sir/madam! Count my work as nothing. Well done to you with the decorum you got from your society! You had better become a celebrity to research and discover about us, not to care what we say. Certainly, it would have been very interesting to you if I could not come to the West so you would see me in a documentary titled, **The Primitive & Inferior Human Race** *by someone from your people. Now, the observation of your own defeat, as a drop of connected seas in my personal life story, should be unpleasant to you. Since, you as a part of a single nation of a multi-national union, drop by drop became connected seas against me, but I defeated the seas. God forbid that you would find yourself as a drop of connected seas or as a particle of successive dust storms against me. You should see yourself as singularly connected seas or successive dust storms.*

Many of them have a strong belief about their racial supremacy.

My white, English Canadian roommate believed in white Supremacy and considered the non-white races as inferior. He attributed all the creativities and innovations of humanity to the white race and said that other races copied from them with low quality and with banality and that they could not copy the real excellent quality invented and produced by them.

I asked him, "Do you know anything about the counting and numbers origin history, including zero, which people invented them first?"

He said, "Yes; they were first invented by Romans."

I said to him, "First study and then answer with such a confidence. You people copied the counting and numbers from South Asia and the Middle East. First you should give us our counting and numbers back so you can go back to the primitive commune and ape-men age, then, with pride and arrogance, claim your racial supremacy over us. If you are humans, you became humans on our counting and numbers."

My roommate also said that the people who do not have the talent to establish a system and manage their society, should not own the land, even if they are natives to that land. To own land, people should either fight or think. He regretted the conflict between the US and Russia and said why should two white, civilized nations be in conflict with each other? They should be friends and coworkers. He hated the non-white immigrants in Canada and said that they made the city dirty and polluted and complained about the immigration policy of the government that accepted them. He called the Native Americans monkey people and was not sorry for their historical genocide. He was opposed to the interracial marriages and mixed generation of white people.

Dear! Your racial supremacy over me is your racial unity, not your racial wisdom. If we are not united races, this is because we do not want to be monsters to other peoples. This is a guarantee for your durability and a threat to my existence.

The Australian government has set up abusive detention camps for refugees in Papua New Guinea to deport the eligible refugees from Australia to there and the ineligible ones back to the countries of their origin as illegal immigrants.

First of all, immigration itself is a natural right for all human-beings and all living-beings, the same as you consider it a right for yourselves, whether before for your ancestors, now for yourself, or in the future for your offspring. Secondly, a refugee is a refugee, whether from human violence, starvation, drought, famine, or a natural disaster.

The legal genocide period of aboriginals in Australia, America, and South Africa for your replacement ended. The legal slavery period of blacks ended. The legal fascism period and the genocide of Jews, Gypsies, Russians and the rest ended. Thus, the racist definition of the 'so-called' illegal immigration and the usurpation of nature will also end. What can be concluded is that greedy humans are so unjust and oppressor that even if they can, they would not hesitate to openly massacre and enslave other people, let alone usurp their nature.

The rest societies who are holding more share of the nature also aren't much different than the Australians in terms of their decency and pudency but with the less or more exculpating them by showing a little modesty—that also maybe for their needs to immigrants.

Since the time I came to Canada, I saw many of the non-aboriginal, Canadian, elderly men and women failing in physical and mental capabilities due to their old age.

Sometimes, when I saw one of them, I said to myself *you might have been one of those who supported the system which was restricting me and depriving me of my own nature, when I was a child and you were younger so that you could benefit more of the nature's wealth. Finally, now I am here and I can enjoy everything of this land but your share of this land is only to breathe. If this land really belonged to you but not to me, why, then aren't you able to enjoy it as I can now?*

I say that all children in the world, especially those starving from deprived nations are as worthy of enjoying the nature's wealth as I am. I am not privileged than anyone else to benefit the wealth of in this vast part of the world for being on this side of the man-made borders.

In these countries the system's and the government's word is the majority's word. But I am not a part of the majority. Most of the newcomer immigrants, after their arrival, forget about their past and become part of the majority, against deprived nations. But I do not collude with the thugs and thieves to get old and die shamefully and disgracefully to the eyes of those who would eventually succeed. I do not forgive those who devoured my allotment in my nature planet willfully. Those may not forgive me if I devour whose allotments in their nature planet willfully.

My question from the Westerners is: *when your grandfathers, by their racial alliance could loot, usurp, and annihilate other peoples around the world, where they finally went that you would finally go? Is keeping work prisoners different than buying one year work price of a labor of deprived nations by your one hour wage? And when the global warming due to your industrial emissions is making our small desert lands more desert, are you conscientious that you still keep restricting us in our own nature planet? While, among each other, you spend half of your lifetimes on tours around the world and dining parties.*
Regardless of your denial of our natural rights in our nature, even in making more ruin of our geographical prisons, your hands are actively and directly or indirectly working. Still, you consider yourselves a gentle race and you misrepresent us!

The last of the Tasmanians, William Laney, died in 1869.

The Tasmanians (100,000 population) was one of the most unique human races due to living in isolation for over 10,000 years from their Australian cousins and for over 50,000 years from the rest of humanity. They became extinct due to genocide by white Europeans.

Too many other tribes and ethnicities faced the same fate as Tasmanians in the main lands of Australia and America. Finally the white Europeans stopped massacring them when they were afraid of their complete extinction and **the stoppage of their anthropological studies and research of them** and losing them as samples of existing human races.

Together with wiping out their generations, the Europeans also with extensive propaganda started demonizing and dehumanizing them. They were claiming that they discovered completely untouched and uninhabited lands.

But the Europeans' biological weapons made from their diseases didn't work against the Asian and African races due to prior exposure and immunity.

This is our nature planet too.

How long would the white Europeans come to make our inabilities spectacular by the giving/receiving of awards on display through our adversities, so that they make us indebted to their favor? It's as if we do not have a tongue, so they become our tongue or as if we do not deserve the same equal rights as them in nature, so they show us generosity.

No, thanks gentleman! I am not an animal so that you can please me by giving me a piece of bone. I know my rights in my nature. I know my stealers. I know my enemies. And I know my onlookers. As long as you do not listen to our voices, your playing movie star will avail us nothing.

Preempt our nature! Starve us to death! Display our miseries! Watch with pleasure! Give and receive awards! When we raise our voice to demand our rights, turn a deaf ear! Well done to your honor!

A likeness of the Hungarian journalist and the sunken Syrian refugee child

Syrian ruins

I think I am successful.

Dear Eastern or Western citizen,
If you still have an arrogant look at me and at my story, *note that you may have been one of the millions of those who stood toughly and stubbornly against me to stop me in my nature, as now you are standing against other immigrants/refugees.*

It is not important if I have not had a luxurious and splendid life so my story can meet your taste and draw your attention. The important thing is that I could take millions of obstacles like you out of my way and I could move forward.

Yes, I do belong to the economical, social, racial, and color group that you tend to evaluate and judge from that perspective; but I am just an individual, unlike you, I have not cowardly been a part of a massive global alliance organized against individuals to usurp their nature and steal their bread.

Yes, I did live in ruins, dessert, poverty, starvation, and deprivation; but I can say you ate my bread—however, you ate in collusion with millions of others and you ate shamelessly.

Maybe you could prevent yourself from getting obese; but the obesity represents your nation(s). Maybe I did not grow up malnourished; but the malnutrition represents my nation(s), which means your nation(s) ate the bread of my nation(s) and you ate mine. **Maybe you are not obese in your body, but you are in your greed.**

I should also add that although you stole my bread, my rights, my freedoms, and the opportunities of my education, recreation, and the growth of my talents, and you killed my talents, but you could not suppress my talent to create this book—however, you would ignore it.

Deported gay Afghanistanis told to 'pretend to be straight'

New Home Office rules would send gay asylum seekers back to Afghanistan, where homosexuality is illegal.
 —The Guardian, 26 February, 2017

The **Home Office** (**HO**) is a ministerial department of the Her Majesty's Government of the United Kingdom, responsible for immigration, security, and law and order.

If the UNHCR and refugee-accepting countries did not continually ascertain their reasoning that Afghanistani gays should willingly live secretly in their country, and that their sexual orientation must never be disclosed, in that case, certainly my book's title *"Overcoming"* and subtitle *"Alone Against the World"* would clearly be an exaggeration.

I am a survivor of the world's discrimination.

> *Go and be strong if you seek comfort of the world,*
> *that in the order of nature the weak is trampled*

At least 50 dead in Orlando Gay Club Shooting
— (News headline, ABC NEWS/Jan 12, 2016)

However, the accuracy of the Orlando Gay club shooting is doubted, since no documentary images of the incident and its victims were released. It more likely looks like fabricated news and a racist propaganda against the background nationality of the accused person rather than a real incident.

But regardless of the veracity or falsity of this news, in this regard my question from the Westerners is: When you arrogantly ignore this book that defends gay Afghanistani rights and you count them all as nothing, what then is your position in relation to these supposedly gay victims that many of them might have been either from your race or gorged themselves like you?

The accused person of this incident was introduced as **a US-born**, Afghanistani-American citizen. I don't go into details how Donald Trump took advantage of this propaganda and how the white supremacists are trying to monopolize the world. **A word** to the wise is sufficient.

A Facebook picture

If we close our eyes to pretend there is no racial and no economical discrimination in the world, it wouldn't change the fact that there is. If we say the poor, deprived nations of color in the world are at least as precious as the Eastern European, backward, white nations to the Western, capitalist, white nations and are welcome to their counties and supported by them, they aren't.

So, whether we act like a highbrow to pretend that everything is okay or not, we cannot conceal the truth from our conscience by conservatism.

If my readers of color first of all, especially those from poor, deprived nations are not in collusion with the master race and do not expose and introduce my book, I will not expect this from my white readers; since, those who are oppressed themselves may submit to end the oppression of others. I have already asked too many of the whites, including those from the LGBT society and activists to review my book. Most of them completely ignored. But for some of them their first question was: "What is my spiritual benefit in reading your book?"

Their spiritual benefit might also have been spiritual to be their material support, as reaching to God to achieve more wealth or to go to paradise.

It was difficult for me to convince them that they would have any benefit. Even after discussion and convincing some of them, they accepted that I could send them free copies of my book, but then, most of them kept silent and did not express their comments.

Culturally they have been educated and nurtured this way in their societies to first of all think of their own personal or group benefits rather than thinking of logic, responsibility, conscience, humanity, rights, or justice.

First they want to know about an author's background and his/her social status with them. They prejudge and ignore my book as unfairly and arrogantly as they deport the 'so-called' illegal immigrants.

If in seeking your own benefits you do not see my starvation, see then your own obesity and be ashamed and stop plundering my quota and devouring my allotment in my nature.

Of course, some of them who think independently, humanely, responsibly, and conscientiously are exceptions and I apologize to them in advance for saying these words.

The election of Donald Trump, with his racist slogans, is proof to the revival of this phenomenon which is being inflamed in the rest of western societies as well. If they are not ashamed of their effrontery, the election of another Adolf Hitler in the mold of another Donald Trump or the history of American and Australian aboriginals to other peoples would likely be repeated.

Some societies of color, including Pakistanis due to their colonial or slavery backgrounds or for some other reasons came to the Western coalition during the cold war. Why, then now, are they not as worthy as the white Eastern Europeans to the farther westerner whites who were against them during that time? And why can't Pakistanis travel to the West unexceptionally, unconditionally, without restriction, and without getting a visa?

If the economies of Japanese, South Koreans, and Arabs are collapsed, their situations would also be no better than Pakistanis.

Certainly, if any of the starving nations were from the white race, the Westerners would grant them some of the natural rights and freedoms.

From the outset their criterion for immigration to the American and the Australian continents was being a white man, with the exception of enslaving purposes. Now it's almost the same condition but under different names, excuses, and processes to exonerate themselves as well as admitting some non-white flattering criminals into their gangs and stealing the talents and capitals of other nations by admitting their professionals and investors.

1- The British royal family
2- The British-blooded people
3- The rest of the white people
4- The outstanding people of color
5- Subservient to the white music
6- Listening to the white music
7- Singing to the white music
8- Dancing to the white music
9- Dreaming to the white music

A Facebook picture

Dear reader of color!

I would be grateful if you would express your opinion of this book and to spread the word so that western authorities could not ignore this message of seeking justice.

But if you are indifferent to the world's injustice or proud for being privileged to the Western society and therefore arrogant towards me, note that sheep are indifferent too and some puppies are admitted with privilege to the houses of their millionaire owners as well; but they still have the prestige of sheep and puppies not of humans. If you only wait for the white music to show any reaction to this book or not you have your option.

I have lived neither dishonorably, nor sheepishly, nor with flattery in my life. If 'you' have any of these character traits, you might not support me to raise my voice as well, as you did not know me before from level zero of my struggle until now. I would have no expectations and no disappointments.

Whenever by the pretext of a small individual crime, whole nations, races, and the original geographies of certain immigrant or refugee groups are conspired against to defamation, millions of people become the media to spread the word of conspiracy. Will anyone come to spread the word of justice for immigrants and refugees, even if they are from the same backgrounds themselves?

If Afghanistan was not a desert land and if there was not starvation, I wouldn't have become a refugee out of there for freedom. I would have fought for freedom there, as now I am fighting for justice here. When I am flexible for defending the rights of others, I wouldn't have been conservative for defending the rights of my own.

Our nature planet is discussed as a solid, indivisible living body.
As long as the poor, deprived nations would fight amongst themselves over the waste of nature and do not claim their rights in the juice of their solid nature, they would have the prestige of the waste in the eyes of those nations who eat the juice of their solid nature.

Last word

The nature is a home to all and it belongs to everyone equally. Immigration is natural and a natural right. No one is privileged to enjoy nature's rights and freedoms above anyone else.

The selfish, racist, opportunistic, and monopolist people say that one reason for their anti-immigrant behavior is that they need to prevent overpopulation. If you say the solution for overpopulation is a global human population control as in China, then they say controlling the population is an interference to other peoples' personal lives. But excessive births in the limited nature with limited resources is not a personal matter, however bullying, obstructing, and encroaching upon other peoples, usurping their nature, and stealing their bread is an interference in their personal lives. Then they say the world is not fair. **But if the world is not fair, you should be fair and you should have honor and a conscience.**

In the end, it's not the words from our enemies that hurt but the silence from our friends.

Appendices

Appendix 1

To Norwegian Embassy in Tehran

Dear Sir or Madam:

I am an Afghanistani refugee. I have a series of social problems in my homeland. I am a 27-year-old homosexual man. Therefore I have recently married an Afghanistani man by the name of Nawaz. Unfortunately the Afghanistani society, without considering exceptional needs of homosexuals, is too prejudiced and violent against homosexual couples. This makes our choice of living as a couple in Afghanistan impossible. This kind of prejudice and violence is based on religious understanding and notions of tribal disgrace and honor.

Prior to this letter to you, I sent three other letters in the course of the past three months to the UNHCR's office, but I did not receive any response from it. When I visited its office to make inquiries about my letters, they told me to wait at least one year before I receive any response from them. Meanwhile the government of Iran has put pressure on the Afghanistani refugees to force them to leave this country as soon as possible. For that reason I decided to present my problems directly to embassies of certain countries having democratic and open-minded societies.

If you examine the circumstances of my life within the framework of Afghanistani social laws, you will observe what a deprived person I am in that society. Moreover, I am extremely despised by the society. I am not capable of marrying a woman. If a person never marries, it is seen as extremely ridiculous by the Afghanistani people. This attitude of people makes me suffer from an inferiority complex.

If my spouse and I return to Afghanistan, we surely will face serious violence by certain people because they consider our marriage as immoral and contrary to religion and traditions of Afghanistan. Separation from my homosexual spouse and isolation are the biggest deprivation in my life on the one hand, and on the other, being perpetually ridiculed and reviled add to my misery.

In order to achieve a lifestyle of my choice—that is, joint living with my homosexual spouse—I need your humanitarian help of accepting us as refugees in Norway. I hope that you will assist us in this respect. Thanking you for your humanitarian help and looking forward to hearing from you.

Yours truly,
Hamid and Nawaz

The Embassy is not able to help you. Please contact the nearest UN office.

Appendix 2

UNCHR
United Nations High Commissioner for Refugees

11-Apr-05

To Whom It May Concern

The below mentioned persons have approached the office of the UNHCR in Ankara asking for assistance as an asylum seeker.

The applicants have been advised to comply with the requirement under Turkish asylum procedure to register with the security directorate foreigners department in his/her area of residence if he/she has a passport, or with the security directorate foreigners department of the city where he/she entered into Turkey, if he/she does not have a passport.

Therefore, he/she was advised to approach the police in Van.

Relationship: Principal Applicant
Family Name: Zaher
Given Name: Hamid
Nationality: Afghanistan
POB: Parwan
DOB: --/--/--

Yours sincerely,

X Y
Representative

Important Note:
This is not a residence permit. Such document can only be obtained from the Turkish authorities. Temporary asylum applications are always to be decided by the Turkish government.

Appendix 3

UNHCR
United Nations Commissioner for Refugees

Full name: Hamid Zaher
UNHCR file number: ———

After careful consideration, our office has determined that you do not meet the criteria for protection as a refugee according to UNHCR's Statute and the 1951 Convention relating to the Status of Refugees.

To qualify for international protection as a refugee, you must demonstrate that you have a well-founded fear of being persecuted on account of your race, or your religion, or your nationality, or your membership of a particular social group, or your political opinion. In our view you do not meet these criteria because:

    The harm you suffered or fear you have is not related to any of the five Convention grounds listed above.

    The events you described to us during your interview do not demonstrate that you have suffered or will suffer treatment so severe as to amount of persecution.

    You are able to obtain adequate protection from the authorities in your country of origin.

    ✓ Your testimony was not credible for the following reasons:

- ✓ Due to material inconsistencies with your own statements or those provided by persons with related claims;
- Due to material inconsistencies with country of origin information available to UNHCR;
- ✓ Your testimony was not found plausible.

Should you wish to have your case reconsidered on appeal:

Please write a letter to our office within the next thirty (30) days. Clearly explain the reasons why you believe you are a refugee. If you wish to present additional facts not provided in your first interview, briefly outline them and explain why they were not mentioned earlier. Your letter of appeal should not exceed two (2) pages in length.

You will only be called for an additional interview if UNHCR considers it necessary for the proper consideration of your appeal. For this reason, please ensure that your letter of appeal contains all the basic information regarding your reasons for leaving your country.

Please note that UNHCR's decision does not affect your temporary asylum application with the government of Turkey, which is subject to a separate procedure.

Yours sincerely,
UNHCR BO Ankara

Appendix 4

Appeal Letter

If you disagree with the UN's decision to reject your claim, you should *exclusively* use this page to write your appeal as instructed. Letters written in forms other than this one will not be considered.

I am an Afghanistani homosexual. In order to prove this, you may satisfy yourself by conducting my medical examination. If you carefully study the circumstances of my life within the framework of religious laws and social and cultural norms of Afghanistan, you will note that any decision that deprives me of the United Nations' protection will be completely unjustified. I consider myself a refugee for the following reasons:

    1. Firstly, I have no sexual freedom in Afghanistan. Every human being in every society enjoys the sexual orientation that he or she has. Why then should I be deprived of this enjoyment of my youth while there are other individuals who achieve what I desire? It is your moral duty not to be negligent in this respect, like the Afghanistani society.

    2. Secondly, do you know that our society, which consists of an absolute majority of traditionalists, always ridicules and reviles homosexuals? This rude habit exists even among the small class of our intellectuals. If you were in my shoes, would you be able to put up with the aggressive behavior and consistent ridicule and revilement by others? I will describe the various aspects

of the grave problems of my life. If one of those problems seems not so serious to you, please do not disregard all of my problems because of this.

You rejected my claim for two reasons, "inconsistencies with my statements or those provided by persons with related claims," and "my testimony was not found plausible."

 1. About inconsistencies: I do not understand what do you mean by inconsistencies?

 2. About your finding that my testimony was not found plausible: I believe that there is nothing better than a medical examination and determination of my sex in justification and support of my statements. If you are not content with the determination of my sex, type of my life, and its comparison to the cultural, religious, and social conditions of Afghanistan, then no evidence will be evidence, and no proof will be proof for you.

In order for you to really understand my situation, I reiterate my problems once again, "Instead of enjoying youth, always suffering from deprivation; instead of love and encouragement, always ridicule and revilement!"

Do you know that sexual deprivation is painful, and harmful to one's health? I am sure you do. Then are you sure that I have minimum sexual freedom in Afghanistan? The fact is that I have not even 1 percent inclination to women.

Upon my conscience and honor, I was forced to leave Afghanistan because of the ever-increasing problems and dangers. It is almost five years that I am living the hardest days of my life in a state of displacement. All the hard work that I did for years in Afghanistan has gone down the drain. But regretfully you, the honorable representatives, deprive me of the United Nations' protection with a closed eye and without hearing my statements. I was forced to leave Afghanistan because I faced inhuman treatment, unreasonable judging, and illogical and unreasonable demands, and I sought asylum from the UN. Thus, I request you, the honorable representatives, to judge my problems in a human, wise, and logical way so as to demonstrate that humanity on earth is not yet dead.

Sincerely,
Hamid Zaher

22-08-2005

Is it true?

Appendix 5

Name & surname: Hamid Zaher
File No.: ———
xx-06-2006

To Whom It May Concern:
    I wish to inform you that I, in the course of my long imposed residence in the city of Van, which is a relatively prejudiced and traditional city, am facing ever increasing problems. I have 180 degrees of sexual deviation and feel the need to make my outer self look like my inner self. But I am attacked and persecuted and tormented everywhere by the prejudiced and traditional people of the city of Van. For instance, among many of these persecutions and torments, I was attacked last Tuesday at 9:30 p.m. by three unidentified individuals. By running away and seeking refuge in a restaurant, I was able to save my life. The restaurant staff has witnessed their attempt on my life. About fifteen days ago I was attacked yet again by two unidentified individuals, and I immediately took refuge in a store. There are many other instances of persecution, torment, and vilification to which I often pay no attention. You may be perhaps one of those who spit on my face upon seeing me, but I completely ignore such reactions.
    It seems certain that something bad will happen to me sooner or later in the city of Van. If your conscience and honor is such that you do not believe my words, then come out on the streets and see for yourself how people react against me. Although my past experience shows that there is no understanding and responsible official here who would pay

attention to the problems of asylum seekers and refugees, other than taking care of his own personal interests, I wish to inform you officials in this respect, before meeting with a dangerous accident, so that if an accident occurs to me, you may see the reflection of your irresponsibility in the mirror of your inhumanity.

The remaining days of my youth, which are still being spent in limitation under your captivity, will never come back. Thus, I will never stop fighting to get my right to live and those of others like me, until I die. Every reasonable person knows, let alone you, the UN representatives and officials, that life for every homosexual is full of limitations and dangers under the Islamic government and the traditional society of Afghanistan. And yet, despite seeking asylum from the UN, so far I have gained nothing but limitations and captivity. In fact I may say that by seeking refuge with the UN, I fell from the frying pan into the fire; my transfer from Istanbul to Van and unlimited indecisiveness testify to my captivity. You are feeding unprotected refugees like me at the UN. Then where is your humanity and honor that you do not understand us? If I lose a part of my body one of these days as a result of being attacked here, rest assured that I will set myself on fire with gasoline right in front of the UN office so that your nature becomes known to the people, so it serves as an example to others, that they may not fall prey to you, human-like spider.

Appendix 6

Name & surname: Hamid Zaher
File No.: ———
xx-07-2006

To the Head of the Mission:

At my security interview last Friday, you suggested that I apply to the police for the transfer of my file. But transfers and useless wanderings, as in the past, from Istanbul to Van and from Van to any other city, will be futile. I do not wish to remain concealed from people's eyes. I want to remain in the shadow of the protection of your hands, like that logo of the UN which has taken a human being under its protection. But I am afraid that these hands, like other hands, may become claws—that is, silence and indifference after the previous clawing. I know that these words will make you more difficult, but I have no control over it. My life has no worth for me anymore. Instead of enjoying a fruitful and humane attention, I expect more horrid violence from life.

In my security interview of last Friday, you told me that my security concerns relate to the police. Why then did the police want to run away from me when a number of people had assaulted me in the middle of the intersection and were throwing kicks and punches on me while the police was present there?

If you think logically, disregarding the indifference by the police, why my security concerns relate to the police in every nook and corner? According to the police itself, the Turkish police had not sent me an invitation card so it could be responsible for protecting me in every nook and corner and every lane and by-lane.

There is no doubt that some obscurantist and barbaric individuals have infiltrated some valuable humane organizations and institutions who are popularizing modern barbarism with their barbaric and inhuman way of thinking. Among them are some at the UN who, on various pretexts, act on their personal beliefs, make some refugees qualified and sell the refugee quota of others, and engage in administrative corruption. Such are their crimes.

In my last Friday's security interview, you said that you were sorry for me. But the word sorry conveys two meanings: firstly, some people use this expression when they hear some sorrowful news. Secondly and conversely, some women use it to mock others. You will prove to me your true intention in acts and deeds. But in any event, I thank you for being sorry for me.

You always deal with people's misfortunes and tragedies. It seems to me that you have developed immunity against the pangs of conscience.

Appendix 7

Name & surname: Hamid Zaher
File No.: ———
xx-07-2006

To Whom It May Concern:
    I wish to inform you that during the period of over one year since I submitted my appeal letter to you, I have received no reply. I am in a bad financial situation here, and due to my homosexuality I am in a bad security situation due to people's prejudices. At the same time, unlimited indecision and waiting has put me in the worst possible psychological condition. In spite of all these pressures, I am not permitted to work and am almost like a prisoner. In circumstances of unlimited waiting, while my precious time is being wasted, I do not enjoy my life.
    From your perspective I may not finally qualify as a refugee. But from my own perspective, I cannot continue to live my life in Afghanistan. Accordingly, I respectfully request the UN officials to decide my case at the earliest so that in the case of rejection, I may make use of my youth and make a decision on my difficult future so I could get out of this ocean of wandering and reach the shores of salvation, if at all possible.

    Thanking you,
    Hamid Zaher

Appendix 8

Name & surname: Hamid Zaher
File No: ———
xx-01-2007

To Case Representative:

In the past I have informed you several times of my many problems, and for the last time I am telling you, as a responsible official, that I am living here in the worst possible psychological, financial, and security conditions. Since I hold you as the singular cause that has created these circumstances for me, I can no longer remain silent against your actions. If you are logical people, I will briefly explain my case for you, and will wait for your immediate decision. Failing this, you will face this time my reaction to your rude actions.

I will briefly refer to the ambiguities or excuses based on which you made your previous decision. You have based your rejection letter on two excuses: one is inconsistencies in my statements, and the other lack of evidence to support my statements.

1. As to inconsistencies, it may be said that such inconsistency that creates doubts does not exist in my statements, but it does in your imagination. As the saying goes, intelligent people do not base their decision on one point. But you are resorting to an excuse on the basis of trivial matters. And this is something beyond reason and logic, because the picture that can be seen requires no explanations. I am putting this picture before your eyes and you will see it with your eyes. When you ignore something that you can see with your own eyes

and pretend as if you have seen nothing, how can you accept something that has happened and is no longer exposed to sight? I am a homosexual, and homosexuality is considered a crime in Afghanistan punishable by death. Sexual orientation and sexual needs are natural inclination and natural needs, not a habit or way of thinking. In these circumstances, do you see the conditions of my life in relation to my sexual needs in Afghanistan? When you ignore my concerns and risks existing at present and in the future and treat them as insignificant, certainly you will make excuses about my past, too.

2. As to supporting evidence, one may say that when my case is a sexual case, I am the body of evidence. I am a homosexual, and homosexuality is considered a crime in Afghanistan and is punishable by death. If you want me to prove this, you may send me to a physician or test me in action with the sexual organs of female representatives in your office, or with the female members of your family. You will see whether or not I am aroused by the opposite sex. In my view, whatever I am saying to you could constitute incontrovertible evidence of the fact that it is not possible for me to live in Afghanistan. Apart from this, it can relate to your own capacity and character whether you can accept it as valid evidence or not. If you give a banknote to a young child, he or she would want to buy something with that money. But if you give it to a baby, it would tear the banknote to pieces since it cannot accept it as a valid proof. You have to have this capacity and capability to accept that Afghanistan is not a place where I can live. But in your case the situation is completely different. You are wiser, more knowledgeable, and more informed than me and anyone else. You know very well why I left Afghanistan and understand it even better what will happen to me if I return to Afghanistan. You are not short of anything in this respect.

But these are just details. The capacity and ability I wish to see in you go back to their roots. First of all, you should have the very basic quality of a living being, i.e., honor. Even the most primitive mono-cell living being lacking intelligence has honor because when it lives in nature, it respects the law of nature and does not act against the law of nature. *The true host and the true home of every living being is nature, and every living being in nature has the equal right to live naturally.* But these border divisions that have been created by force of arms and by force of swords are the false hosts and false homes. Thus, everyone must live where they enjoy their natural right. If you think like humans, you must treat me like yourself, with the sexual needs that you have and the sexual freedom that you want for yourself. If you think not like a human being but like a living being, you must treat me like yourself, a living being with its own sexual orientation and the way that it must live.

As a human being, you must agree that it is not possible for me to live in Afghanistan. As a living being, you must accept that living in Afghanistan is not possible for me. But if you do not have the first and foremost attribute of a living being, a dead donkey has more dignity than you, for when the dead donkey was alive, it respected the law of nature. Even after death it respects the law of nature. If you do not respect the law of nature and my sexual requirements, you are so rude and dishonorable as if you live in the womb of your mother but sink your teeth in your mother's womb. In such case a negative multiplier has been placed before your attributes. The more wise, knowledgeable, and aware you are, the more is added to your weight (responsibility). So far you have done me no good; but you have hurt and humiliated me to a great extent. You have wasted two years of my valuable time; if I was a homeless person, you have made me even more displaced. I have no hope that you will review my case favorably in the future, since honor is not a bird that comes back home after taking flight. If one dies, one dies forever and does not come back to life. Are you aware of the situation of homosexuals in Afghanistan? Can you give me even one example of a person who lives in Afghanistan as a homosexual? If that is not the case, then why don't you judge me correctly if you are not dishonorable? Why do you hurt and humiliate me so much? Why do you waste so much of my time? You who sell my right of asylum to others, at least should not hurt me. If you wanted to give me any reply, you could have done it in these two years. But you do not wish to give me any reply.

    I have informed the police of Turkey, Amnesty International, and the Human Rights Organization of this matter. If you are not dishonorable, do not do anything to prompt me to react disrespectfully against your disrespectful action.

With hatred,
Hamid Zaher

Appendix 9

Name & surname: Hamid Zaher
File No: ———
xx-02-2007

To Case Representative:

Finally you have forced me to go on strike. Since you are the cause for the beginning of my strike, you will be the cause of its end as well. You have assumed responsibility here at your own initiative. Why do you play with the lives of people and your own reputation? If you are being obstinate and difficult with me, you are being difficult not only with my life but also with your own reputation.

I am now a prisoner of two years of wasted time and a prisoner of your obstinacy, but why? Finally, there is a limit to obstinacy too! Do you not believe that a homosexual faces all kinds of dangers in Afghanistan, including death, and this fact is as clear as the sun? Why do you try to hide the sun with two fingers? You who have closed your eyes do not see others, but do not think that others do not see you. Finally, for how long do you wish to keep your eyes closed? You have put me under such tremendous mental pressure so as to force me to leave this place; rest assured that I'll never leave this place unless you arrange my expulsion. But it takes two to tango. Before I die gradually under your silent pressure, I'll do something to make you respond. Before your reputation is damaged, please take action. You should know that I am not somebody who will always remain silent under your constant pressure; I'll reveal the curtain of your intangible and depraved violence at your own hands.

> We are waves whose rest is their death.
> We are alive because of our restlessness.

Appendix 10

Letter of Complaint

Respecting the rights of fellow human beings is tantamount to understanding oneself.
To err is human, but to repeat it is a sin.

It is a human duty to bring to the attention of you, the UN representatives, that homosexuals are considered as a neuter gender, because naturally they cannot reproduce. It is only you, the males and females, who bring them into this world. Thus, do not subject the effects, of which you are the cause, to prejudice and violence. All homosexual refugees who do not have sexual freedom in their own countries, whose sexuality is a source of pain and danger, and who are deprived of their natural right deserve your support without any exception, excuse, or humiliation, and deserve to be accepted as refugees; do not separate them from others. Do not make the whole world as another court and another infinite prison for those who are condemned in their own countries, whose countries are tantamount to a large prison or a solitary cell for them.

We hope that humanity and logic should suffice for you and, unlike the past, there will be no need for violent reactions by each individual applicant against you and no need for hatred and anger. Do you like illogical reciprocal conduct toward you?

We hope that all of you UN representatives and officials would condemn your past, respond positively to this proposal, and prove your humanness and humanity, and we would witness you put this into practice soonest.

You UN officials are educated and worldly wise people. When a small number of you cannot be convinced by reason and logic to give up your stubbornness against homosexuals, how then can one convince huge, superstitious, and uneducated populations who have their own beliefs and who follow the flock like sheep with their heads down? How can one silence their prejudice and violence against homosexuals?

You witness the problems of homosexuals in Islamic societies as clearly as the sun; then why your stubbornness against them? Do you think that stubbornness is logical? Do you think there is a difference between the logic with which you treat homosexuals and the logic of the Taliban and the reactionary regime of Iran and other reactionary regimes? Perhaps the only difference between them and you is the pen that you are carrying instead of arms; but there is no difference between your logic and ideal and theirs.

There are many people for whom you schedule an early appointment date and accept them within a week or two after the interview and determine a country for them. Why then should a homosexual wait for months or years? Why is a homosexual rejected by you? Perhaps you may say that your decision-making differs on the basis of intensity of danger that threatens a refugee. But are the great and lasting dangers that threaten a homosexual less than the ones that threaten others? Do those who formally celebrate their sexual union, and for whom others dance and dally to honor their sexual union, face greater danger than a homosexual who is condemned to death because of his or her sexual union? Do those who are sheltered against danger at least by their own families face greater danger than a homosexual who has only enemies but no friends? Do those who pride themselves on their sexuality face greater difficulty than the homosexuals who always conceal their sexuality and have broken hearts? Are the problems of political, religious, and ideological people, who made their choices consciously, greater than the problems of homosexuals, whose sexual orientation is not their choice and their only crime is that they were born like this? Do you respect only those who are respected by everyone else, but disrespect the homosexuals who are disrespected by everyone else? If you do not disrespect them, then why do you not accept homosexuals sooner who actually face real problems?

For whatever reason you reject a homosexual or force him to appeal, first and foremost you must understand the meaning of reason. Reason is something that indicates the issue under consideration, not illogical words and blind obedience that you call logic. There exists no logical reason to reject the refugee status to a homosexual refugee who has no sexual freedom in his country of birth; presenting illogical grounds for rejecting his claim is a great disrespect and rudeness. The fact that you should be able to accept each and every one of them quickly, without excuses and without harassment, as a refugee subject to your protection relates directly to your own honor, capacity, and humanity, not to that subjective interview and test from which you get no real answers. Conducting long interviews, asking stupid questions, and examining cases and wasting time are completely illogical and inhuman acts. If you are a human being and naturally feel sexual needs in yourself and seek sexual freedom for yourself, you should naturally treat them as a human being with sexual needs like yourself. But if you think that you are an animal, not a human being, then you should treat them like an animal with the same sexual needs that you see in yourself. Only the basic honor and integrity in your being is enough for you to accept homosexuals at the first meeting, on the very first day, without any foolish excuses as refugees deserving your protection.

Can one reach the top rung without stepping on the lower rungs? When you cannot prove the basic integrity of your being alive in the course of months and years, it is indeed strange that you speak of politics, religion, ideology, job, belief, and so on, and sooner than that! Isn't it shameful that with such a mysterious way of thinking and dealing with homosexuals, you present yourself as lesser than an animal without logic?

Please give an honorable and logical answer to all of the sixteen questions raised in this letter, and explain clearly like a human being why you neglect homosexuals and why you make them wait longer than other individuals.

In order to reassure yourself in respect of homosexual refugees whose homosexuality you doubt, you may test them with the sexual organs of female representatives in your office or female members of your own family, instead of wasting their time, because time is valuable and you will get no satisfactory result from wasting their time.

Thanking you,
Hamid Zaher

xx-10-2007

Appendix 11

VALİLİK MAKAMINA

Afganistan uyrukluyum. 38 ay dır Türkyede mülteci olarak oturmaktayım. Birleşmiş Miletler ve Türkiye cumhuryetin arasındaki sözleşmesine göre, mülteciler bir geçici ikamet süresinden sonra Türkiye den üçüncü bir ülkeye yerleştilirler. O yüzden Kanada ülkesi benim için giriş vizesi vermiş. Ama Türkiye den ayrılmadan önce yabancıların şubesi çıkış vizesi veriliş için benden 1,850 YTL ikamet parası istemiş.

Ben Afganistan fakir ülkesinden gelmişim. Ailemiz fakir olduklarından dolayı beni yardım edemiyorlar. Üstelik Türkiye de oturduğum süresinin boyunca, çalışma izin olmadığından dolayı çalışamamaktaymışım ve kendi harçlarımda hep sıkıntıdaymışım.

Boyla bir durumdayken bütün bu tutarı ödeyecek gücüm yoktur ve çıkış vizesi verilişin konusunda, bu parayı ödemeden muaf olmak ya da en azından yarısını indirim ettirmek istiyorum. Yapılmasının gereğini saygılarımla arz ederim.

Teşekkürler;
Hamid Zaher

11/03/2008

Appendix 12

To the Governor's Office:

I am an Afghanistani citizen. I have been living for the last thirty-eight months as a refugee in Turkey. According to a treaty between the UN and the Republic of Turkey, refugees are placed in third countries after their temporary stay in Turkey. Accordingly Canada has issued me an entry visa. But prior to leaving Turkey, the Foreign Citizens' Department has asked me to pay 1,850 Turkish liras to issue an exit visa for me.

I come from the poor country of Afghanistan, and my family cannot help me because they are poor too. Moreover, during my stay in Turkey I did not have a job because I was not allowed to work. I was always in difficulty in respect of my expenses.

Under these circumstances I am not able to pay the entire amount. Accordingly, I request that either I be exempted from paying the exit visa fee, or at least half of it be discounted. Thanking you in anticipation.

Truly yours,
Hamid Zaher

11/03/2008

Endnotes

Endnote 1

Farsi or Dari?

Some foreign readers became curious and they asked me why I wrote this book in Farsi (Persian) rather than Dari, while, I am from Afghanistan and Dari is spoken in Afghanistan, but Farsi is spoken in Iran.
In fact, Farsi or Dari either is the same language with different dialects in many parts of Iran, Afghanistan, and Tajikistan. It is traditionally called Farsi in the all three countries.
The term 'Dari' was formerly used as an honorific title of Farsi language during the past centuries by the poets and writers of this language, in all of its territories, including Iran.
In Afghanistan since 1964 for political reasons the name Farsi was officially replaced by Dari and it was declared as a separate language from Farsi. Then, in the educational, media, and governmental systems too many of its original former words were replaced by new the exotic words, in order to be practically distinguished from Farsi. Its former original words were declared as the exotic or Iranian words and their usage was forbidden and became punishable.
At the time, the Afghanistani government was a Pashtun ethnically dominated government which was a tough rival of the

Farsi language and its policy was to weaken the Farsi language so that the Pashtu language was strengthened as a result.

Dari (Farsi) and Pashtu are both the formal languages of Afghanistan. Farsi is spoken by about 50% of the population as their first language and also serves as lingua franca. Pashtu is spoken by about 38% of the population.

Although the Afghanistani government succeeded to differentiate this language from its original mode to some extent through a long-term educational, media, and governmental systems, but from the outset, this policy of the government was opposed by the Persian littérateur and their opposition with the government is still continues.

The limitations and changes which were imposed on Persian language in Afghanistan, caused it not only separation from its Iranian trunk but also many imperfections, weaknesses, and inefficiencies.

Presently some of the foreign governments and media, including the BBC, are practicing the original Farsi version of this language for their Afghanistani audience; while, some others, including the U.S. and Canadian governments and their media, are practicing the falsified Dari version for their Afghanistani audience.

The U.S. anti Farsi policy is attributed to an Afghan-American politician who is said an ethno-nationalist Pashtun and has been involved in the U.S. policy-making at the White House, State Department, and Pentagon.

The Canadian anti-Farsi policy is also attributed to some Pashtun ethno-nationalists who have been the pioneers of Afghanistani politician ns in Canada.

The involvement of superpowers and their allies, with the policy of 'divide and rule', is not unthinkable in this issue.

There is another reason too that the interpreters list them to the government as separate languages to show their proficiency of more than one language. For the same language they list Farsi, Dari, and Tajik as mastering three different languages.

Endnote 2

Related to Part 3/The Ugly Truth

The *Ariana Encyclopedia*, and the *Ethnography Atlas of Non-Afghan Ethnic Groups Living in Afghanistan*, after being approved by Hamid Karzai, the President of Afghanistan, were published in June 2012, through the Science Academy of Afghanistan. In those books in addition to minimizing the percentages of non-Afghan ethnic groups, many insults were added to their injury, i.e.

- *Hazaras, the descendants of Mongolian and Tatar tribes, are immigrants in Afghanistan... They are brave warriors, hospitable and generous people. Because of the lack of knowledge and the existence of ignorance, they are stubborn, spiteful, bad-tempered, liar, and militant.*

- *The author of "Da Pashtano Qabilo Shajare Aw Mineh," quoting one of his Hazara friends, without naming him, states: Among us, the Hazara people, the original ones and of the supreme lineage are those who can see one of their eyes with the other. It means that the curvature of their noses is deeper than the sockets of their eyes. Their names have the suffix Ali; and while walking they shuffle once to one side and once to the other. He adds, there are some other specifications too, but without the permission of his friend, he cannot mention them.*

- *All the womenfolk of this ethnic group are fat, with white skin, and smooth and nice faces; but their eyes, eyebrows and noses are similar to their men folk and except the top of their head, all of their bodies are smooth and hairless.*

- *Hayat Afghani writes: The Hazaras are unfaithful and unkind, and they do not avail their close friends in bad times... and they have no bearing for the words unlike their temper. Except this weakness, they are good in nature.*

— Ethnography Atlas of Non-Afghan Ethnic Groups Living in Afghanistan, pp. 653, 667, 672—published by, Afghanistani Academy of Sciences, June 2012